Faith in Foreign Aid

The United States contributes more foreign aid than any other state in the world, and it is often recognized as a leader in engaging religious organizations in aid delivery. *Faith in Foreign Aid* is the first book to closely examine how the relationship between religious organizations and USAID plays out in practice.

Faith in Foreign Aid relies on an original dataset to trace faith-based funding patterns in US foreign aid from 2001 to 2021. The findings show that despite America's push to engage religious organizations in aid, the total number of religious organizations it funds is relatively low, especially when compared with the number of USAID's secular partners. These faith-based organizations (FBOs) also represent the minority of US-based development FBOs broadly. Relying on extensive original survey and interview data, the book suggests that many religious organizations are deterred from applying for public funding because they perceive the government as biased against them, or fear their religious mission might be challenged. In addition to investigating why some FBOs eschew government funds, the book also examines why some FBOs choose to partner with USAID and what this relationship can look like. *Faith in Foreign Aid* highlights the voices and experiences of FBOs, showing a way for more effective engagement between religious organizations and government actors.

The book will be of interest to researchers across public policy, development, religion, and political science, as well as to practitioners at USAID and development organizations.

Susan Turner Haynes is an Associate Professor of Political Science at Lipscomb University in Nashville, TN, USA. She teaches International Development, Constitutional Law, American Foreign Policy, and International Security, among others. Her first book, *Chinese Nuclear Proliferation,* was published in 2016.

Routledge Research in Religion and Development

The *Routledge Research in Religion and Development* series focuses on the diverse ways in which religious values, teachings and practices interact with international development.

While religious traditions and faith-based movements have long served as forces for social innovation, it has only been within the last ten years that researchers have begun to seriously explore the religious dimensions of international development. However, recognising and analysing the role of religion in the development domain is vital for a nuanced understanding of this field. This interdisciplinary series examines the intersection between these two areas, focusing on a range of contexts and religious traditions.

Religious Organisations in Sub-Saharan Africa and South Asia
Connections to Society and the State
Carole Rakodi

Faith in Foreign Aid
Religious Organizations' Engagement with USAID
Susan Turner Haynes

For more information about this series, please visit: www.routledge.com/Routledge-Research-in-Religion-and-Development/book-series/RRRD

Faith in Foreign Aid

Religious Organizations' Engagement with USAID

Susan Turner Haynes

Routledge
Taylor & Francis Group
LONDON AND NEW YORK

First published 2025
by Routledge
4 Park Square, Milton Park, Abingdon, Oxon OX14 4RN

and by Routledge
605 Third Avenue, New York, NY 10158

Routledge is an imprint of the Taylor & Francis Group, an informa business

British Library Cataloguing-in-Publication Data
A catalogue record for this book is available from the British Library

ISBN: 9781032598758
ISBN: 9781032598796
ISBN: 9781003456704

DOI: 10.4324/9781003456704

Typeset in Sabon
by Newgen Publishing UK

To Claire, Luke, and Lucy—*I'm sorry it isn't a picture book.*

To Michael—*I'm sorry it isn't a bestseller.*

Contents

Figures

Tables

Acknowledgments

A heavy course load at a primarily undergraduate institution may seem to some to sound the death knell of a professor's research. In my case, however, the opposite is true. This book emerged precisely because I was teaching, and learning about, several different subjects at once, and because I had intelligent and curious students with which to engage. The following is a comprehensive but not exhaustive list of all those who helped bring this book to fruition.

First and foremost, I extend my gratitude to God, the source of all wisdom and inquiry. I owe to Him this beautiful life, where I can do what I love surrounded and supported by people I love. I am also thankful for the particular people He put in my path for this project.

This book would not have been started had it not been for many early conversations with Stephanie Shackleford, who graciously agreed to speak to my International Development class in the spring of 2018, and who first drew my attention to the likely disconnect between religious organizations and USAID. Stephanie and I met regularly in the summer and fall of 2018 with a key group of students, who were instrumental in getting the project off the ground. Without their work coding and collating aid recipient data and conducting pilot phone interviews, the empirical puzzle would not have come to light. Carrie Cowart, Jake Guerrero, and Payman Beduhe—thank you for your work and early interest in my research.

I also want to thank the many students who collected data for later stages of the project. This includes Debra Zhang, Ben Hemby, Kalli Close, Andrew Daffron, Cavin Jacobson, Eden Melles, Abby Komistek, Veronika Jones, Nicole Hemphill, Brian Hendrickson, Merry Holland, Zach Laws, Christian Layne, Jackson Stubblefield, Dexter Woods, Kayla Wood, Austin Travis, Dane Mortensen, Brenna Wolfe, Allison Cozart, Sara Malham, Daniel Taft, John Gill, Addison Gross, David Iskander, Luke Jenkins, Hamilton Jones, Madeline Knight, Mackenzie McConnell, Huy Nguyen, Kiley Sayre, and Elena Walker. Three students, in particular, also served as my research assistants at various points, and I am especially grateful for the work they did and the conversations we had. Konnor Gottfred, Antonina Lucido, and Lauren Bailey—thank you for your dedication to the project.

The heavy involvement of undergraduate students in my research was made possible by my institution, Lipscomb University, which has always sought to provide students with opportunities in and outside of the classroom to deepen their skills and knowledge. In addition to prioritizing student research, Lipscomb also supported me by providing me with a Faculty Research Grant in the summer of 2021 and a sabbatical in fall 2023.

This project also benefited from the generous financial support of the American Political Science Association, which provided me with a Centennial Center Research Grant in the summer of 2022. I also want to thank Guidestar, Inc. (now Candid) for supplying a complimentary custom data list that helped with the survey phase of the project.

I also want to express my sincere appreciation to the individuals who participated in this research, including those who completed the online survey and those who took the time to speak with me on Zoom. It is because of you this book exists. I respect the hard and important work you do, and I am honored to try to share your perspective and experience.

Lastly, I extend a heartfelt thank you to my friends and family for their patience and support and for bringing much-welcomed levity and love to my life. I am blessed to have you.

1 Introduction

America is the world's top financier of foreign aid, providing more money, in absolute terms, than any other country.[1] In 2021, this amounted to nearly 50 billion dollars, less than one percent of the federal budget and less than half a percent of the country's gross national income.[2] Surveys show that most Americans believe this expense is justified and favor maintaining the status quo in US aid spending.[3] A majority of religious individuals feel similarly.[4] Donald Trump did not. Instead, President Trump proposed significant cuts to foreign assistance every year he was in office.[5] Congress never obliged, but the president's announcements nevertheless served as a repeated litmus test for the public's commitment to foreign aid. Each of his proposals faced significant opprobrium. Among the constituencies most concerned were America's Christian leaders, over 100 of whom registered their dissent in an open letter to Congress in 2017.[6] These leaders argued that American abundance comes incumbent with a moral responsibility to assist countries less fortunate. Hence, the United States should not abrogate or mitigate its aid commitments but lean in, assist others, and strive to be "a shining city upon a hill."[7]

The letter's signatories held significant political and moral weight. Two of the individuals had spoken at the president's inauguration.[8] Others were presidents and CEOs of large Christian organizations—the kind typically supported by the Republican base and also that spent millions of their own funds on international assistance.[9] Their support of foreign aid did not represent mere lip service but was born out in the missions and operations of the organizations they helmed.

Many of these individuals spent their lives serving "the least of these," and they considered beneficence a moral obligation of both the faithful *and* the federal government. Yet, the leaders refrained from suggesting the two work *in tandem* to pursue this objective. On this point, there is less consensus. Faith-based organizations (FBOs), the vast majority of which are Christian, make up nearly 60% of all US-based humanitarian and development organizations in the United States.[10] Yet, they account for approximately 13% of the US government's implementing foreign aid partners.[11] This statistic is especially

DOI: 10.4324/9781003456704-1

curious considering the repeated overtures of the American government to engage FBOs in aid delivery.

FBOs have had the legal clearance to apply for federal funds in the United States for over 20 years now, thanks primarily to George W. Bush. President Bush wanted to make it easier for the US federal government to outsource services to FBOs, in part, because he thought FBOs were sometimes better situated than secular nongovernmental organizations (NGOs) to "save and change lives."[12] At the time, there was little evidence to support the president's claims, but more evidence has since accumulated. Today, while FBOs are shown to have their disadvantages, such as sometimes being less transparent, accountable, and communicative with donors vis-à-vis secular NGOs, there is also an emerging consensus regarding their strengths.[13]

Why does the United States (and other countries) continue to prioritize partnering with FBOs in international development? In part, it's because they often share common features that can positively impact development outcomes. This includes greater geographic access, deep community relations, sprawling infrastructure, and a spiritual connection with beneficiaries.[14] A leading scholar in the study of religions and development, Katherine Marshall, puts these in terms of access capital, relational capital, social capital, and spiritual capital.[15] Another key feature born out in research is what Marshall calls "moral capital," which she refers to as the ability of FBOs to engender trust in the communities they serve.[16] Adam Nicholas Phillips explains this further:

> faith communities can be first responders in times of hardship, the last to leave when emergencies subside, or a permanent entity embedded in communities coping with crises. As a result, faith-based organizations often hold positions of special trust—and provide essential social support—particularly in societies wary of outsiders and even their own governments. Their unique, embedded presence makes these organizations indispensable components in the international development community mosaic.[17]

Phillips served as the Executive Director of the Local, Faith, and Transformative Partnerships Hub at the United States Agency for International Development (USAID)—America's premier aid agency.[18] The center has survived four presidential administrations and has had the same mission under each—to expand and deepen the government's partnerships with FBOs. Curiously, however, the center has published very little data on how many FBOs it funds and how much money it allocates to them. This remains true even though the center, and Phillips specifically, recently underscored the importance of USAID's FBO partners with its first Strategic Religious Engagement Policy.[19] This book provides answers by detailing the faith affiliation of all USAID award recipients from 2008 to 2021. In addition to presenting quantitative statistics, this book also explores the qualitative nature of FBO–USAID relations. In particular, I rely upon survey and interview data to share the perspectives of FBOs—both those that eschew and those that choose USAID funding. The accumulated evidence leads me to conclude that while faith *in* US foreign aid remains high among many faith leaders, their engagement *with* foreign aid remains relatively minimal. This paradox is examined further by exploring three related sets of questions:

1 First, what are the trends in USAID funding FBOs over the past 20 years? Has the number of funded organizations fluctuated significantly over time? To what extent has the *amount* of US funding to FBOs varied? Do funding patterns emerge depending upon who occupies the Oval Office?
2 Second, what accounts for the relatively few FBOs receiving USAID grants? Is this explained by the government discriminating against FBO applicants, or do FBOs choose not to apply? If fewer FBOs are applying for funds, why is this the case? Are these organizations unaware of their eligibility, or are they aware and choosing not to apply? If the latter, why do they rebuff this opportunity?
3 Third, what has been the experience of the few faith-based humanitarian and development organizations that *have* received grants from USAID? Are their stories a testament to the agency's successful engagement with religious organizations, or do they evince a strained marriage of competing interests?

As the above questions suggest, the overarching aim of this book is to explain why and how some FBOs have engaged in US foreign aid and why others have chosen not to do so. Exploring this subject in depth requires operationalizing several fairly nebulous concepts, including foreign aid, engagement, and FBOs. The next three sections provide more detail on these terms and explain how they are defined and measured in this study. This is followed by a discussion of the book's methodology and the importance of its findings. The conclusion lays out the structure of the book and summarizes subsequent chapters.

Foreign Aid

Foreign aid colloquially is taken to mean assistance provided from one country to another.[20] Less discussed are the critical questions of *who* within a given country provides the aid, *what* the aid funds, and *how* the aid is implemented. In the United States, the answers to these questions have shifted over time. As the amount of monetary assistance has burgeoned, so too has the number of people involved. American aid in the 21st century involves more administrating entities, funds more projects, and includes more implementing partners than ever before.

Initially, America sent money abroad at the behest of the president through a singular executive entity, the Department of State. Today, however, American foreign aid encompasses a constellation of actors, including but not limited to

USAID, the Department of Health and Human Services, the Department of State, and the Department of Treasury, as well as the President's Emergency Plan for AIDs Relief and the Millennium Challenge Corporation. This book restricts the ambit of analysis specifically to USAID as the primary steward of American foreign assistance.[21] In 2022, USAID spent over $41 billion on projects in over 100 countries and addressed a variety of issue areas, including natural disasters, agriculture, education, governance, human rights, women's empowerment, and global health, to name a few.

The geographic and programmatic diversity of modern US aid stands in stark contrast to the singularly focused aid of the past. When the United States first announced its intent to provide foreign assistance, its sole aim was to help European states with recovery and reconstruction following World War II. The United States had long-term goals of building political allies and trade partners, but the influx of cash was relatively time-bound and targeted to an immediate need. It wasn't until later that the United States began providing continued assistance, looking to promote long-term change. Today's foreign aid portfolio includes both types of assistance.

"Humanitarian assistance" refers to aid intended to ameliorate suffering and save lives in the face of or in the aftermath of immediate exigent crises. This type of aid comprised over a quarter of USAID's budget in 2022.[22] This money went to people affected by everything from floods and famine to conflict and war, and it purchased immediate necessities like food, water, soap, and shelter. One of the most pressing issues in 2022 was the war in Ukraine, to which the United States allocated an additional $2 billion. Beginning in February 2022 and continuing through the duration of the year, the war left thousands of civilians dead, tens of thousands injured, and millions displaced. America sent food directly to those in the hardest hit areas and sent cash transfers and vouchers to people in other parts of the country where they could still purchase food and other necessities. It also sent medicine and medical supplies to aid the sick and injured. In total, US humanitarian relief in Ukraine in 2022 reached over 13 million people.[23]

In addition to providing war relief for Ukraine and responding to various other international crises, the United States also spent $11 billion on economic development.[24] In contrast to humanitarian relief, which is more reactive, development assistance refers to proactive aid meant to grow and stabilize a country's economy. More specifically, development aid aims to enhance other countries' standard of living (and buoy them against external shock) by investing in key economic sectors like agriculture, energy, and innovative technologies, as well as contributing to critical social services like healthcare and education.[25] An example of work in this area includes USAID's investment of $150 million to enhance electricity, cell coverage, and internet access in hospitals across sub-Saharan Africa.[26] Currently, the erratic nature of the power supply in many sub-Saharan African states forces hospitals to provide suboptimal patient care. When the power goes out, hospitals are sometimes forced to cancel scheduled procedures or, more alarmingly, deny someone an emergent procedure. Power outages also impact the ability of hospitals to keep life-saving vaccines refrigerated. The absence or instability of an internet connection is similarly problematic, as it prevents hospitals from keeping electronic medical records and maintaining continuity of care. These are problems USAID hopes to fix, starting with 10,000 hospitals over the next five years.[27] Its vision is both large and long term, and it will require a consortium of other actors.

USAID used to channel the majority of its aid directly to foreign governments, but now the vast majority is distributed through third parties.[28] These parties are responsible for the on-the-ground work in another country. USAID's Health Electrification and Telecommunications project, described earlier, relies substantially on several businesses in the energy sector, including industry giants Apt and Bechtel.[29] In addition to for-profit businesses, USAID also channels funds to individuals, foundations, universities, multilateral organizations, and nonprofit organizations (which include FBOs).

This book investigates foreign aid by looking specifically at the money spent by USAID. These funds go toward projects associated with both humanitarian relief and development assistance, though going forward, I'll follow convention and use the term "development" to refer to both.[30] I also focus my analysis on FBOs as a separate subgroup of nonprofit NGOs. The US government, and USAID specifically, has repeatedly stated that it wishes to engage more with this sector. But what does "engagement" really mean?

Engagement

In 2002, USAID established the Center for Faith-Based and Community Initiatives to "eliminate barriers to faith and community-based organizations" and to "serve as a bridge" between such organizations and the government.[31] It has recently renewed and expanded upon this commitment by instituting its "Partnership Incubator," which, Administrator Samantha Power claims, will help diversify the agency's partnership base. "It is crucial," said Power, "that we engage more frequently and more intensely and sustainably with the broader range of partners."[32] This includes FBOs.

Engagement with USAID can take many forms, but the present analysis is limited to the financial aspect of engagement and looks specifically at the partnerships between FBOs and USAID forged through financial agreements. This is because, unlike other interactions between FBOs and USAID, the exchange of money between the two necessitates an ongoing relationship with multiple touchpoints. There is also greater demonstrated intentionality in entering the relationship since both sides must invest significant time and resources before the official start of a project.

The competitive nature of USAID awards means organizations must apply for funds associated with projects that align with USAID's strategic objectives.[33] Applications can include up to 150 supplemental documents and often require a dedicated team of individuals working overtime to meet deadlines.[34] Successful teams often include legal, accounting, and grant-writing professionals. On the government's side, program officers and technical teams, comprising internal and external experts, evaluate each proposal. Further interactions are required once an organization wins an award to negotiate and finalize terms.[35] Project implementation also requires additional communication and multiple financial transactions.[36] The number and nature of these transactions, as well as the expectations surrounding them, differ depending upon the type of award received.

USAID funds private organizations through three mechanisms: contracts, cooperative agreements, and grants.[37] Contracts are classified as "acquisitions" and are used when an organization wants to directly provide a good or service to USAID. Many of the largest recipients of USAID contracts are for-profit entities providing USAID with consultative or technical services.[38] Generally, interested companies bid for open funding opportunities, and the government selects the most competitive offer.[39] Cooperative agreements and grants are different. Unlike contracts, cooperative agreements and grants fall under the umbrella of "assistance," and they represent USAID's primary funding channel. The work carried out under grants and cooperative agreements directly benefits other countries rather than the US government. The amount of involvement expected of the US government also differs.

With contracts, the US government expects to have regular interactions and to provide technical direction to the fund recipient. With grants and cooperative agreements, recipients remain accountable but enjoy greater autonomy. The government takes a relatively "hands-off" approach with grants and collaborates with the recipients of cooperative agreements in key planning and implementation decisions. A final point of distinction involves the nature and geography of award recipients. In contrast to contracts, which are mostly awarded to US businesses, grants and cooperative agreements are typically carried out by nonprofit organizations that have operations or partners abroad.[40]

In addition to monetary awards, USAID also provides organizations with in-kind food commodities and freight assistance through its Food for Peace Program.[41] This process begins, similar to others, with an organization applying for a specified project. Once the application is accepted, the US government then works with the implementing partner to select appropriate and available commodities. It also arranges shipping to the intended country.[42] The prime distributors of food aid are international organizations and NGOs. Among the latter, FBOs form a distinct subset.

Faith-Based Organizations

The term "faith-based organization," or FBO, officially entered the political lexicon in 2000 when US President George W. Bush introduced the Faith-Based and Community Initiative. While the term has appeared in at least six executive orders across four administrations, it still lacks a legal definition. Academics also have not reached a consensus on the term. Most scholars agree that "faith-based" is a more capacious term than "religious" when describing organizations since the former can cover a broader range of actors, including those not affiliated with or inspired by an established or recognized religious tradition. It can also be perceived as more appropriate for organizations whose operations do not explicitly include religious activities like worship or religious instruction.[43] Nevertheless, some scholars still have an issue with the term. They argue that "faith-based" remains too narrow a descriptor because it fails to encompass the diversity of spiritual beliefs. Thomas Jeavons and Carole Rakodi, for instance, argue that the word "faith" has an inherent Western bias, and Evelyn Bush claims it is likely to preclude specific living, nontraditional religions.[44] Others find the term faith-based organizations too restrictive because it suggests motivation and not a mere affiliation. To include the latter, they suggest using the broader term "faith-related organizations."[45] Practitioners have also weighed in, with the cofounder of Islamic Relief stating that his organization might best be conceived of as a "value-based organization."[46]

This book uses the term faith-based organization, because it is the most commonly accepted term among development scholars and practitioners, and, more importantly, it is part of the nomenclature of USAID.[47] Since USAID does not offer a definition, I adopt the definition advanced by Susan Dicklitch and Heather Rice, who define faith-based NGOs as "non-state actors that have a central religious or faith core to their philosophy, membership, or programmatic."[48]

FBOs represent a wide range of faith traditions, including, but not limited to, Christianity, Islam, Judaism, Buddhism, Baha'ism, Hinduism, and Jainism. Many humanitarian and development organizations also identify as "spiritual" or "multi-religious."[49] There are also a smaller number of organizations associated with indigenous beliefs. In addition to the variation among FBOs in what they believe, FBOs also differ in *how* these beliefs manifest in an organization's funding, structure, staffing, practices, and programs. Depending on how one defines an FBO, it can include everything from a house of worship to an organization financially supported by a religious body to an organization that exists independently from such institutions but is founded upon or currently operates with religious motivations or provides certain services associated with religion.[50] It may require its staff or board to hold certain beliefs, or it may not. Similarly, it may engage in proselytization, or it may subscribe to the adage *acta non verba* and prefer to preach by doing.

The diversity of FBOs has prompted several researchers to develop detailed typologies.[51] Ronald Sider and Heidi Unruh, for instance, delineate the differences among FBOs concerning their expression of faith.[52] They suggest that in lieu of treating faith as a dichotomous variable, researchers should think of faith as a continuous variable. They base their typology on how overtly an FBO expresses its faith and how much its faith identity shapes its everyday operations. The bookends of this continuum are the categories of "faith-permeated" and "secular," and in between are organizations with different levels of expressed faith, including organizations considered "faith-centered," "faith-affiliated," and those that have a "faith background." The finer delineations are made by looking at how faith is reflected in an organization's mission statement and programs and the rules and norms associated with an organization's staff, board, and donors. A few examples serve to illustrate the point:

- *HOPE International* is an international nonprofit that best fits Sider and Unruh's "faith-permeated" category. Founded in 1997 by Christian businessman Jeff Rutt, HOPE began and remains a ministry dedicated to "Helping Other People Eternally." It is avowedly evangelical in its approach to development and does not separate its religious activities or messaging from its financial services. The two are considered integrally linked. Staff members, who are required to be Christian, thus share the Gospel with the same fervor and in the same context as they do business acumen. This is made explicit in HOPE's mission statement and promotional material.[53] Though not affiliated with a specific denomination, HOPE relies heavily upon local churches to facilitate saving groups and financial training.[54] Its operations and microloans are sustained by private donations, and the organization does not rely on public funding. HOPE selects board members who demonstrate a strong Christian faith, and it seeks to build the faith of all those who encounter the organization—from board members to employees to service beneficiaries—through regular prayer and devotions.[55]
- *World ORT* is another example of a "faith-permeated" FBO—though one that does not proselytize. ORT was founded in the 19th century to provide vocational training to Jewish Russians. Its programs now reach over 40 countries, and its focus is primarily on science and technology, yet its fundamental values remain the same. The organization uses education as a conduit to strengthen Jewish identity and community.[56] Like HOPE, ORT's faith is easily identifiable in its mission and messaging. Faith is also the unifying factor among ORT's staff, board, and donors (with the Jewish Foundation of North America being a primary contributor). Its operations and activities are also heavily infused with religion, with both its Jewish and non-Jewish students expected to learn about Jewish history and read from the Hebrew Bible and Talmud.[57]
- *Sarvodaya* (formally the Sarvodaya Shramadana Movement of Sri Lanka) most closely aligns with what Sider and Unruh describe as a "faith-centered" organization. Sarvodaya is a national FBO in Sri Lanka whose mission includes the Total Awakening and Well-being of All. Drawing inspiration from the teachings of the Buddha and Gandhi,

the organization combats wealth inequality and conflict through a network of volunteers who can be of any (or no) faith. Meetings begin with optional meditation.
- *The Indus Hospital and Health Network* (IHHN) is best described as an NGO with a "faith-background." IHHN began as the Indus Hospital with a solitary donated building from the Islamic Mission Trust and now consists of a constellation of medical facilities across Pakistan. IHHN's mission statement explains that its facilities provide free medical care in the name of Allah, and the majority of its donations come from individual donors in the form of Zakat.[58] Unlike many faith-permeated and faith-centered organizations, however, IHHN does not include an individual's faith among its hiring criteria and does not expect its nearly 10,000 staff members to engage in spiritual practices or training. IHHN also does not offer separate spiritual services or intertwine religious programs or activities with its medical operations.[59]

The organizations mentioned earlier are representative but not inclusive of the universe of FBOs, and Sider and Unruh admit that their typology does not neatly accommodate all FBOs. As a result, they suggest their framework is best conceived of as a spectrum. "The reality," says Sider and Unruh, "is that many organizations and programs will fall in the gray area between the types or will combine elements of different categories."[60] In fact, many of the world's largest development FBOs reside somewhere between the "faith-permeated" and "faith-centered" categories or between "faith-centered" and "faith-background." This includes organizations whose mission statements or names clearly include religious wording but who offer secular services, such as Islamic Relief, the Mennonite Central Committee, Christian Aid, Catholic Relief Services, World Vision International, the Aga Khan Foundation, and Caritas Internationalis.[61]

The diversity of FBOs makes a common definition difficult, and operationalization more difficult still. As a result, some eschew the quandary altogether. USAID, for instance, has historically not attempted to identify FBOs among its applicants or fund recipients.[62] As a result, we lack aggregate information on the number of FBOs USAID has partnered with, the number of grants and cooperative agreements USAID has distributed to FBOs and the amount of money USAID has provided to FBOs. When the Government Accountability Office (GAO) wanted answers to this effect, it had to conduct independent research. More specifically, the GAO examined the list of USAID award recipients and identified FBOs by reviewing organization websites, mission statements, aims, and values to see if they directly mentioned a religious affiliation or used religious terminology.[63]

Christopher Scheitle suggests this kind of content analysis can be ideal for researching FBOs, not least because mission statements and similar verbiage are less likely to change than other online text.[64] It can also be more objective than an individual's survey or interview response. At the same time, this methodology has its limitations. Relying on an external text, like a website, to determine an organization's religious identity runs the risk of both over- and under-inclusion or committing a type I and type II error, respectively. If a researcher employs strict textual analysis, for instance, they may fallaciously identify organizations like the Red Cross, which is decidedly secular, as an FBO due to "cross" being in the organization's name and online material. One could also incorrectly code an organization as Jewish if its online statements reference Jews when, in fact, the organization is secular and only involves issues relating to ethnic Jews. A similar error can occur in situations where an organization's website references a *previous* religious motivation or affiliation of the organization. In such cases, strict textual analysis could lead one to misclassify an organization as an FBO, when, in fact, the organization no longer considers itself faith-based.

In general, as Evelyn Bush points out, the problem of possible over-inclusion in identifying FBOs via content analysis is largely ameliorated by careful coding.[65] One can train researchers to be mindful and attentive to context. The error of under-inclusion is more difficult to correct. Not all FBOs disclose their religious association online. In some cases, this may be because doing so would present a security risk, such as when organizations operate in environments more hostile or suspicious of religion.[66] In other cases, secular verbiage may be adopted to appease specific organization constituencies. Research by Ebaugh et al. suggests strict textual analysis is likely to capture at least 80% of FBOs.[67] Other methods that may allow for greater representation include analyzing website imagery and examining an organization's board composition.[68] If one can gain access to internal documents, such as an organization's annual reports, this, too, could help discern an organization's faith status.

Another way to identify FBOs is to rely upon self-identification via surveys or interviews, yet this approach also has problems. One issue is that an organization may be sensitive to accepting the label of being "faith-based"—especially to a researcher with whom they do not have an established relationship. Faith and religion, generally, can be sensitive subjects, and sometimes it is perceived that the label could hurt an organization's chances for funding.[69] (This perception is tested in Chapter 5 and discussed further in Chapter 6.) Moreover, since there is sometimes a stigma in international development against organizations that proselytize, a development organization otherwise motivated by or affiliated with religion may eschew being called "faith-based" in an attempt to disassociate with organizations that evangelize.[70] A final issue with relying upon individual respondents to identify FBOs is that, unlike an organization's mission statement, the responses one receives using this methodology may vary depending on the individual. One person may believe the organization qualifies as an FBO, while another may not.

The lack of a common definition of FBOs or a common standard in their operationalization does not mean that modern scholars must begin de novo. Instead, they can and should build upon and refine the work of others. They can also mix methods. This is the approach I take in this book, using online content analysis to identify the FBOs accepting USAID funds and using survey self-identification to hear from FBOs who have not received USAID funds. The next section details my process in more detail.

Methodology

This book addresses the question of FBO–USAID engagement using a mixed-method approach. More specifically, I use online coding, surveys, and interviews to tell the story of who among FBOs applies for USAID funding and who does not, what they generally receive and when, and how funded FBOs perceive their relationship with USAID. The final narrative is the product of research collected from coding over 3,000 organization websites, surveying over 400 NGOs, and interviewing 44 FBOs.[71] The process involved three imbricated stages.

The first stage involved using quantitative content analysis to code the websites of nonprofit USAID award recipients. This is the same approach taken by the GAO and other researchers to identify FBOs.[72] For our purposes, the initial list was acquired from USASpending.gov, a website that houses all US major federal contracts, grants, and cooperative agreements.[73] The list contained all USAID assistance above $25,000 provided to nonprofits between 2008 and 2021. The information included, inter alia, the amount promised and provided to each organization, the date the amount was awarded, the reason for the award, primary geographic information associated with award activity, and the name and address of the implementing organization. I also culled a list of subprime awards for the same years, though this information was not required to be entered until 2010.[74]

Once the lists were organized and cleaned, over two dozen student researchers were trained on how to identify FBOs using online content analysis and provided a common codebook. Each student coded several hundred organizations over several weeks. This involved them locating an organization's website and then using the codebook to identify the presence or absence of specific keywords in an organization's mission and values statements.[75] Table 1.1 shows nine different codes for faith affiliation, each with operational definitions and a specific word list.

In addition to identifying FBOs based on strict textual analysis, researchers also considered website imagery, including organization logos and images appearing on an organization's homepage. The codebook provided visual examples to aid students in this endeavor. Upon the conclusion of coding, the primary investigator reviewed all organizations identified as FBOs to confirm their inclusion in the study.

Table 1.1 Specified Terms for Identifying the Religious Status of USAID-Funded Organizations

Code	*Religious Affiliation*	*Words*
30	Secular	Absence of any of the below references
40	Secular with religious roots	Religious reference only in a historical context (i.e., "Founded by missionaries in 1990 …")
41	Jewish	Jewish[a], Judaism, Jewry, Torah, Halakha, Tanakh, Haredi, synagogue
42	Buddhist	Buddhism, Mahayana, Vajrayana, Theravada, Sanskrit, Buddha, sangha, shingon
43	Islamic	Allah, Islam, Quran, Muslim, Sharia, Sunni, Sunnah, Muhammad, Moslem, shahada, Imam, Sufi (Sufism), Taswwuf
44	Christian	Christian, Bible, Gospels, Christ, Jesus, Cross, Scripture, Baptist, Disciple, Evangelical, Apostle, Protestant, Catholic, Pentecostal, Episcopalian, Evangelical, Presbyterian, Anglican, Lutheran, Quaker, Nazarene, Seventh-Day Adventists (Adventists), Coptic[a], ecumenical, nondenominational, church, Bible verse, scripture, Holy Spirit, Reformation, apostolate
45	Spiritually Ambiguous/ Indigenous	God, Monotheism, polytheism, Lord, Deity, the Divine/Divinity, Spirit, Heaven, Angel, Meditation, holy, divine, mystical, faith, faith-based (language indicating animal or ancestor worship)
46	Hindu	Hinduism, Dharma, Vishnu, Shakti, Veda, Upanishad, Bhakti
47	Interfaith	Multi-religious, interfaith, interreligious, or includes two or more terms identified with codes 41–44.

Note: [a]Organizations whose websites mentioned "Coptic" or "Jewish" were further evaluated by the Primary Investigator to distinguish if the organization considered these in religious or strictly in ethnic/cultural terms.

Coding FBOs among USAID's grant recipients allowed me to aggregate and analyze the data to reveal funding trends. These trends are discussed further in Chapter 4. It also posed further questions. Why, for instance, do FBOs comprise 13% of all NGOs receiving USAID assistance when they comprise 59% of the US-based NGOs involved in international development?[76] To answer this question, further analysis was necessary.

The second stage involved conducting pilot phone calls and fielding an online survey to find out why FBOs were *not* applying for USAID funds.[77] Since a complete list of FBOs in development does not exist, a team of student researchers worked from a general list of NGOs in development obtained courtesy of Guidestar (now Candid).[78] This list included all US-based nonprofit organizations registered with the Internal Revenue Service (IRS) under the National Tax-Exempt Entities (NTEE) Code of Q for which there was available contact information in the database.[79] A "Q" code is associated with organizations involved in "International Affairs, Foreign Affairs, or National Security" and includes the subcategories of international development and relief services, international human rights, global peace and security, and the promotion of international understanding.

Student researchers conducting the pilot phone survey contacted 304 organizations and completed 57 phone surveys in the fall of 2018. The data from these calls helped refine the online surveys that were emailed to organizations in the spring and summer of 2019.[80] Approximately 2,200 organizations were contacted and 405 organizations responded to our survey, with screener questions eliminating those that were outside our sampling frame.[81] Our FBO responses suggest that, in addition to the general obstacles facing development vis-à-vis obtaining government funds (such as the administrative burden of applying for and managing funds), faith-based development organizations also avoid funds because they perceive they might be discriminated against due to their religious nature, or their acceptance of funds would lead to the loss of donors or the shift of their religious mission.

In the third stage, we sought to test these assumptions by contacting organizations that had accepted USAID funds to discuss their experiences. Two student researchers and I undertook the first phase of the project, interviewing a total of 34 organizations.[82] Another ten organizations were interviewed in a second phase to ensure greater representativity.[83] The interviews consisted of approximately ten open-ended questions and took approximately 20–50 minutes, depending upon the length of respondent answers. Individuals were contacted via both phone and email and interviewed via Zoom. Most of the individuals interviewed represented high-level executives at their organization. Organizations interviewed varied significantly in terms of size, program area, and area served. (These details are provided in Chapter 5.)

While diverse in many respects, the organization representatives I had the opportunity to speak with all expressed appreciation for someone listening to their perspective. My research is about amplifying their voices and sharing their stories. It is also about leaning in and better understanding how FBOs are engaging with USAID. I do this by tracking and analyzing the financial data and also using surveys and interviews to fill in the gaps. The picture that emerges is important for everyone to see, including those in academia, government, and development.

Importance

This book presents both quantitative and qualitative data on USAID's FBO partnerships. Both types of data are crucial to telling the whole story, and the entire story is important for several reasons. First, since no comprehensive FBO funding data currently exists for USAID, this book fills a significant gap in the religions and development literature. It also provides practitioners and government officials with data that helps to clarify the current state of religious engagement at USAID. In addition to contributing necessary information to a critical conversation, this book also serves the important function of potentially correcting current misunderstandings that may be stymieing future engagement between FBOs and USAID. It does this in two ways: by showing government officials some of the nonlegal barriers keeping FBOs from applying for government funds and by sharing with the FBOs that have not yet considered or sought USAID funds more information about what engagement might look like from the perspective of other faith-based implementing partners.

The first and primary contribution of this volume is the financial data it presents. In an article immediately following USAID's 2021 Summit on Strategic Religious Engagement, Katherine Marshall, Sudipta Roy, Chris Seiple, and Hugo Slim emphasized that researchers were still no closer to having comprehensive quantitative data on USAID's financial flows to FBOs. This remains, they said, one of the "important [unanswered] questions." Why does such information matter? Because without it, there is no transparency and accountability. If no published data is available on the extent to which the US government partners with FBOs to deliver foreign aid, then we lack even a baseline indicator of USAID's efforts to engage with FBOs. Worse still, the lack of empirical data leaves room for policymakers and leaders (well-meaning and otherwise) to take license in their descriptions of the government's current engagement efforts. Lee Marsden describes how this played out in the early years of the Faith-Based Initiative under Bush. "Different figures are quoted to different audiences," he said, "for example, when seeking to attract applications from FBOs ... considerable emphasis is placed [by administrative officials] on the 'extra' resources available."[84] In fact, Marsden says that FBOs were applying for the same funds as secular NGOs. Similar criticism followed the Bush administration's first comprehensive report on faith-based funding, which some amounted to nothing more than "a lot of smoke and mirrors."[85] By presenting the financial data for FBO funding over the past 20 years, this book adds clarity to the conversation.

Having accurate numbers makes obfuscation more difficult. This is true in policy as well as scholarship. Katherine Marshall elaborates: "Data on the overall level of financial flows both from and to religious institutions and communities are especially incomplete," leading sometimes to a "muddiness of estimates" and "lack of solid consensus" among scholars.[86] Solid information on the funds channeled to FBOs would help build consensus and advance further research on FBOs. For example, if we know that FBOs comprise 13% of all USAID-funded nonprofit organizations, we are then in a position to ask why more do not apply, and we can develop and test select hypotheses. We also have data that is ripe for comparative analysis since USAID is not the only state aid agency to try to engage FBOs.[87]

In addition to filling a gap in the literature, this book also provides a necessary corrective to the common portrayal of religious engagement. When USAID and others speak of "strategic religious engagement," for example, the emphasis is placed on USAID engaging with religious (faith-based) actors rather than the other way around. But a relationship involves two people. FBOs also have agency. They, too, have a perspective. They have a choice. As a result, says Olivia Wilkinson, the Director of Research for the Joint Learning Initiative on Faith and Local Communities, one should not only inquire about how USAID engages FBOs but also ask how FBOs engage with USAID.[88] There is less scholarship focusing on this aspect of the relationship and more is needed.

The scholarly contributions of this book are supplemented by its practical import. FBOs are no longer sidelined in development, but, in some cases, thrust into the limelight. Put another way, one scholar noted: "If you want to get ahead in international development policy today, you've got to use the F-word: faith-based."[89] USAID and many other development donors now prioritize engaging faith-based actors, yet *how* to best achieve this is unclear. The information revealed in this book indicates that USAID only partners with a minority of the FBOs involved in international development. It also shows that engaging more FBOs may require addressing some of the assumptions some FBOs hold. This includes the perception that the acceptance of government funds would result in a loss of individual donors and the perception that funds come with conditions that may force an organization to compromise its religious beliefs. If USAID seeks to engage more faith-based partners, knowing these concerns and working to assuage them would benefit its efforts. On the other side of the equation, the FBOs who have such concerns could benefit from reading the experiences of other FBOs who have already worked with USAID on development or humanitarian relief projects. This presents them with more information with which to choose whether or not to engage with USAID.

Approach

This book amplifies the voice of FBOs through social scientific research. Through survey data, I share why many FBOs choose not to pursue government funding. I am also able, through personal interviews, to tell the stories of the organizations that choose to partner with the government. The book is structured as follows: Chapter 2 situates the case of the United States in the broader global story of religion and development. It discusses the separate yet parallel efforts of faith-based actors and organizations and public development donors in the latter half of the 20th century and how the second millennium saw the two merge and religion resurge. It also explains how America's efforts at religious engagement are not sui generis but represent only one example of a broader international trend that has taken hold of many state and multilateral aid organizations in the 21st century.

Chapter 3 supplements the breadth of the preceding chapter with a necessary in-depth discussion of the domestic context of religious engagement in the United States. It begins by recounting the United States' early partnerships with religious organizations in aid and tracks the money that flowed to these organizations in the late 20th century. It then discusses the details of President George W. Bush's Faith-Based and Community Initiative and its manifestation at USAID. While the United States' efforts were not altogether dissimilar from those of other states, the chapter shows that the United States *was* unique in the domestic controversy it faced in light of FBO funding. This stemmed in large part from America's constitutional doctrine regarding the separation of church and state and its polarizing politics. As the chapter explains, many scholars, policymakers, and practitioners called into question whether the US Constitution permitted the government to fund FBOs at all, and the Court had to be the final arbiter. Others found qualms with what they saw to be the political agenda of FBO funding. (A debate this book helps settle with data.) There were also critiques specific to how funded FBOs shaped US foreign policy. The chapter outlines these various debates in more detail.

Chapter 4 outlines USAID's FBO funding by first reviewing and synthesizing the available data on USAID's funding of FBOs under the Bush administration and then presenting original FBO-funding data for 2008–2021. It shows that the Faith-Based Initiative and the subsequent regulatory changes at USAID led the agency to fund a greater number of FBOs and that USAID has continued to partner with FBOs over the past 20 years, with no measured differences between presidential administrations. Still, the total number of USAID-funded FBOs, especially relative to the number of USAID's secular partners, remains low. It is also clear that USAID partners with only a minority of the development FBOs in the United States.

Chapter 5 seeks to better understand this discrepancy using empirical evidence from a survey of over 400 NGOs involved in humanitarian assistance and international development. The collected data reveals there is likely an underrepresentation of FBOs among US government award recipients *and* applicants, suggesting that FBOs differ from secular organizations in their willingness to apply for government funds. When asked why this was the case, the most commonly expressed concern among the surveyed FBOs was the perception of anti-religious government bias. A lesser number of FBOs also expressed concerns about the perceived negative effects of government funding, including the potential loss of organizational autonomy, diminution of an organization's religious mission and identity, and exit of individual donors.

Chapter 6 examines what evidence is available to support these fears. I interviewed 44 FBO representatives and asked if they have ever experienced government discrimination or if they have experienced mission drift or loss of donors due to accepting government funds for development projects. Many of the FBOs interviewed indicated they had an overall positive experience working with USAID, though they also shared some of their frustrations and recommendations for improving future partnerships.

The final chapter summarizes the book's primary findings and explores how the value of FBOs has manifested in the context of the COVID-19 pandemic. It also discusses the value USAID brings to FBOs, again using COVID-19 as an example. It examines USAID's 2023 Strategic Religious Engagement Policy and provides further recommendations informed by the FBOs surveyed and interviewed.

Notes

1 While the top contributor of aid in terms of volume, the United States ranks considerably lower (25th in 2022) when considering aid as a share of gross national income. Organisation for Economic Cooperation and Development (OECD, 2023), Net ODA (indicator). DOI:10.1787/33346549-en, accessed August 21, 2023.
2 ForeignAssistance.gov.
3 A 2022 Development Engagement Lab Survey revealed that 67% of Americans favor foreign aid, with 53% supporting maintaining or increasing US foreign aid spending and only 34% expressing a desire to decrease aid spending. Fergal Raftery and Jennifer Hudson, "Foreign Aid and America's Middle Class," *Development Compass*, February 25, 2022, https://developmentcompass.org/blog/campaigning/foreign-aid-and-america-s-middle-class
4 Results from the 2018 General Social Survey reveal that while individuals identifying as religious are slightly more likely than those without a religious affiliation to think America spends too much on foreign aid, those holding this viewpoint remain in the minority. Across all religious affiliations, most individuals aver that America should continue to maintain or even increase its foreign aid spending. Smith, "General Social Survey, 2018." Moreover, a 2017 National Association of Evangelicals survey revealed that 95% of evangelical leaders believed the United States should continue foreign aid for the extreme poor. See "US Should Continue Foreign Aid," *National Association of Evangelicals*, April 2017. www.nae.org/u-s-continue-foreign-aid/
5 Following his "America First" policy, President Trump proposed cutting foreign aid in 2017, 2018, 2019, 2020, and 2021. Proposed reductions ranged from slightly over a quarter to a little less than one-third of obligated funding. Morgenstern et al., "Selected Trump Administration Foreign Aid Priorities," 2.
6 "100+ Christian Leaders Tell Congressional Leadership: Protect Foreign Assistance," March 16, 2017, *World Vision*, www.worldvision.org/about-us/media-center/100-christian-leaders-tell-congressional-leadership-protect-foreign-assistance
7 Ibid.
8 This included the president of the National Hispanic Christian Leadership Conference, Samuel Rodriguez as well as Cardinal Timothy Dolan. Kate Shellnut, "Evangelical Leaders Challenge Trump's 'America First' Budget," *Christianity Today*, March 16, 2017, www.christianitytoday.com/news/2017/march/evangelical-leaders-trump-america-first-budget-foreign-aid.html

9 Some of the humanitarian relief organizations represented include Habitat for Humanity, World Vision International, Catholic Relief Services, Compassion International, World Relief, Medical Teams International, the Mennonite Central Committee, Living Water International, Food for the Hungry, MAP International, World Renew, and Convoy of Hope.

10 Heist and Cnaan, "Faith-Based International Development Work," 9.

11 Chapter 4 details the underlying data. The full dataset is available in Lipscomb University's Carolyn Wilson Digital Collections at https://digitalcollections.lipscomb.edu/hpp_fac/1/.

12 George Walker Bush, "President Bush Attends Office of Faith-Based and Community Initiatives' National Conference" (Omni Shoreham Hotel Washington, DC, June 26, 2008). The White House. Office of the Press Secretary. https://georgewbush-whitehouse.archives.gov/news/releases/2008/06/20080626-20.html

13 On the limitations of FBOs, see Lipsky, "Evaluating the Strength of Faith," 26.

14 FBOs, because of their faith, can sometimes have greater access to places than secular organizations. This can be for security reasons (i.e., operating in Afghanistan under the Taliban) or due to physical infrastructure (with FBOs located in more remote areas, far away from access roads). For example, see "Missed Again: Making Space for Partnership in the Typhoon Haiyan Response" (London: Christian Aid; CAFOD; Oxfam GB; Tearfund; Action Aid, 2014), https://shorturl.at/ijrB0; Wilkinson et al., "Faith in Localisation?" 4.

15 Marshall, Roy, Seiple, and Slim, "Intrinsic and Strategic Leverage of Religion," 34.

16 This was among the first identified strengths of FBOs, initially disclosed by the World Bank in its "Voices of the Poor" study. The study showed that those in the world's poorest countries were generally more inclined to trust religious organizations than governments or secular organizations. Narayan and Petesch, *Voices of the Poor*, 94; a Gallup survey similarly found that in sub-Saharan Africa, 82% of people trust religious organizations over secular organizations. Jones and Petersen, "Instrumental, Narrow, Normative?" 1305.

17 Phillips, "One Year Later," 100.

18 Phillips was appointed to this position by President Joe Biden and served from March 2021 to September 2023. The Local, Faith, and Transformative Partnership Hub is one of five hubs under USAID's Bureau for Development, Democracy, and Innovation.

19 United States Agency for International Development (USAID), "Building Bridges in Development."

20 The formal definition, as provided by the US Foreign Assistance Act of 1961, is

> any tangible or intangible item provided by the United States Government [including "by means of gift, loan, sale, credit, or guaranty"] to a foreign country or international organization under this or any other Act, including but not limited to any training, service, or technical advice, any item of real, personal, or mixed property, any agricultural commodity, United States dollars, and any currencies of any foreign country which are owned by the United States Government.
>
> (§634(b))

21 USAID spent over $41 billion in foreign aid in 2022, compared to the $11 billion spent by the State Department, $3.75 billion spent by the Treasury Department,

and $2 billion spent by the Department of Health and Human Services. All other federal agencies involved in dispensing foreign aid handled amounts in the millions. Data retrieved from ForeignAssistance.gov.

22 Data from ForeignAssistance.gov.

23 United States Agency for International Development, "Fact Sheet #5: Ukraine – Complex Emergency," December 23, 2022, www.usaid.gov/sites/default/files/2022-12/2022-12-23_USG_Ukraine_Complex_Emergency_Fact_Sheet_5.pdf

24 Data from ForeignAssistance.gov.

25 The United States also uses development assistance to promote neoliberal economic and political policies.

26 "Power Africa Announces More Than a Dozen New Partners to Electrify 10,000 Health Facilities Across sub-Saharan Africa," Office of Press Relations, USAID, December 12, 2022, www.usaid.gov/news-information/press-releases/dec-14-2022-power-africa-announces-more-dozen-new-partners-electrify-10000-health-facilities-across-sub-saharan-africa

27 Ibid.

28 The United States spent only $199 million in direct government-to-government aid transfers in 2022. United States Agency for International Development, "Moving Toward a Model of Locally Led Development, FY 2022 Localization Progress Report," 5. www.usaid.gov/sites/default/files/2023-06/FY%202022%20Localization%20Progress%20Report-June-12-23_vFINAL_1.pdf

29 "Power Africa Announces More Than a Dozen New Partners to Electrify 10,000 Health Facilities Across sub-Saharan Africa."

30 This follows the convention of the OECD, which defines "Official Development Assistance" (ODA) as "flows of official financing administered with the promotion of economic development *and welfare* of developing countries as the main objective, and which are concessional in character with a grant element of at least 25%" (ital. added). This is taken to include humanitarian aid but excludes military assistance. OECD Glossary of Statistical Terms. https://doi.org/10.1787/9789264055087-en

31 USAID, "U.S. Agency for International Development Administrator Mark Green's Remarks at the Ministerial to Advance Religious Freedom," July 26, 2018. www.usaid.gov/news-information/press-releases/ jul-26-2018-usaid-administrator-mark-green-remarks-ministerial-advance-religious-freedom

32 United States Agency for International Development, "Administrator Samantha Power on a New Vision for Global Development," November 4, 2021, Georgetown University, Washington, DC. www.usaid.gov/news-information/speeches/nov-04-2021-administrator-samantha-power-new-vision-global-development

33 USAID's five strategic objectives are peace and security, investing in people, governing justly and democratically, economic growth, and humanitarian assistance.

34 Siobhan McDonough, "The US Spends Billions on Foreign Aid. But It Doesn't Know How Much Good Our Money Is Doing," *Vox*, August 1, 2022, www.vox.com/future-perfect/23274306/usaid-foreign-aid-effectiveness-evidence-grants

35 The Automated Directive System (ADS), Chapter 300: 303.3.6.1 "Eligibility Requirements."

36 Justin Sandefur, "USAID Localization by the Numbers," Center for Global Development, November 17, 2022, www.cgdev.org/blog/usaid-localization-numbers

37 These are outlined in the Federal Grant and Cooperative Agreement Act (31 U.S.C. 6301–08). Most USAID assistance to private organizations takes the form of direct funding, though it also provides noncash assistance in the form of food and freight assistance (PL 480).

38 Though most contracted organizations are for-profit, nonprofit organizations are eligible to apply. Rules governing contract eligibility and conditions include the Federal Acquisition Regulation (FAR), USAID's Supplement to the FAR (AIDAR), and USAID's Policy – ADS 302.

39 This is typically done in response to a formal request for proposals (RFP), though USAID accepts a limited number of unsolicited proposals.

40 Most of these remain US-based, though USAID seeks geographic diversity. More specifically, USAID's localization agenda (discussed more in Chapter 7) prioritizes partnerships with non-US-based NGOs local to the areas they serve. On the number of US-based USAID partners, see Sandefur, "USAID Localization by the Numbers.

41 This program is authorized under the Food for Peace Act of 1954 (FFPA; PL 83–480), which provides that funds be requested by the Department of Agriculture and administered by USAID.

42 The Agricultural Cargo Preference (ACP) requires at least 50% of US food aid commodities ship on US-flag vessels.

43 Walker et al. emphasize that the term "religious" is most often used to describe organizations associated with the Abrahamitic faiths of Christianity, Judaism, and Islam. There is also the perception among some that a "religious organization" engages specifically and perhaps exclusively in teaching or ministry. This is the observation Ajaz Ahmed Khan makes of surveyed Muslim donors, which I also found evidence for in my surveys (discussed in more detail in Chapter 5). Walker, Mazurana, Warren, Scarlett, and Louis, "Chapter Five: The Role of Spirituality in Humanitarian Crisis Survival and Recovery," 117; Khan, "Chapter Four: Religious Obligation or Altruistic Giving?" 107; Bush, "What Is a Religious NGO?" 265–266.

44 Jeavons, "Religious and Faith-Based Organizations," 141; Rakodi, "Religion and Development," 640; Bush, "What Is a Religious NGO?" 265–266.

45 Smith and Sosin, "The Varieties of Faith-Related Agencies." Other terms also appear for FBOs outside of the development literature. Ebaugh, Chafetz, and Pipes, for example, examine what they call "faith-based social service coalitions," defined as those that self-identify as faith-based but that do not necessarily affiliate with a religious congregation (2006, 382).

46 Benthall, "Chapter Three: 'Cultural Proximity' and the Conjecture of Islam with Modern Humanitarianism," 84.

47 Jones and Petersen contend that the use of "faith-based organization" is so ubiquitous in international development and nonprofit studies that it should be considered a "relatively unproblematic category." Jones and Petersen, "Instrumental, Narrow, Normative?" 1298.

48 Dicklitch and Rice. "The Mennonite Central Committee (MCC) and Faith-Based NGO Aid to Africa," 662; I prefer this definition to the more commonly used definition used by Clarke and Jennings because it is slightly more inclusive. Clarke and Jennings define FBOs as "any organisation that derives inspiration and guidance for its activities from the teachings and principles of the faith or from a particular interpretation or school of thought within that faith." Clarke and Jennings, *Development, Civil Society and Faith-Based Organizations*, 6.

49 Berger, "Religious Nongovernmental Organizations," 15.
50 Some scholars exclude congregations from the definition of an FBO. Jeavons, "Religious and Faith-Based Organizations," 144.
51 Monsma, *When Sacred and Secular Mix*; Monsma, "Non-Profit and Faith-Based Welfare-to-Work Programs"; Clarke, "Faith Matters"; Clarke, "Faith-Based Organizations and International Development"; Olarinmoye, "Faith-Based Organizations and Development."
52 Sider and Unruh, "Typology of Religious Characteristics of Social Service."
53 HOPE International, homepage, www.hopeinternational.org, accessed September 5, 2022.
54 HOPE International, "What We Do," www.hopeinternational.org/what-we-do, accessed September 5, 2022.
55 While it seeks to convert people to Christianity, HOPE does not make loans or participation in its program contingent upon conversion. It provides services to people of all faiths and races.
56 Tova Kantrowitz, "Education for Life": World ORT head Dan Green describes priorities, challenges of past two years, *Jewish News Syndicate*, January 12, 2022, www.jns.org/education-for-life-world-ort-head-dan-green-describes-priorities-challenges-of-past-two-years/
57 ORT America, "Enriching Jewish Experience," Information Sheet, https://ortamerica.org/wp-content/uploads/2021/08/JewishExp-2pg-Flyer-final.pdf
58 Zakat is the charitable obligation of all Muslims set forth in the Quran, and it constitutes the third of the five pillars of Islam. Contributions vary depending upon individual wealth and primarily go toward other indigent and destitute Muslims, with the specific conditions of eligibility delineated in Surat Al-Tawbah, 9:60. Indus Hospital and Health Networks Financial Statements for the Fiscal Year Ended June 30, 2022, https://indushospital.org.pk/wp-content/uploads/2023/05/Audited-Financial-Statements-2021-22.pdf
59 The peripheral position of the Islamic faith in IHHN operations is exemplified by its scant attention in the organization's most recent annual report, which is mentioned once in the report's introductory letter. See the Indus Hospital and Health Network Annual Report, 2021–2022, https://indushospital.org.pk/wp-content/uploads/2023/08/AR_2021-22.pdf
60 Sider and Unruh, "Typology of Religious Characteristics of Social Service," 119.
61 All of these organizations, though they employ a majority of co-religionists, primarily focus on the universalist provision of humanitarian and disaster relief and avoid proselytization. However, some, like Islamic Relief, may also offer services or goods more specifically geared toward co-religionists, such as the processing and canning of meat sacrificed during the Islamic month of *Dhul Hijjah* for the poor and delivering iftar meals during Ramadan.
62 There is a request for "business type" which derives from the System for Award Management (SAM) data and includes values A-X assigned, corresponding with State Government, County Government, City or Township Government, Special District Government, Regional Organization, US Territory or Possession, Independent School District, Public/State Controlled Institution of Higher Education, Federally Recognized Indian/Native American Tribal Government, Indian/Native American Tribal Government, Indian/Native American Tribal Designated Organization, Public/Indian Housing Authority, 501C3 Nonprofit, non-501C3 Nonprofit, Private Institution of Higher Education, Individual, For-Profit Organization, Small Business, Hispanic-serving Institution, Historically

Black College or University, Tribally Controlled College or University, Alaska Native and Native Hawaiian Serving Institutions, Non-domestic Entity, and Other. Codes are not mutually exclusive except when specified. "Faith-based organization" is not included.

63 General Accounting Office, "Foreign Assistance," Appendix I.

64 Scheitle, "Chapter Seven: From Documents to Data," 215.

65 Bush, "What Is a Religious NGO?" 266.

66 Hopgood and Vinjamuri, "Chapter Two: Faith in Markets," 58.

67 Ebaugh, Pipes, Chafetz, and Daniels, "Where's the Religion?" 422.

68 Scheitle, "Chapter Seven: From Documents to Data," 2017.

69 Tomalin, "Thinking about Faith-Based Organisations in Development," 694.

70 This bias is due, in part, to the prohibition against proselytization included in the Code of Conduct of the International Red Cross and Red Crescent Movement and NGOs in Disaster Relief, drawn up in the mid-1990s. Among the Code of Conduct's signatories are Catholic Relief Services, Caritas Internationalis, and the Lutheran World Federation. I encountered this also in my survey of NGOs (explored more in Chapter 5) when a respondent selected that their organization was best described as "faith-based," but they clarified in the comments that they did not fund "evangelizing projects."

71 The total number of coded organizations was actually over 10,000 since the project initially hoped to include an analysis of USAID's subprime recipients. However, this data was found to be too unreliable to include in the study.

72 General Accounting Office, "Foreign Assistance"; Ebaugh, Pipes, Chafetz, and Daniels, "Where's the Religion?"; Vander Zaag, "Canadian Faith-Based Development NGOs and CIDA Funding"; Schroeder, "Religion and Secularism in Development: Trends in the Approaches of Bilateral Donors in Canada and the United Kingdom." This method is also employed by MinistryWatch.com, a watchdog group that publishes reports for Christian donors. The site lists "legitimate" FBOs by reviewing mission statements and memberships in Evangelical organizations. Hopgood and Vinjamuri, "Chapter Two: Faith in Markets," 46.

73 The Federal Funding Accountability and Transparency Act 2006 (FFATA) required this information to be published online by January 2008.

74 USAID mandated all prime award recipients to report certain subawards and subcontracts in the Subaward Reporting System (FSRS) created under the Federal Funding Accountability and Transparency Act of 2006. The subprime data, though analyzed, is not included in this study due to it being found unreliable.

75 Researchers generally followed the same process for primary fund recipients (primes) and secondary recipients (subprimes). However, since the subprime list generally includes smaller organizations, researchers were allowed to reference sources other than websites, such as social media pages, when a website could not be located. With both the prime and subprime lists, if a researcher encountered an inactive URL, they were instructed to use the Wayback Machine to find and code an archived version of the website. If they encountered a website in a language other than English, every attempt was made to have a student fluent in that language code the website. Alternatively, students would rely upon the organization's secondary translated website. As a last resort, they used Google Translate.

76 This calculation excludes multilateral and undisclosed award recipients.

77 This survey was developed over the course of a semester in the fall of 2018 with myself and a team of students conducting a pilot telephone survey to a selected

sample of Q code organizations. Of the 57 completed phone interviews, 43 respondents self-identified as secular, and 14 self-identified as religious. Answers provided in this phase of the project helped generate testable hypotheses regarding the relationship between international secular NGOs, FBOs, and US government funding.

78 Guidestar, a nonprofit company that provided public and subscriber access to information for over two million US nonprofits, merged with the Foundation Center in February 2019 to form Candid. My contact list, provided by Guidestar in 2018, included all US-based nonprofit organizations registered with the IRS under the NTEE Code of Q for which there was available contact information in the database. (A "Q" code is associated with organizations involved in "International Affairs, Foreign Affairs, or National Security." Subcodes under this broader category include international development and relief services, international human rights, global peace and security, and the promotion of international understanding.) This list excludes congregations and organizations with gross receipts under $50,000, both of which are exempt from IRS filing requirements.

79 Our selection method likely excludes any FBO considered "an integrated auxiliary of a church" because such organizations are exempt from filing IRS 990 forms. FBOs fitting this description might be closely connected to a church body, incorporated within a religious denomination, or separately incorporated but still closely related to a religious sect. FBOs that identify themselves as religious but operate independently are not exempt and thus included in the study.

80 Since the Guidestar data did not include email addresses, students collected these independently using the information provided.

81 Using procedures recommended by the American Association of Public Opinion Research, the survey eligibility rate was 89%. Based on the survey eligibility rate, the survey response rate was 16%. Examples of organizations that were outside our sampling frame are those that focus primarily on domestic issues (and must have selected an incorrect NTEE code when filing their IRS 990 form) and those that focus on international issues but do so without having offices overseas (such as organizations dedicated to increasing awareness of international issues in the United States or those involved in lobbying for global issues). I pulled another seven surveys from the final analysis because the respondent indicated the organization pursued ministry exclusively (and therefore should have indicated "X" on their IRS form rather than "Q").

82 The two student researchers interviewed a total of nine organizations as a part of their senior seminar projects.

83 Thirty-four organizations were contacted in the summer of 2020, and an additional ten organizations in the summer of 2022 to have better representation from non-Christian organizations. The second phase benefited substantially from a Centennial Center Summer Research Grant from the American Political Science Association. In both rounds of interviews, organizations were contacted first by email and phone and informed of the intent and scope of the study and the reason for their organization's inclusion. This information was provided verbally, if possible, and always in written form within a consent document.

84 Marsden, "Bush, Obama and a Faith-Based US Foreign Policy," 964.

85 Alan Cooperman, "Bush Touts Grants to Religious Charities," *Washington Post*, March 10, 2006. www.washingtonpost.com/archive/politics/2006/03/10/bush-touts-grants-to-religious-charities/87c3f0d2-29df-43c4-a1a7-2d57cffcb985/

86 Marshall, "Impressions & Indications of Religious Engagement in Development," 20.
87 The aid agencies of Germany, Canada, Switzerland, the Netherlands, Denmark, and Sweden, for instance, all engage with FBO at various levels and have all deepened the conversation on the role of religion in development by hosting workshops, sponsoring research, and publishing papers on the subject. (This is discussed further in Chapter 2.)
88 Wilkinson, "Putting the 'Strategic' into Strategic Religious Engagement," 81.
89 Balchin, "The F-Word and the S-Word," 532.

Bibliography

Balchin, Cassandra. "The F-Word and the S-Word: Too Much of One and Not Enough of the Other." *Development in Practice* 17, no. 4/5 (2007): 532–538.

Benthall, Jonathan. "Chapter Three: 'Cultural Proximity' and the Conjecture of Islam with Modern Humanitarianism." In *Sacred Aid: Faith and Humanitarianism*, edited by Michael Barnett and Janice Gross Stein (New York: Oxford University Press, 2012): 65–89.

Berger, Julia. "Religious Nongovernmental Organizations: An Exploratory Analysis." *VOLUNTAS: International Journal of Voluntary and Nonprofit Organizations* 14 (2003): 15–39. DOI:10.1023/A:1022988804887

Bielefeld, Wolfgang and William Suhs Cleveland. "Faith-Based Organizations as Service Providers and Their Relationship to Government." *Nonprofit and Voluntary Sector Quarterly* 42 (2013): 468–494.

Bush, Evelyn. "What Is a Religious NGO? Conceptual and Classificatory Challenges in Research on Transnational Religion." In *Faithful Measures: New Methods in the Measurement of Religion*, edited by Christopher Bader and Roger Finke (New York: New York University Press, 2017): 260–286.

Clarke, Gerard. "Faith-Based Organizations and International Development: An Overview." In *Development, Civil Society and Faith-Based Organisations*, edited by Gerard Clarke and Michael Jennings. (Basingstoke: Palgrave Macmillan, 2008): 17–45.

Clarke, Gerard. "Faith Matters: Faith-Based Organisations, Civil Society and International Development." *Journal of International Development* 18, no. 6 (2006): 835–848. DOI:10.1002/jid.1317

Clarke, Gerard and Michael Jennings. *Development, Civil Society and Faith-Based Organizations: Bridging the Sacred and the Secular* (Basingstoke: Palgrave Macmillan, 2008).

Dicklitch, Susan and Heather Rice. "The Mennonite Central Committee (MCC) and Faith-Based NGO Aid to Africa." *Development in Practice* 14, no. 5 (2004): 660–672. www.jstor.org/stable/4029894

Ebaugh, Helen Rose, Paula F. Pipes, Janet S. Chafetz, and Martha Daniels. "Where's the Religion? Distinguishing Faith-Based from Secular Social Service Agencies." *Journal for the Scientific Study of Religion* 42, no. 3 (2003): 411–426. www.jstor.org/stable/1387743

Ebaugh, Helen Rose., Janet S. Chafetz, and Paula F. Pipes. "The Influence of Evangelicalism on Government Funding of Faith-Based Social Service

Organizations." *Review of Religious Research* 47, no. 4 (2006): 380–392. www.jstor.org/stable/20058105

General Accounting Office. "Foreign Assistance: USAID Relies Heavily on Nongovernmental Organizations, but Better Data Needed to Evaluate Approaches," GAO 02-471 (Washington, DC: April 25, 2002).

Heist, Dan and Ram A. Cnaan. "Faith-Based International Development Work: A Review." *Religions* 7, no. 19 (2016): 1–17.

Hopgood, Stephen and Leslie Vinjamuri, "Chapter Two: Faith in Markets." In *Sacred Aid: Faith and Humanitarianism*, edited by Michael Barnett and Janice Gross Stein. (New York: Oxford University Press, 2012): 37–64.

Jeavons, Thomas H. "Religious and Faith-Based Organizations: Do We Know One When We See One?" *Nonprofit and Voluntary Sector Quarterly* 33 (2004): 140–145.

Jennings, Michael Simon Feeny, Gill Westhorp, and Cara Donohue. "A Potent Fuel? Faith Identity and Development Impact in World Vision Community Programming." *Journal of International Development* 33 (2021): 70–85.

Jones, Ben and Marie Juul Petersen. "Instrumental, Narrow, Normative? Reviewing Recent Work on Religion and Development." *Third World Quarterly* 32 (2011): 1291–1306. DOI:10.1080/01436 597.2011.596747

Khan, Ajaz Ahmed. "Chapter Four: Religious Obligation or Altruistic Giving? Muslims and Charitable Donations." In *Sacred Aid: Faith and Humanitarianism*, edited by Michael Barnett and Janice Gross Stein, 90–114 (New York: Oxford University Press, 2012).

Lipsky, Alyson B. "Evaluating the Strength of Faith: Potential Comparative Advantages of Faith-Based Organizations Providing Health Services in Sub-Saharan Africa." *Public Administration and Development* 31, no. 1 (2011): 25–36.

Marsden, Lee. "Bush, Obama and a Faith-Based US Foreign Policy." *International Affairs* 88, no. 5 (2012): 953–974.

Marshall, Katherine. "Impressions & Indications of Religious Engagement in Development." *The Review of Faith & International Affairs* 19, sup1 (2021): 12–30.

Marshall, Katherine, Sudipta Roy, Chris Seiple, and Hugo Slim. "Intrinsic and Strategic Leverage of Religion in Development." *The Review of Faith & International Affairs* 19, sup1 (2021): 31–41. DOI:10.1080/15570274.2021.1983356

Mitchell, Bob. *Faith-Based Development: How Christian Organizations Can Make a Difference* (Maryknoll, NY: Orbis Books, 2017). DOI:10.1002/jid.3512

Monsma, Stephen V. "Non-Profit and Faith-Based Welfare-to-Work Programs." *Society* 40, no. 2 (2003): 13–18. DOI:10.1007/s12115-003-1047-3

Monsma, Stephen V. *When Sacred and Secular Mix: Religious Nonprofit Organizations and Public Money* (Lanham, MD: Rowman & Littlefield, 1996).

Morgenstern, Emily M., Nick M. Brown, Luisa Blanchfield, Shayerah I. Akhtar, Nicolas Cook, Thomas Lum, and Peter J. Meyer, "Selected Trump Administration Foreign Aid Priorities: A Wrap Up." *Congressional Research Service*, R4666, January 21, 2021, https://crsreports.congress.gov/product/pdf/R/R46656

Narayan, Deepa and Patti Petesch. *Voices of the Poor: From Many Lands* (Washington, DC: World Bank and Oxford University Press, 2002).

Olarinmoye, Omobolaji Ololade. "Faith-Based Organizations and Development: Prospects and Constraints." *Transformation an International Journal of Holistic Mission Studies* 29, no. 1 (2012): 1–14. DOI:10.1177/02653788114279851 4/04/2021

Phillips, Adam Nicholas. "One Year Later: Reflections on USAID's 2020 Evidence Summit on Strategic Religious Engagement." *The Review of Faith & International Affairs* 19, sup1 (2021): 98–101. DOI:10.1080/15570274.2021.1983359

Rakodi, Carole. "Religion and Development: Subjecting Religious Perceptions and Organisations to Scrutiny." *Development in Practice* 22, no. 5–6 (2012): 621–633. DOI:10.1080/09614524.2012.686602

Scheitle, Christopher P. "Chapter Seven: From Documents to Data." In *Faithful Measures: New Methods in the Measurement of Religion*, edited by Roger Finke and Christopher Bader (New York: New York University Press, 2017): 201–226.

Schroeder, Kristy Bergman. "Religion and Secularism in Development: Trends in the Approaches of Bilateral Donors in Canada and the United Kingdom." A thesis submitted to the Faculty of Graduate Studies, The University of Manitoba, The University of Winnipeg, 2016.

Seidel, Timothy. "Development, Religion, and Modernity in Palestine-Israel." *CrossCurrents* 62, no. 4 (2012): 424–441.

Sider, Ronald J. and Heidi Rolland Unruh, "Typology of Religious Characteristics of Social Service and Educational Organizations and Programs." *Nonprofit and Voluntary Sector Quarterly* 33, no. 1 (March 2004): 109–134.

Smith, Steven Rathgeb and Michael R. Sosin. "The Varieties of Faith-Related Agencies." *Public Administration Review* 61, no. 6 (2001): 651–670.

Smith, Tom W. "General Social Survey, 2018." *The Association of Religion Data Archives*. 2020. DOI:10.17605/OSF.IO/7JF94

Tomalin, Emma. "Thinking about Faith-Based Organisations in Development: Where Have We Got to and What Next?" *Development in Practice* 22, no. 5/6 (2012): 689–703. www.jstor.org/stable/41723132

United States Agency for International Development (USAID). "Building Bridges in Development: USAID's Strategic Religious Engagement Policy," September 2023. www.usaid.gov/sites/default/files/2023-09/USAID-Strategic-Religious-Engagement-Policy-9-6-23_1.pdf

Vander Zaag, Ray. "Canadian Faith-Based Development NGOs and CIDA Funding." *Canadian Journal of Development Studies* 34, no. 2 (2013): 321–347.

Walker, Peter, Dyan Mazurana, Amy Warren, George Scarlett, and Henry Louis. "Chapter Five: The Role of Spirituality in Humanitarian Crisis Survival and Recovery." In *Sacred Aid: Faith and Humanitarianism*, edited by Michael Barnett and Janice Gross Stein (New York: Oxford University Press, 2012): 115–139.

Wilkinson, Olivia. "Putting the 'Strategic' into Strategic Religious Engagement." *The Review of Faith & International Affairs* 19, sup1 (2021): 78–84.

Wilkinson, Olivia, Kuyang Harriet Logo, Emma Tomalin, Wani Laki Anthony, Florine de Wolf, and Asha Kurien. "Faith in Localisation? The Experiences of Local Faith Actors Engaging with the International Humanitarian System in South Sudan." *Journal of International Humanitarian Action* 7, no. 1 (January 11, 2022): 40–52.

Wuthnow, Robert, Conrad Hackett, and Becky Hsu. "The Effectiveness and Trustworthiness of Faith-Based and Other Service Organizations: A Study of Recipients' Perceptions." *Journal for the Scientific Study of Religion* 43, no. 1 (2004): 1–17.

Zehavi, Amos. "The Faith-Based Initiative in Comparative Perspective: Making Use of Religious Providers in Britain and the United States." *Comparative Politics* 40, no. 3 (2008): 331–351.

2 Global Religious Engagement

Introduction

The spring of 1891 brought a severe drought to Imperial Russia in which nearly a million acres of parched land produced little vegetation. Without reserves, 300,000 peasants died of starvation. In telling the plight of survivors, newspapers recounted stories of those forced to boil grass for sustenance.[1] No states sent aid, though the US government did consider the matter.[2] Fast forward 130 years, and the same soil bears witness to another tragedy—the Ukrainian war. The two crises share few similarities. In the Ukrainian conflict, death is not wrought by an indiscriminate force of nature but by a power-seeking despot. The Russian government's role in inflicting suffering is not dubious but definitive. The world's response is not reticent but robust, with an international aid apparatus emerging in the interim. The United States is not quiescent but among the most vocal critics and generous donors. Standing over a century apart, the two crises are juxtaposed on nearly every front, save one—the prominent role of religious groups in providing humanitarian relief.

Faith-based organizations have a long history of offering humanitarian aid. In the case of the 1891 famine, Christian organizations and congregations paid for over one-fifth of all food commodities shipped from the United States to Russia.[3] Today, FBOs continue to respond to natural disasters and the varied calamities caused by man—war chief among them. The need can be overwhelming. In the war between Russia and Ukraine that began in February 2022, tens of thousands of people were killed or injured, and millions were displaced in the first year of the conflict.[4] The international aid community sent billions of dollars in humanitarian relief.[5] Among the sea of contributions was $700,000 in food aid sent from Islamic Relief, $75 million from American Christian charities, and $85 million from the Jewish Federations of North America.[6] FBOs, while not among the top donors, nevertheless continue to mobilize substantial resources.

This chapter details the evolution of FBOs' overseas operations, from their early missionary and humanitarian work to war relief to economic development. It also explains when and how public actors began to do parallel work

DOI: 10.4324/9781003456704-2

and at what point the two enterprises intersected. This larger international backdrop is critical to contextualizing the US case and USAID's efforts over the past quarter century to reinscribe faith in foreign aid.

Missionary Outreach

All major religions encourage altruism.[7] Some religions exhort believers to extend benevolence and charity to those of the same faith, while others widen the imperative to include all humanity.[8] In either case, proximity is less relevant than need. As a consequence, religious individuals and organizations have historically traveled long distances to attend to the needs of the impoverished, sick, hungry, and homeless, as well as those cast as benighted.[9] Missionaries set the earliest example, followed by FBOs whose primary purpose was humanitarian assistance. Today, while states and multilateral institutions are the actors most associated with international aid, FBOs remain powerful players—not least because their involvement long predates their public counterparts.

The story of FBOs in international development began over two millennia ago with missionaries. Among the missionary religions, Buddhism has the earliest origins, with Buddhist monks and nuns disseminating the Dharma and establishing monasteries as early as the 5th century BC.[10] In contrast to Buddhism, which remained relatively concentrated in Asia, Christianity emerged in the 1st century AD and quickly spread across several continents.[11] Centuries later, the work of Christian missionaries would imbricate with the companions and subsequent followers of Muhammed, who were following the Qur'anic injunction to invite people into the truth of Islam (*da'wah*).

The interlaced efforts of early missionaries led to a steady increase of religious converts, especially throughout Eurasia. Further growth occurred as these efforts were married to the machinations of the state. Many of the great powers expanded their territories through conquest and colonization, with the hope of realizing the dictum *cuius regio, eius religio*, or "whoever rules, his is the religion." One of the strategies states used to achieve this objective was to either deploy or abet missionaries to preach throughout their respective territories.[12]

In addition to preaching, missionaries would also often provide a multitude of social services. They would distribute food and medicine as well as Bibles. They would teach farming and forestry and also provide religious instruction. They would establish asylums and schools as well as churches and mosques.[13] In some cases, the quality of education in missionary schools far exceeded that of the schools established by the colonial government.[14] In others, missionary schools were the *only* schools available.[15] From the perspective of the missionaries, such institutions served the dual purpose of addressing a worldly need while also serving as conduits through which they could more easily share their spiritual truths. From the perspective of the state, missionary schools and services had the effect of "civilizing" those under colonial control and, therefore, could serve as convenient auxiliaries in the advancement and consolidation of imperial power.[16] In some cases, states could even use missionaries to quell anticolonial rebellion.[17] Only rarely did missionaries register any kind of opposition to the state agenda.[18]

In the main, the colonial and missionary enterprises had parallel, if not auspiciously conjoined objectives. Both sought global hegemony, be it political or spiritual, and both would find relative success in their pursuit. European powers controlled 84% of the world's states by 1914. At the same time, Christianity reached over 92% of states, thanks in part to over 600 foreign mission agencies and 62,000 deployed missionaries.[19]

Concomitant to the outreach of Christian missionaries were the efforts of Muslim missionaries or *da'is*. Muslim *da'is* also benefited from state expansion. The Ottoman Empire provides a prominent example. At the height of its power, the Empire encompassed the Balkans, Middle East, Northern Africa, and Arabian Peninsula—much of which it acquired by conquest. Though the Empire ruled under Islamic authority (and sultans took the title of Caliph), it did not subject its newly acquired subjects to Islamic law nor persecute people of other religious beliefs. Instead, it generally accepted its religious heterogeneity, even condoning the presence of early Protestant and Latin missionaries and schools.[20] This tolerance waned, however, as the Empire expanded, due to the fear that increased diversity would foment fragmentation.

Marshal Süleyman Hüsnü advocated that the Ottoman Empire should respond to the threat of alterity in its outlying areas by forming a Muslim "missionary society" that would train members of the ulema and articulate an official Sunni orthodoxy. This took the form, under Abdülhamid II, of having all Ottoman Muslim missionaries trained under the Empire's chief mufti in Istanbul and sending them on "civilizing missions" to teach at Muslim schools in the provincial periphery. The intended effect was to shore up the Empire's religious identity and consolidate its power. Ultimately, the strategy failed, and the Ottoman Empire collapsed in 1922. Yet, while religion proved an insufficient political sinew, it left a lasting legacy in education. Over 500 Qur'anic schools survived Ottoman rule.[21]

Faith-Based Humanitarianism

The success and salience of some of the earliest missionary societies in the area of education foreshadow the effects of many modern FBOs. However, the *raison d'être* of these earlier organizations also differs from many of their contemporary successors. Missionary societies generally prioritized cultivating the soul and mind above improving one's physical and material circumstances.[22] It wasn't until the mid-19th century that this began to change, and separate organizations arose aiming to address the spiritual *and* social conditions of the communities they served.[23]

Two of the most prominent organizations adopting this approach include the Young Men's Christian Association (YMCA), established in 1844, and the Salvation Army, established in 1865. These organizations operated under the assumption that deeds can supplement words in the demonstration of Christian love.[24] The *Christian Herald*, a US-based periodical, also subscribed to this ethos. However, in contrast to the YMCA and The Salvation Army, which both focused initially on serving those at home, the relief work of the *Christian Herald* began by addressing the needs of those abroad. In justifying the newspaper's entrée into international humanitarianism, the paper's editor framed overseas crises as ripe for Christian charity, not least because it presented a striking opportunity for evangelism. "... When the hungry people ask ... how it is that the stranger and the foreigner have come to their help in their extremity," the paper told readers, "they will ... hear that Jesus loves them and that because he loves them, his people are giving them food ... [this] may lead many to love him, too."[25] This perspective was also exemplified by several contemporaneous Christian relief committees.[26]

The understanding undergirding these organizations was that humanitarian relief and evangelism were separate yet imbricate objectives, with the former *amplifying* and not denigrating the latter.[27] The resultant harmony was reflected in the Christian response to several international crises, including the Chinese Famine of 1876–1879, the Russian Famine of 1891, the Hamidian massacre and Spanish persecution of Cubans in the mid-1890s, the Indian and Finland famines in the early 1900s, and the Balkan War in 1912. In the face of foreign starvation, disease, disaster, and war, American Christians donated millions.[28] Yet the true test of their beneficence was yet to come.

World War I saw the death of between 7 and 15 million soldiers due to battle- and war-related famine and disease. An additional 21 million soldiers were wounded. The world's premier humanitarian aid organization, the International Red Cross, attended to the needs of combatants, as did the The Salvation Army and YMCA. But the war also threatened the lives of millions of civilians. Among other things, civilians were in dire need of food and healthcare. More help was needed than the established humanitarian organizations could provide, and newly formed NGOs stepped in to fill the lacuna.

Among the many NGOs formed during and after World War I were those established by people of faith. This included organizations established by Jewish Americans, like the American Jewish Joint Distribution Committee, World Jewish Relief, and Hadassah, as well as other organizations such as the Quaker-affiliated American Friends Service Committee and other Christian organizations like Christian Science Relief and the Mennonite Central Committee.[29] These organizations were *motivated* by faith but not necessarily dedicated to promoting it.[30] Their target audience was also different than the humanitarian organizations that preceded them. Rather than reaching out to the unchurched, the primary aim was to alleviate the suffering of co-religionists.[31]

By 1939, there were 41 registered faith-based humanitarian NGOs in the United States. This number increased substantially in the coming years as World War II began and the need for humanitarian assistance burgeoned.

By the time the United States entered the war, the number of FBOs had already increased by 50%. Still more were formed in the latter years of the war, including some of the most well-known and largest organizations in existence today, including Catholic Relief Services (1943) and World Relief (1944). By the war's conclusion, religious organizations comprised almost a third of all US-registered humanitarian organizations.[32] Still more FBOs formed in the years that followed, including Church World Service (1946) and Lutheran World Relief (1946).[33] These were among the 200 NGOs established in the immediate postwar period to assume the Herculean task of European reconstruction.[34]

Faith-Based Development

In the three decades following World War II, the imperial powers contracted, and over 50 states in Asia and Africa achieved independence. This power shift and the shift of the international issue du jour from humanitarianism to development presented missionaries and humanitarian FBOs with the opportunity to grow both operationally and geographically.

Missionaries who had served under colonial governments faced a choice upon independence. They could ride the imperial coattails back home or stay and see the building of a new state. Most chose the latter. In light of the vacuous welfare structures inherited by the new governments, missionaries were welcome to continue providing social services. They could continue to run schools and asylums and even expand their operations according to demonstrated need and available funds. In some cases, this meant also providing transportation, electricity, water, medical care, youth programming, and housing. While these services were necessary, the uncomfortable truth remained that FBOs were the progeny of colonialism and often inherited (and typified) the very paternalism the state wished to shed. A similar paradox existed with the additional Western NGOs that came to "help."

In the latter half of the 19th century, the "development" of decolonized states became a political zeitgeist. Many NGOs, including FBOs, thus shifted their operations from Europe to the newly independent nations of Asia and Africa. They also shifted their modus operandi from war relief or disaster relief to long-term development. Even some of the names of organizations reflect this programmatic shift, including two of today's most well-known FBOs: Catholic Relief Services, which began as War Relief Services, and Adventist Development Relief Agency, which began as the Seventh-day Adventist Welfare Service. The dominance of FBOs on the African continent, in particular, is reflected in newly released data from the International Council of Voluntary Agencies (ICVA). According to the ICVA Repository, by 1968, FBOs accounted for nearly a third of all NGOs in 16 African countries. In seven African countries, half or more of the state's NGOs were faith-based.[35] Even this, some aver, may be an underestimate, since it likely excludes some of the smaller churches that were nonetheless "NGO-ized" and participatory in the development agenda.[36]

As the "nervous system" of aid shifted from humanitarianism to development and from Europe to the Global South, the composition of global FBOs changed as well.[37] Most notable was the reduction in the number of Jewish FBOs. While Jewish organizations dominated during World War I, many of these organizations disbanded after World War II (Hadassah, World Jewish Relief, and the Jewish Joint Distribution Committee being notable exceptions).[38] Muslim FBOs were virtually nonexistent, though this would change in subsequent years.[39]

The 1970s and 1980s saw a third wave of NGOs, including a greater number of Muslim organizations. Some of these, like the International Islamic Charitable Organization, were founded to directly counter the influence of Christian FBOs in Africa.[40] Others, like the International Islamic Relief Organization, were established to address newly emergent crises in Muslim-majority nations, such as the famines that affected countries in the Horn of Africa. Still others emerged in response to the Soviet occupation of Afghanistan and the later Bosnian conflict.[41] The primary thrust of many of these FBOs was to assist fellow Muslims, an aim that Marie Juul Petersen says pushed them to "the margins of the mainstream aid system."[42] Yet this description is also befitting of FBOs in general—at least until recently. This is because, while FBOs were among the earliest players to engage in international outreach and service, their efforts were largely eclipsed—and ignored—by other actors. Today, what some call "the foreign aid regime" consists primarily of state aid agencies and multilateral institutions—all of which emerged in the waning years of World War II.[43]

The Foreign Aid Regime

World War II took the lives of over 60 million people and left entire cities buried in detritus. With the majority of Europe's transport infrastructure decimated, much of its industrial production ground to a halt. Rampant inflation and buckling debt, in addition to trade deficits, made the complete economic (and political) collapse of Europe seem a fait accompli. The resuscitation of Europe would require outside intervention—and significant munificence. It was in this environment that the modern foreign aid regime was born.[44]

Delegates from 44 nations convened at Bretton Woods in July 1944. While the reconstruction of Europe was top-of-mind, the attendees sought a larger objective. In anticipation of the war's cessation, they sought to construct a new international order—one that would promise enduring peace and greater economic stability. The meeting ended with a solid blueprint. Two new multilateral institutions, the International Reconstruction and Development Bank (IRDB) and the International Monetary Fund (IMF), would buttress the coming order. The IRDB, under the aegis of the newly created World

Bank (WB), would provide nations with low- or no-interest loans, and the IMF would establish a fixed but adjustable exchange rate. A year later, the United Nations (UN) would serve as the third pillar by promoting economic development among member nations.

The new architecture of the international economy allowed the world's industrial production to largely recover by 1947.[45] However, not every country recovered quickly. That same year, Germany had only reached a third of its previous capacity, and Austria and Greece were both at least 25% behind their prewar production levels.[46] America offered another approach. It would provide $13 billion, not in loans, but in unconditional aid.[47] In justifying this expenditure, US Secretary of State George Marshall explained that no less than the "entire fabric of the European economy" was at stake, and the failure of these economies augurs ill for the entire world.[48] He extrapolated:

> Our policy is directed not against any country or doctrine but against hunger, poverty, desperation and chaos. Its purpose should be the revival of a working economy in the world so as to permit the emergence of political and social conditions in which free institutions can exist. Such assistance, I am convinced, must not be on a piecemeal basis as various crises develop. Any assistance that this Government may render in the future should provide a cure rather than a mere palliative.[49]

Marshall was clear that the beneficiaries of American funds were in no position to repay their benefactor. That was not the expectation. Rather, the expectation was to use funds to help European nations recover and strengthen the world capitalist market through strategic aid. The United States took a long-term approach, preferring to build the agricultural and industrial capacity of nations they hoped would be future trading partners—and political allies. To this end, shipments of fertilizer, petroleum, coal, cotton, and nonferrous metals were more plentiful than shipments of food. The United States also provided technical assistance, both by sending teams to Europe and their territories and by accepting and training Europeans in the United States. The emphasis was on recovery over relief. The United States soon extended this strategy beyond Europe. President Truman explained the program in his famous Four Points Speech: "Only by helping the least fortunate of its members to help themselves can the human family achieve the decent, satisfying life that is the right of all people." America, with its "store of technical knowledge," was cast as uniquely situated to help.[50] With that, foreign aid became a mainstay of US foreign policy. Other countries followed suit.

The latter half of the 20th century saw many of the world's most developed nations incorporate aid into their foreign policies. Motivated by a mix of altruism and self-interest, these nations pursued different strategies in selecting their beneficiaries. The former imperial powers channeled aid predominately to their prior colonized countries (which had often inherited a weakened infrastructure from colonial rule), while the United States and the

Soviet Union used aid as a tool to win allies during the Cold War. Even Japan and Germany, the two countries most devastated by World War II, became major donors by 1960. In Japan's case, it directed aid primarily to its Asian neighbors following the reparation payments it made in the years immediately after the war.

The institutionalization of bilateral aid led in 1960 to the establishment of the Development Assistance Group (DAG), an organization intended to track and monitor official aid flows. DAG became the Development Assistance Committee (DAC) under the aegis of the Organization for Economic Cooperation and Development (OECD) the following year, and what began as a coalition of 10 countries grew to 15 within a decade. Concomitantly, the WB expanded by adding another lending mechanism, the International Development Association (IDA), to provide no- and low-interest concessional loans and grants specifically to developing countries. This momentum led the UN to dub the 1960s "The UN Development Decade." It also set a global aid target of 1% of the Gross National Incomes of all economically advanced nations. Though this goal was later adjusted—and remained aspirational—subsequent decades saw a substantial increase in bilateral aid, as well as an increase in aid oversight and coordination among donor countries.[51] This culminated in 1995 in the DAC countries seeking to engage with multilateral development institutions to articulate regime-wide development goals.

The Millennium Development Goals (MDGs), published in 2000, were the result of these efforts. With the MDGs, the WB, IMF, UN, and OECD had collectively identified eight areas of critical importance in the fight for global equity and articulated what progress the international aid regime wanted to see in the next 15 years. The targets included, inter alia, the end of extreme poverty and hunger, the mitigation of child mortality, and the promotion of gender equity.[52]

The MDGs were at once impressively (and ambitiously) expansive and shallowly rooted. Their formulation required significant coordination and consensus-building, yet the conversation was largely kept among the top public donors. Most NGOs, including FBOs, did not participate (though they were later solicited for implementation).[53] This was not necessarily surprising, for while the development work of many FBOs paralleled that of the UN and other public agencies, coordination among the two had historically been minimal. Omobolaji Ololade Olarinmoye even describes the humanitarian and development work of FBOs as largely "invisible" to the foreign aid regime.[54] This followed the growing skepticism surrounding religion in the postwar period. The 21st century would see this change.

A Religious Resurgence

The prevailing theory during the latter part of the 20th century was that religion would likely decline as societies modernized and technologies advanced.[55] This did not come to fruition. Instead, to the extent secularism followed modernity, the results were uneven and nonlinear. The advanced industrialized societies of Western Europe followed the expected pattern, while the United States, the world's premier economy, maintained a religious majority. Meanwhile, many of the emerging economies were not quick to shed their religious identities but instead hosted growing religious populations.[56] As a result, the start of the 21st century saw more people in more countries prioritizing God and attending religious services.[57] By 2012, over 80% of the world's citizens claimed to be religiously affiliated.[58] The secularization thesis had been effectively upended by what some scholars called a "religious resurgence" or a "turn to religion."[59] Some also suggested it marked the beginning of a post-secular society.[60] Much to the posthumous chagrin of Nietzsche, God was not dead but had become globalized, weaponized, and politicized.

One of the answers proffered for religion's renewed relevance is globalization. As societies across the globe became increasingly interdependent, religion became unmoored from territory and culture—set free to grow in the ever-expanding space of cross-cultural connections.[61] According to Scott Thomas, this means "Religion is increasingly, if unevenly, becoming a matter of [individual] choice—about whether to believe [and] whether to embrace one particular kind of religion" rather than a product of one's environment.[62] In short, as political, economic, and cultural forces become further intertwined, religious encounters—and adherents—increase. The opening of the post-Soviet space and China at the turn of the century provide poignant examples. As isolationist regimes and policies ended, people within these states enjoyed greater freedom and access to outside ideas. Contrary to secularization theory, this resulted in *more* people subscribing to religion, not less.

The modernization of the post-Soviet states and China enabled people from inside these states to have greater access to information and also allowed those from elsewhere to have greater access to come in and evangelize. This follows Thomas's argument that the growth of religion globally is also due to religious groups capitalizing upon the new (flattened) global landscape.[63] The modalities for missionary activity have increased. The internet allows for instant communication and connection. International travel is both more accessible and affordable. The effect is what some have called an "unprecedented expansion" in the evangelical missionary enterprise.[64]

Another force contributing to the increased relevance of religion is its *weaponization*. Missionaries were not the only religious actors galvanized by globalization. There were also those more nefarious, including groups using violence to advance religious aims.[65] These included Islamic terrorist organizations like Hezbollah and Al Qaeda, as well as Christian terrorist organizations like the Aryan Nations and the Hindu and Buddhist-inspired Aum Shinrikyo in Japan.[66] Between 1980 and 1995, the number of such religious terrorist groups increased tenfold.[67] Religion quickly became the primary ideological driver of terrorism.[68] The majority of the violence was associated with groups claiming to represent Islam.[69] These trends evidenced what some perceived as a coming shift in the world order. Globalization, they averred, would continue to erode national loyalties, making the intransigent demarcations of religion more pronounced. The full thesis, proffered by Samuel Huntington, held that the new fault line of global conflict would be between Islam and the Judeo-Christian West.[70]

Some saw the attacks of September 11 as a harbinger for this coming "clash of civilizations." Huntington's argument provided a convenient, if fallacious, explanation that greatly enhanced the perceived importance of religion in international affairs.[71] Yet even as his theory fell into disrepute, interest in religion and its effect on international relations remained high.[72] 9/11 had shown the power of religious actors to violently challenge the authority of the state. The subsequent decade furthered the point, with the world seeing an additional 5,000 religiously motivated terrorist attacks.[73]

At the same time that some groups violently challenged state authority by weaponizing religion, others used the state's political machinery to gain power, exemplifying the *politicization* of religion.[74] The Taliban's reign in Afghanistan following the Afghan war and the electoral victory of the Muslim Brotherhood after the ousting of Egypt's Hosni Mubarak provide notable examples. The influence of religion's rise was also apparent in several established secular democracies. India's Bharatiya Janata Party, with its hallmark of Hindu Nationalism, saw a meteoric rise in Parliament, ultimately achieving majority-party status by 1996.[75] A similar trend occurred in Turkey, where the Justice and Development Party, a moderate Muslim party, won over a third of the seats in Parliament in 2002.[76]

Religion was also shown to be a prominent political force in the United States, primarily with the rise of the "Religious Right." Emerging as a political force in the late 1970s, the Religious Right comprised a constellation of primarily evangelical and Pentecostal individuals and organizations who believed the United States' domestic and foreign policies needed a moral refashioning.[77] The group became a stalwart constituency of the Republican Party, proving instrumental in the election of President Ronald Reagan in 1980 and the takeover of both the US House and Senate in 1994.[78] The definitive victory for the Religious Right was the election of President George W. Bush in 2000.

President Bush was a self-proclaimed born-again Christian who promised to bring his faith to the White House. He also pledged to pursue a humble foreign policy.[79] He was able to keep only one of these promises. After 9/11, the United States waged war against Afghanistan, intending to extinguish Al Qaeda. Two years later, it also waged war against Iraq, justifying its aggression under the banner of the greater "War on Terrorism."[80] The volte-face in America's political priorities under Bush and in the aftermath of 9/11 meant religion was, for the first time, in the foreground of American foreign policy.

In the wake of 9/11, President Bush made overt efforts not to vilify the Muslim faith, but his foreign policy was nonetheless heavily influenced by Samuel Huntington's thesis on the "clash of civilizations." This was directly evidenced in the 2002 National Security Strategy (NSS), which described the world as engaged in a "struggle of ideas" with nothing less than the "future of the Muslim world" at stake.[81] The enemy, explains Gregorio Bettiza, was not Islam, but specifically "Islamofascism," and the battle was not necessarily between the "West and the Rest" (a la Huntington), but between "violent/extremist and peaceful/moderate Muslims" in the Middle East.[82] The United States, for its part, would fight back with both hard and soft power, the latter infused with conservative evangelism.[83]

Far from an epitaph for religion, the 2002 NSS highlighted religion's continued relevance, a point made even stronger by America's adoption of a broader "faith-based foreign policy." In development, this manifests into an increasing emphasis on religious freedom and a push to use FBOs to deliver foreign aid.

Religious Engagement

The increased prominence of religion in international affairs highlighted the myopia of the foreign aid regime's neglect of religious actors. Clearly, religion and religious actors were of greater importance than once perceived. America's "faith-based foreign policy" and specifically its engagement of FBOs in aid highlighted America's recognition of this fact. However, America was not the first player among the foreign aid regime to try to engage FBOs. That distinction goes to the WB.

WB President James Wolfensohn met with the Archbishop of Canterbury in 1993 to discuss how the Bank might engage religious institutions to alleviate poverty. Out of this meeting came several interfaith conferences. This culminated in 1998 into two institutionalized dialogues at the WB: The World Faiths Development Dialogue and the Development Dialogue on Values and Ethics. The WB further elevated religion's role in development upon releasing its "Voices of the Poor" report. The report, published in 2000, featured survey responses from over 40,000 individuals across 50 countries and revealed that many people in the developing world often trust religious organizations more than governments or secular organizations.[84]

The report underscored the value of FBOs in development. This point was further exemplified by the Jubilee 2000 campaign. What started as an idea—tying together the Biblical mandate of debt forgiveness and the Catholic celebration of jubilee every 50 years—evolved into a robust advocacy campaign galvanizing hundreds of religious actors, NGOs, political leaders, and celebrities to protest the accrued debt of developing countries to bilateral and multilateral aid institutions.[85] The campaign, which began in 1996, ultimately succeeded in acquiring 24 million signatures across 166 countries.[86] It also pressured the IMF, WB, and the world's top bilateral donors to cancel over $100 billion in debt held by developing countries.[87]

The WB report and the Jubilee 2000 campaign represent important early examples of faith intersecting with the foreign aid regime. Further convergence was made possible by the latter's reconceptualization of development. Wolfensohn explained: "... we've been confronted with the reality that no amount of work on governance, no amount of work on economic planning is adequate if we don't understand these underlying forces of culture and history."[88] Ultimately, the Bank and others began reevaluating their ideas of development and strictly economic analyses of poverty gave way to the idea of holistic and sustainable development, highlighting the importance of individual identity and social connections.[89] As thought shifted, the ever-present but overshadowed role of religion came to the fore, and FBOs transitioned from being marginalized to *legitimized* actors in development. This is evidenced, inter alia, by the Bank's regular engagement with the World Council of Churches from 2002 to 2008 and its Faith and Development Leaders Meeting in 2009, which convened 85 faith leaders across 28 countries.[90] Since 2010, the Bank has also regularly engaged FBOs through its membership on the steering committee of the United Nations Interagency Task Force on Religion and Sustainable Development (UNIATF-R).

Other parts of the UN also gradually came to engage FBOs. UN's nominal recognition of the role of religious actors in development began in 1972 with the establishment of the UN "Committee of Religious NGOs." FBOs occupied this quiet corner of the UN until the 1990s when they began attending the various UN conferences leading up to the Millennial Summit.[91] A select few FBOs were also involved in the creation of the UN's Millennium Development Goals revealed at the Summit. Many more were involved in their implementation. Over the lifespan of the MDGs (2000–2015), the number of FBOs registered with the United Nations Economic and Social Council (ECOSOC) went from 180 to at least 320.[92] At the same time, more of the UN was paying attention to religion and religious actors. The growth of the UNIATF-R is a case in point. When UNIATF-R was first established in 2010, it comprised only eight UN entities (including the WB). Ten years later, its membership had more than doubled to include 27 entities. The quantitative increase in FBOs involved at the UN paralleled the increase in FBOs' qualitative contribution. While only a few FBOs had any say in the formation of the MDGs, many more were involved in the UN's next round of development targets, the Sustainable Development Goals, including all UNIATF-R members.[93]

In addition to multilateral institutions, over the past two decades, most of the world's top bilateral aid donors have expanded their engagement with faith-based communities and organizations.[94] These efforts range from the more systematic to the ad hoc. In many cases, the state's attention to religion in development manifests into donor workshops, research groups, and dialogues, with FBOs invited to share their perspective. Many states also enhanced their funding of FBOs and developed more formal partnerships through strategic agreements. Sometimes, the government appointed a personal interlocutor or established a specialized office or division to manage these relations. In a few cases, states produced official documents outlining the state's commitment to engaging FBOs and the steps it expected to take to further its FBO relations.

When placed along a spectrum, the United States stands out as the bilateral donor with the most institutionalized form of FBO engagement. USAID has had a Center for Faith-Based and Community Initiatives (CFBCI) since 2002.[95] This Center has typically included an appointed director and several civil service staff. The United States also has written regulations governing USAID's relations with FBOs.[96] The primary distinction between the United States and other countries is how it formed its institutional and legal infrastructure. The CFBCI resulted from a top-down process rather than a bottom-up collaboration with FBOs. In other cases, the state government created faith-focused centers or appointed interlocutors due to a sustained conversation with faith-based stakeholders. The same is true for written guidelines for donor–FBO relations.

In Britain (arguably the most analogous case to the United States), formal conversations concerning the nexus of religion and development began in 2000, yet the state was slow to translate rhetoric into action. It was not until 2005 that the British Department for International Development, or DFID (now the Foreign, Commonwealth & Development Office), embarked upon a collaborative research project with the University of Birmingham to further investigate the role of religion in development. Lasting six years and costing 3.5 million pounds, the project has been described as "one of the most ambitious efforts to build ... evidence-based analysis and research [on religion and development]."[97]

Alongside the theoretical contributions of the Birmingham research collaborative, DFID also authorized a Faith Working Group to produce a practical document for FBOs seeking to partner with the state in pursuing development objectives. This became the 2012 "Faith Partnership Principles Paper." Though the Faith Working Group terminated upon publication of the paper, DFID sustained its attention to religion through a handful of dedicated personnel on the Civil Society Team within the Department's Inclusive Societies Department.

The only other country to assign specific staff as interlocutors to the faith community is Germany. In 2014, Germany's Federal Ministry for Economic Cooperation and Development (BMZ) established the Sector Programme Values, Religion and Development. Like Britain, Germany also published a strategy paper detailing how the state and FBOs could best work together to achieve development outcomes.[98]

Elsewhere, the attention to religion can seem relatively ephemeral. A working group is established, a project is pursued, a dialogue begins, and just as soon as it starts, it appears to have finished, producing a report soon forgotten amidst other pressing issues.[99] Canada, for instance, published a strategy document similar to Britain and Germany—20 years ago and has not revisited it since. Examples of European donor countries that fit this trend include Switzerland, the Netherlands, Denmark, and Sweden.[100] Exemplars outside the OECD include Japan, which established the "Japan Religion Coordinating Project for Disaster Relief" in 2011 following the Great East Japan Earthquake.

Clearly, the work of FBOs is no longer "invisible." Neither do FBOs have the "lowly status" once ascribed to them among institutions in the foreign aid regime.[101] Instead, the history of FBOs' humanitarian work and their geographic expanse, as outlined in this chapter, have become more appreciated. From their early missionary work to humanitarian relief to modern development, FBOs have been fundamental drivers of personal and societal change. Even the foreign aid regime, which arose after World War II and came to eclipse FBOs in resources and impact, now readily acknowledges the legitimacy of religious actors in development. This is largely due to the growing realization that religion is not fading into obsolescence as once predicted but becoming increasingly salient—especially to those living in the Global South. The added effect of this "religious resurgence" is an attempt by many public donors to try and engage FBOs in development. Chapter 4 will show that such efforts, at least in the case of the United States, have been lackluster. Prior to examining this data, however, it is necessary to fully explore the unique political and legal context of faith-based aid in the United States and examine the controversies surrounding its introduction and implementation.

Notes

1 Curtis, *Holy Humanitarians*, 27.

2 The Senate passed a resolution "to transport contributions for the relief of the suffering poor of Russia," but the measure languished in the House and ultimately died in committee. Queen, "American Relief in the Russian Famine," 144.

3 "Famine Fleet: American Relief to Russia in 1891–92," *Hoover Institution Library and Archives*, www.hoover.org/shorthand-story/17

4 Tobi Thomas, "Russia-Ukraine War in Numbers: Casualties, Refugees and Aid," *The Guardian*, March 11, 2022, www.theguardian.com/world/2022/mar/11/russia-ukraine-war-numbers-casualties-refugees-aid

5 The US Congress allocated $113 billion in aid, and the UN received $3.4 billion in commitments or donations primarily from state governments.

6 "Islamic Relief Offers over $700,000 to Support Families Affected by Ukraine Crisis," *Islamic Relief Worldwide*, March 18, 2022, https://islamic-relief.org/news/islamic-relief-offers-over-700000-to-support-families-affected-by-ukraine-crisis/; Jill Foley Turner, "Ukraine Update: 20+ Charities on the Frontlines," *National Christian Foundation*, March 25, 2022, https://rb.gy/um8qsd; "One Year In: Jewish Federations Assess Impact of $85M in Ukraine Aid," *FedBeat*, February 21, 2023, www.jewishfederations.org/fedworld/jewish-federations-release-impact-of-85m-in-ukraine-aid-432298

7 Batson, Schoenrade, and Ventis, *Religion and the Individual*.

8 In Judaism, there are discrepant beliefs about the most appropriate beneficiary of Jewish charity. Many in traditional Judaism argue that the priority is to serve fellow Jews first, a concept known as *tikkun Yisrael*, while most contemporary Jews subscribe to the concept of *tikkun olam*, or "heal the world."

9 Sometimes, missionaries were motivated to address a physical need, but often, in tandem with this motivation, there was the desire to "enlighten" those seen as intellectually and morally inferior. Brantlinger, "Victorians and Africans."

10 Judaism, Hinduism, and Zoroastrianism are considered non-missionary religious traditions. In contrast, Buddhism, Christianity, and Islam are all considered to have a missionary component, where "the spreading of the truth and the conversion of unbelievers are raised to the rank of a sacred duty." Muller, *Lectures on the Science of Religion*, 318.

11 The original apostles saw the global dissemination of the Gospel as a spiritual mandate, and according to Eusebius, each was assigned a specific region in which to preach. This is known by Christians as "The Great Commission," and it is a command Jesus relays to his disciples in Galilee. The full passage, appearing in Matthew 28:18–20, reads:

> Then Jesus came to them and said, "All authority in heaven and on earth has been given to me. Therefore go and make disciples of all nations, baptizing them in the name of the Father and of the Son and of the Holy Spirit, and teaching them to obey everything I have commanded you. And surely I am with you always, to the very end of the age."

Though the Bible references the apostles' dispersion, Eusebius of Caesarea ("the Father of Church History") provided a more detailed account in the 2nd century. In Book 3, Chapter 1 of *Ecclesiastical History*, Eusebius explains that Thomas went to Parthia; Andrew to Scythia; John to Asia (and then Ephesus); Peter to Pontus, Galatia, Bithynia, Cappadocia, Asia, and Rome; and Paul from Jerusalem to Illyricum.

12 Spain and Portugal were the prime contributors to the spread of Christianity in the 16th, 17th, and 18th centuries, with their monarchs directly financing Roman Catholic missionaries and sending them throughout their respective territories. With the exception of the Dutch in the late 18th century, which employed missionaries in Ceylon and the East Indies, most states did not directly employ Protestant missionaries. This included Britain, which was the primary colonizer in the 19th century. Instead, independent Protestant missionary societies emerged, often enjoying legal protections and state subsidies. Some of the oldest and most prominent protestant missionary societies include the London Society (established in 1795), the Church Mission Society (established in 1799), and the American Board of Commissioners for Foreign Missions (established in 1812). Latourette, "Colonialism and Missions."

13 Latourette, "Colonialism and Missions," 339.

14 George E Urch, "Education and Colonialism in Kenya," *History of Education Quarterly* 11, no. 3 (Autumn 1971): 249–264.

15 Nunn, "Gender and Missionary Influence," 490.

16 King, *God's Internationalists*, 10; Oliver, Balbier, Krabbendam, and Schafer, "Special Issue," 1027.

17 During the "Kenya Emergency," for example, Kenyan missionaries (in addition to the British Red Cross and Save the Children) engaged in rehabilitation campaigns in partnership with the British colonial government to quell the threat of the Mau Mau and sustain British control of the colony. In this instance, the Gospel was seen as a kind of salve for the sickness of insurgency and religious instruction in prisons, a tactic in the state's larger strategy to " 'cleanse' suspected Mau Mau of

their anti-colonial beliefs." Baughan, "Rehabilitating an Empire"; Elkins, "The Struggle for Mau Mau Rehabilitation," 30.
18 Fields, "Christian Missionaries as Anticolonial Militants"; Woodberry, "The Missionary Roots of Liberal Democracy."
19 Zurlo, Johnson, and Crossing, "World Christianity and Mission 2021," 17.
20 Cagri Erhan, "Ottoman Official Attitudes Toward American Missionaries," *Turkish Yearbook of International Relations* 30 (2000): 191–212. https.//doi.org/10.1501/Intrel_0000000017
21 There were also over 400 Bible schools. Rogan, "Missionary Rivalries in Ottoman Transjordan," 47.
22 In fact, some wanted nothing to do with humanitarian service, seeing such works as trivial relative to the salvific mission. "… [T]he highest kind of Christian work," explained the president of the Christian Missionary Alliance, is "the winning of souls, [and] the evangelization of nations." "Let the world take care of [the rest]," he urged. See Curtis, *Holy Humanitarians*, 144.
23 Another example is the Medical Missionary Society of China, established in 1838, which marked the beginning of the medical mission movement and the formation of similar organizations. Lazich, "Seeking Souls Through the Eyes of the Blind," 59.
24 The YMCA began as a Bible study specifically for the unchurched and overworked young men of London. While still focused primarily on the *spiritual* needs of men, it nevertheless was unique in its attention to their social condition. In 1866, the New York YMCA added physical improvement to its mission and added training facilities, camps, and organized sports.
25 "The Societies Feeding the Famine Sufferers," *Christian Herald and Signs of our Times* 15, May 11, 1892, 298, https://archive.org/details/christianheralds15unse/
26 China Famine Relief Fund Shanghai Committee, *The Great Famine.*
27 The parable of the Good Samaritan in the Gospel of Luke was often highlighted as justifying this position. The Bible records Jesus as instructing his followers to love God and love their neighbor. When asked to clarify who, in fact, constituted a "neighbor," Jesus responded with the Parable of the Good Samaritan, which describes a Samaritan who comes across a man recently beaten and robbed. The Samaritan attends to his wounds and pays for his keep until he recovers.
28 The *Christian Herald* alone raised $3.3 million (over $110 million in today's currency). Heather D. Curtis, "The Crusading Newsman Who Taught Americans to Give to the Poor," *Zocalo Public Square*, October 20, 2019, www.zocalopublicsquare.org/2019/10/20/the-crusading-newsman-who-taught-americans-to-give-to-the-poor/ideas/essay/
29 The Salvation Army and YMCA were also prominent religious organizations involved in the war efforts, but like the International Red Cross, their operations were primarily aimed at aiding combatants.
30 In some cases, these organizations were completely new; in others, they represented a reconceptualization of previous missionary agencies. Six of the seven largest evangelical mission agencies eventually assumed humanitarian objectives and became development organizations. King, *God's Internationalists*, 7.
31 While the foundational intent of religious humanitarian organizations was often to help co-religionists, they could not limit their assistance to such individuals in times of war because of the impartiality agreement in the Geneva Conventions. During periods of reconstruction, state governments had similar requirements.

32 McCleary, *Global Compassion*, 16.
33 World Relief originated as the National Association of Evangelicals in 1944 and assumed the name World Relief in 1950.
34 Davey, Borton, and Foley, "A History of the Humanitarian System," 6.
35 Cullen, McCorriston, and Thompson, "The 'Big Survey,' " 737.
36 Ibid., 742.
37 O'Sullivan, "A 'Global Nervous System.' "
38 McCleary, *Global Compassion*, 22.
39 Less than 1% of all the FBOs operating in Africa in 1968 represented the Muslim faith. See Cullen, McCorriston, and Thompson, "The Big Survey," 738.
40 Petersen, "Trajectories of Transnational Muslim NGOs," 767.
41 These included the royal Saudi Committee for Support of Afghanistan, the Islamic Call Committee, the Benevolence International Foundation, the Al Haramain Islamic Foundations, the Arab Doctor's Union's Human Relief Agency, the International Islamic Council for Da'wa and Relief, Human Concern International, and Mercy Relief International. See Petersen, "Trajectories of Transnational Muslim NGOs," 768.
42 Petersen, "Trajectories of Transnational Muslim NGOs," 771.
43 Lumsdaine, *Moral Vision in International Politics*, 253.
44 Ghani and Lockhart, *Fixing Failed States*, 13.
45 United Nations, *World Economic and Social Survey 2017*, 27.
46 Ibid., 28.
47 America had already contributed $11 billion in aid to Europe prior to the end of the war.
48 The "Marshall Plan" speech at Harvard University, June 5, 1947, www.marshallfoundation.org/the-marshall-plan/speech/
49 Ibid.
50 Inaugural Address of Harry S. Truman, Yale University, January 20, 1949.
51 The target was later changed to .7% of a country's Gross National Income—where it remains today. This time period also saw the implementation of so-called structural adjustment programs (SAPs) by the IMF and IDA, where developing countries would have to adopt specific macro- and micro-economic policies before securing a desired loan or grant. The IDA and IMF were the primary implementers, but regional multilateral banks such as the Inter-American Development Bank (IDB) also took this approach.
52 The full list includes (1) The eradication of extreme poverty and hunger, (2) the provision of universal primary education, (3) the promotion of gender equality and the empowerment of women, (4) the reduction of child mortality, (5) the improvement of maternal health, (6) the mitigation of HIV/AIDS, malaria, and other diseases, (7) the promotion of environmental sustainability, and (8) the establishment of a global partnership for development.
53 The exceptions include the World Council of Churches, United Methodist Church, Religions for Peace, and CARITAS. Haynes, *Faith-Based Organizations at the United Nations*, 123.
54 Olarinmoye, "Faith-Based Organizations and Development," 3.
55 Berger, *The Sacred Canopy*.
56 Inglehart and Baker, "Modernization, Cultural Change, and the Persistence," 31.
57 Moghadam, "*A Global Resurgence of Religion?*"

58 Conrad Hackett et al., "The Global Religious Landscape," *Pew Research Center* (Washington, DC: Pew Research Center, 2012).
59 Peter L. Berger, "Secularism in Retreat," *The National Interest* 46 (1996/97): 3–12.
60 de Vries and Sullivan, eds., *Political Theologies*; Haynes, *Faith-Based Organizations at the United Nations*; Bettiza, *Finding Faith in Foreign Policy*. For a critique of the post-secular concept, see Tomalin, "Religions, Poverty Reduction and Global Development Institutions."
61 Roy, *Holy Ignorance*.
62 Thomas, "A Globalized God," 98.
63 The idea of globalization "flattening" the world is attributed to Thomas Friedman. Friedman, *The World Is Flat*.
64 Bettiza, *Finding Faith in Foreign Policy*, 59. This is evidenced, inter alia, by the growing number of individuals involved in short-term mission trips, as well as the increased number of full-time missionaries. (There were over half a million Christian missionaries in 2000 and over 140,000 Muslim missionaries.) Wuthnow, *Boundless Faith*, 167–168; Johnson, Zurlo, Hickman, and Crossing, "Christianity 2015," 29; Johnson and Scoggins, *Christian Missions and Islamic Da'wah*, 10.
65 For an early account of how globalization accelerated religious terrorism, see Ranstorp, "Terrorism in the Name of Religion."
66 Al Qaeda, a Sunni terrorist group, emerged in 1988 after the Soviet occupation of Afghanistan. The Aryan Nations, an American white supremacist terrorist group, began in 1977 but reached its zenith in the late 1980s and 1990s. Aum Shinrikyo was founded in 1987 in Japan. Lesser known of the three, Aum Shinrikyo specialized in attacking civilians using chemical and biological weapons. It was responsible for the sarin subway terrorist attack in Tokyo that killed 12 and injured over 1,000 in March 1995.
67 Bruce Hoffman, "Old Madness, New Methods," RAND, www.rand.org/content/dam/rand/www/external/congress/terrorism/phase1/hoffman.pdf
68 Institute for Economics and Peace. Global Terrorism Index 2014: Measuring the Impact of Terrorism, Sydney, 2014, 31, www.economicsandpeace.org/wp-content/uploads/2015/06/Global-Terrorism-Index-Report-2014.pdf
69 Anthony H. Cordesman, *Islam and the Patterns in Terrorism and Violent Extremism*, October 17, 2017, Center for Strategic and International Studies, https://csis-website-prod.s3.amazonaws.com/s3fs-public/publication/171017_Report_Islam%20and%20the%20-War_on_Terrorism_.pdf
70 Huntington, "The Clash of Civilizations?"
71 Numerous quantitative studies were published testing Huntington's theory and all failed to find significant results in favor of the thesis. Henderson and Tucker, "Clear and Present Strangers;" Chiozza, "Is There a Clash of Civilizations?"; Fox, "Paradigm Lost."
72 An estimated 90% of all academic works on terrorism were written in the years following 9/11. See Silke, "Research on Terrorism," 28.
73 Institute for Economics and Peace. Global Terrorism Index 2020: Measuring the Impact of Terrorism, Sydney, November 2020, http://visionofhumanity.org/reports (January 22, 2022).
74 I frame this in terms of the "politicization" of religion, but the "religionization" of politics is an equally valid construct. The appropriateness of both phrases

exemplifies that neither religion nor government has been "co-opted" by government or religious actors, respectively. Instead, their interests have aligned and evolved due to the active participation of members from both camps.

75 Mohak Gupta, "BJP Foundation Day: Party's Rise to Power from 2 MPs in 1984 to 282 in 2014," *India Today*, April 6, 2017, www.indiatoday.in/fyi/story/bjp-foundation-day-modi-vajpayee-1984-congress-969890-2017-04-06

76 The characterization of the AKP (Justice and Development Party) as a "Muslim party," though now accepted, was initially contested. Alev Cinar, "The Justice and Development Party: Turkey's Experience with Islam, Democracy, Liberalism, and Secularism," *International Journal of Middle East Studies* 43, no. 3 (2011): 529–541.

77 The primary organizational actors in the movement were the Moral Majority, led by Jerry Falwell; the Council for National Policy, led by Tim LaHaye; the Concerned Women for America, led by Beverly LaHaye; and the Religious Roundtable, led by Ed McAteer.

78 Jacobson, "The 1994 House Elections in Perspective," 211.

79 The Commission on Presidential Debates, "The Second Gore-Bush Presidential Debate," October 11, 2000, www.debates.org/voter-education/debate-transcripts/october-11-2000-debate-transcript/

80 The White House, "President Addresses the Nation" (September 7, 2003), www.whitehouse.gov/news/releases/2003/09/20030907-1.html

81 The 2002 NSS also, for the first time, included *development aid* alongside defense and diplomacy as a means to enhance national security. White House, 2002. *National Security Strategy of the United States of America*. Washington, DC: White House, 31, https://georgewbush-whitehouse.archives.gov/nsc/nss/2002/

82 Bettiza, *Finding Faith in Foreign Aid*, 144.

83 Gregorio Bettiza explains that though this was not the initial view of President Bush, influential members of the administration persuaded the president to take this position. See Bettiza, *Finding Faith in Foreign Policy*, 149.

84 Naranyan and Petesch, *Voices of the Poor.*

85 Among the most notable advocates were Pope John Paul II, the Dalai Lama, and U2's lead singer Bono. Roodman "Creditor Initiatives in the 1980s and 1990s," 25.

86 Pettifor, "The Jubilee 2000 Campaign," 305.

87 Ibid.

88 James D. Wolfensohn, "Faith and Development – The Link Yet Tapped for Global Poverty Reduction," The World Bank Group, Washington, DC, May 2, 2002, https://rb.gy/td4vh

89 This is best evidenced by the World Bank's pivot away from structural adjustment programs and the adoption of the UN Millennium Development Goals in 2000.

90 Haynes, *Faith-Based Organizations at the United Nations*, 129.

91 This included the UN Conference on Environment and Development (Earth Summit) in 1992, the International Conference on Population and Development (ICPD) in 1994, and the Fourth World Conference on Women in 1995.

92 Haynes, *Faith-Based Organizations at the United Nations*, 54; Jeffrey Haynes, "What Do Faith-Based Organizations Seek at the United Nations?" *E-International Relations*, November 15, 2013, www.e-ir.info/2013/11/15/what-do-faith-based-organisations-seek-at-the-united-nations/

93 Tomalin, Haustein, and Kidy, "Religion and the Sustainable Development Goals," 102, 107.

94 This discussion of bilateral aid donors precludes Saudi Arabia, which, as of 2021, is the eighth-largest bilateral donor of humanitarian aid. As an Islamic theocracy, Saudi Arabian aid is funneled only through Islamic NGOs.

95 Though it has changed names multiple times under different presidents, it began as the Center for Faith-Based and Community Initiatives (CFBCI) under President George W. Bush in 2002 via Executive Order 13279 following the establishment of an earlier White House Office of Faith-Based and Community Initiatives (OFBCI). The Center was continued under Obama, though effectively changed names in 2009 under Executive Order 13199 when the White House Office changed to the Office of Faith-Based and Neighborhood Partnerships. In 2018, via Executive Order 13831, Trump changed the name of the White House Office of Faith-Based and Neighborhood Partnerships to the White House Faith and Opportunity Initiative and also changed the names of subsidiary centers to match the White House Office. President Biden then changed the White House Office and Centers back to the Office of Faith-Based and Neighborhood Partnerships via Executive Order 14015 in 2021.

96 See *69 FR 61715*.

97 Petersen, "Exploring and Working with Faith-Based Organizations," 46.

98 *Bundesministerium für wirtschaftliche Zusammenarbeit und* Entwicklung (BMZ). (2016). Religionen als Partner der Zusammenarbeit [Religions as partners in cooperation]. Berlin. www.bmz.de/de/mediathek/publikationen/reihen/strategiepapiere/Strategiepapier363_02_2016.pdf

99 Ibid., 53.

100 The Swiss Agency for Development Cooperation hosted a conference on religion and development in 2002 and held several workshops with FBOs soon after. The Dutch Foreign Ministry worked closely with the Knowledge Center for Religion and Development from 2010 to 2014. The Danish International Development Agency did not organize a group but intermittently consulted with the Danish NGO Working Group on Religion and Development. The Finnish Ministry of Foreign Affairs participated in the donor–UN–FBO policy roundtable in New York in 2015. None of these countries have an institutionalized element addressing religion and development, nor have they produced any guidelines for FBO engagement. For a more thorough overview of the efforts of these states and the UK, see Petersen, "Exploring and Working with Faith-Based Organizations."

101 Haynes, *Faith-Based Organizations at the United Nations*, 2.

Bibliography

Balchin, Cassandra. "The F-Word and the S-Word: Too Much of One and Not Enough of the Other." *Development in Practice* 17, no. 4/5 (2007): 532–538.

Batson, Daniel C., Patricia Schoenrade, and W. Larry Ventis. *Religion and the Individual: A Social-Psychological Perspective* (New York: Oxford University Press, 1993).

Baughan, Emily. "Rehabilitating an Empire: Humanitarian Collusion with the Colonial State During the Kenyan Emergency, ca.1954–1960." *Journal of British Studies* 59, no. 1 (2020): 57–79.

Berger, Peter L. *The Sacred Canopy* (Garden City, NY: Doubleday, 1967).

Bettiza, Gregorio. *Finding Faith in Foreign Policy: Religion and American Diplomacy in a Postsecular World* (New York: Oxford University Press, 2019).

Brantlinger, Patrick. "Victorians and Africans: The Genealogy of the Myth of the Dark Continent." *Critical Inquiry* 12, no. 1 (1985): 166–203. www.jstor.org/stable/1343467

Chatelard, Géraldine and Mohammed Tarawneh. *Antonin Jaussen, sciences sociales occidentales et patrimoine arabe* (Beyrouth: Presses de l'Ifpo, 1999): 37–49. http://books.openedition.org/ifpo/5317

China Famine Relief Fund Shanghai Committee. *The Great Famine: Report of the Committee of the Chine Famine Relief Fund* (Shanghai: American Presbyterian Mission Press, 1879).

Chiozza, Giacomo. "Is There a Clash of Civilizations? Evidence from Patterns of International Conflict Involvement, 1946–97." *Journal of Peace Research* 39, no. 6 (2002): 711–734.

Cullen, Poppy, Steve McCorriston, and Andrew Thompson. "The 'Big Survey': Decolonisation, Development and the First Wave of NGO Expansion in Africa After 1945." *The International History Review* 44, no. 4 (2022): 721–750. DOI:10.1080/07075332.2021.1976810

Curtis, Heather. *Holy Humanitarians: American Evangelicals and Global Aid* (Cambridge, MA: Harvard University Press, 2018).

Davey, Eleanor, John Borton, and Matthew Foley. "A History of the Humanitarian System, Western Origins and Foundations." *HPG Working Paper*. Overseas Development Institute, London, 2013. www.odi.org/publications/7535-global-history-humanitarian-action

Elkins, Caroline. "The Struggle for Mau Mau Rehabilitation in Late Colonial Kenya." *International Journal of African Historical Studies* 33, no. 1 (2000): 25–57, 30.

Fields, Karen E. "Christian Missionaries as Anticolonial Militants." *Theory and Society* 11, no. 1 (1982): 95–108. www.jstor.org/stable/657286

Fox, Jonathan. "Paradigm Lost: Huntington's Unfulfilled Clash of Civilizations Prediction into the 21st Century." *International Politics* 42 (2005): 428–457.

Friedman, Thomas. *The World Is Flat: A Brief History of the Twenty-First Century* (New York: Farrar, Straus, and Giroux, 2005).

Ghani, Ashraf and Clare Lockhart. *Fixing Failed States: A Framework for Rebuilding a Fractured World* (1st ed.). (New York: Oxford University Press: 2009).

Haynes, Jeffrey. *Faith-Based Organizations at the United Nations* (New York: Palgrave Macmillan, 2017).

Henderson, Errol A. and Richard Tucker. "Clear and Present Strangers: The Clash of Civilizations and International Conflict." *International Studies Quarterly* 45, no. 2 (2001): 317–338.

Huntington, Samuel P. "The Clash of Civilizations?" *Foreign Affairs* 72, no. 3 (Summer 1993): 22–49.

Inglehart, Ronald and Wayne E. Baker. "Modernization, Cultural Change, and the Persistence of Traditional Values." *American Sociological Review* 65, no. 1 (2000): 19–51.

Jacobson, Gary C. "The 1994 House Elections in Perspective." *Political Science Quarterly* 111, no. 2 (1996): 203–223.

Johnson, Todd M. and David R. Scoggins. "Christian Missions and Islamic Da'wah: A Preliminary Quantitative Assessment." *International Bulletin of Missionary Research* 9, no. 1 (2005): 8–12. DOI:10.1177/239693930502900102

Johnson, Todd M., Gina A. Zurlo, Albert W. Hickman, and Peter F. Crossing. "Christianity 2015: Religious Diversity and Personal Contact." *International Bulletin of Missionary Research* 39, no. 1 (2015): 28–29.

King, David J. *God's Internationalists: World Vision and the Age of Evangelical Humanitarianism* (Philadelphia: University of Pennsylvania Press, 2019).

Latourette, Kenneth Scott. "Colonialism and Missions: Progressive Separation." *Journal of Church and State* 7, no. 3 (1965): 330–349.

Lazich, Michael C. "Seeking Souls Through the Eyes of the Blind: The Birth of the Medical Missionary Society in Nineteenth-Century China." In *Healing Bodies, Saving Souls: Medical Missions in Asia and Africa*, edited by David Hardiman, 58–86. Welcome Series in the History of Medicine, Clio Medica 80 (Amsterdam and New York: Rodopi, 2006).

Lumsdaine, David Halloran. *Moral Vision in International Politics: The Foreign Aid Regime, 1949–1989* (Princeton, NJ: Princeton University Press, 1993).

McCleary, Rachel. *Global Compassion: Private Voluntary Organizations and US Foreign Policy Since 1939* (New York: Oxford University Press: 2009).

Moghadam, Assaf. "A Global Resurgence of Religion?" Paper No. 03-03, Weatherhead Center for International Affairs, Harvard University, Cambridge, MA, August 2003.

Muller, Max. *Lectures on the Science of Religion* (New York: Charles Scribner's Sons, 1893).

Narayan, Deepa and Patti Petesch. *Voices of the Poor: From Many Lands* (Washington, DC: World Bank and Oxford University Press, 2002).

Nunn, Nathan. "Gender and Missionary Influence in Colonial Africa." In *Africa's Development in Historical Perspective*, edited by Emmanuel Akyeampong, Robert H. Bates, Nathan Nunn, and James A. Robinson (New York: Cambridge University Press, 2014): 489–512.

Olarinmoye, Omobolaji Ololade. "Faith-Based Organizations and Development: Prospects and Constraints." *Transformation* 29, no. 1 (2012): 1–14.

Oliver, Kendrick, Uta A. Balbier, Hans Krabbendam, and Axel Schafer, "Special Issue: Exploring the Global History of American Evangelicalism Introduction." *Journal of American Studies* 51, no. 4 (2017): 1027.

O'Sullivan, Kevin. "A 'Global Nervous System': The Rise and Rise of European Humanitarian NGOs, 1945–1985." In *International Organizations and Development, 1945*–1990, edited by Marc Frey, Sonke Kunkel, and Corinna R. Unger (London: Palgrave Macmillan, 2014): 196–219.

Petersen, Marie Juul. "Exploring and Working with Faith-Based Organizations: An Analysis of Practices in Selected EU Member States." DEVCO, European Commission, and Agora on Religion and Development, 2018. www.humanrights.dk/sites/humanrights.dk/files/media/migrated/juul_petersen_2019._working_with_fbos.pdf

Petersen, Marie Juul. "Trajectories of Transnational Muslim NGOs." *Development in Practice* 22, no. 5/6 (2012): 763–778.

Pettifor, Ann. "The Jubilee 2000 Campaign: A Brief Overview." In *Sovereign Debt at the Crossroads: Challenges and Proposals for Resolving the Third World Debt Crisis,* edited by Chris Jochnick and Fraser A. Preston (New York: Oxford University Press, 2006): 297–318.

Queen, George S. "American Relief in the Russian Famine of 1891–1892." *The Russian Review* 14, no. 2 (1955): 140–150. DOI:10.2307/125573

Ranstorp, Magnus. "Terrorism in the Name of Religion." *Journal of International Affairs* 50, no. 1 (1996): 41–62. www.jstor.org/stable/24357404

Rogan, Eugene "Missionary Rivalries in Ottoman Transjordan at the Turn of the 20th Century". In *Antonin Jaussen, sciences sociales occidentales et patrimoine arabe*, edited by Géraldine Chatelard and Mohammed Tarawneh (Beyrouth: Presses de l'Ifpo, 1999): 37–49.

Roodman, David. "Creditor Initiatives in the 1980s and 1990s." In *Sovereign Debt at the Crossroads: Challenges and Proposals for Resolving the Third World Debt Crisis*, edited by Chris Jochnick and Fraser A. Preston (New York: Oxford University Press, 2006): 25.

Roy, Oliver. *Holy Ignorance: When Religion and Culture Part Ways* (New York: Oxford University Press, 2014).

Silke, Andrew. "Research on Terrorism: A Review of the Impact of 9/11 and the Global War on Terrorism," in *Terrorism Informatics: Knowledge Management and Data Mining for Homeland Security*, edited by Hsinchun Chen, Edna Reid, Joshua Sinai, Andrew Silke, and Boaz Ganor (New York, Springer: 2008): 27–50.

Thomas, Scott. "A Globalized God: Religion's Growing Influence in International Politics." *Foreign Affairs* 89, no. 6 (November 2010): 93–101.

Tomalin, Emma. "Religions, Poverty Reduction and Global Development Institutions." *Palgrave Communications* 4, no. 132 (2018). www.nature.com/articles/s41599-018-0167-8.pdf

Tomalin, Emma, Jorg Haustein, and Shabaana Kidy. "Religion and the Sustainable Development Goals." *Review of Faith & International Affairs* 17, no. 2 (2019): 102–118.

United Nations. *World Economic and Social Survey 2017: Reflecting on 70 Years of Development Policy Analysis*, 2017. www.un.org/development/desa/dpad/wp-content/uploads/sites/45/publication/WESS_2017-FullReport.pdf

de Vries, Hent and Lawrence E. Sullivan, eds. *Political Theologies: Public Religions in a Post-Secular World* (New York: Fordham University Press, 2006).

Woodberry, Robert D. "The Missionary Roots of Liberal Democracy." *The American Political Science Review* 106, no. 2 (2012): 244–274. www.jstor.org/stable/41495078

Wuthnow, Robert. *Boundless Faith: The Global Outreach of American Churches* (Berkeley, CA: University of California Press, 2009).

Zurlo, Gina A., Todd M. Johnson, and Peter F. Crossing, "World Christianity and Mission 2021: Questions About the Future." *International Bulletin of Mission Research* 45, no. 1 (2021): 15–25.

3 America's Religious Engagement

Introduction

The religious resurgence that emerged at the turn of the 21st century manifested differently across the world. Religiosity in America did not decline as expected but remained strong, with two-thirds of the country regularly attending religious services.[1] This was matched by an increasing number of people willing to accommodate religion in the public square. The idea that government could *partner* with religious organizations to address social ills was gaining appeal. By 1999, over three-quarters of Americans approved of the government outsourcing social services to religious organizations.[2] This "emerging consensus" on faith-based funding, as described by President Clinton, brought about an electoral opportunity for his hopeful successors.[3]

Both Democratic candidate Al Gore and Republican candidate George W. Bush promised to extend federal funding opportunities to faith-based organizations (FBOs) during their presidential campaign.[4] In general, the idea had broad bipartisan support. "The only thing politicians seemed to want to fight about," says Dennis R. Hoover, "was who was more in favor of it."[5] Enter the tumultuous 2000 election and a divided government, and this consensus quickly deteriorated into contention. By the time George W. Bush entered the White House and began implementing his so-called Faith-Based Initiative in 2001, he faced a cacophony of criticism.

Understanding the political milieu surrounding the Faith-Based Initiative is critical to understanding the current state of FBO engagement in American foreign aid. This chapter provides a necessary prelude to subsequent chapters by describing the historical context of FBOs and American foreign aid, the genesis of the Faith-Based and Community Initiative, its manifestation at the United States Agency for International Development (USAID), and the various legal and political debates it engendered. From a legal standpoint, the primary question surrounding the initiative was whether the federal funding of FBOs violates the Establishment Clause of the US Constitution. The political controversies involve whether President Bush and his successors used the initiative to buy political loyalty and to what extent FBO funding impacted American foreign policy. This chapter addresses each of these debates in turn.

DOI: 10.4324/9781003456704-3

Even though the political maelstrom surrounding the initiative has largely subsided, the lingering malaise of many FBOs to federal funding attests to the ripple effect and relevancy of many of these earlier debates.

Early American Aid

When President George W. Bush began the Faith-Based and Community Initiative (hereafter shortened to "the Faith-Based Initiative"), one of his primary talking points involved the discrimination FBOs faced in applying for federal funding.[6] The president sought to put an end to such discrimination. Put another way, the president described his goal as "leveling the playing field" for FBOs vis-à-vis secular nongovernmental organizations (NGOs) pursuing government grants.[7] But was the field actually uneven, and if so, why and how? The answer depended, in part, upon the agency in question. In foreign aid, FBOs had, at one time, been the government's primary implementing partners, but by the time Bush came to office, US foreign aid was primarily carried out through secular NGOs. This transition paralleled the increasing prioritization of development in American aid.

The modern era of American foreign aid began in the aftermath of World War II when the United States spent $12 billion to forestall Europe's economic collapse.[8] The majority of US aid initially took the form of direct bilateral cash transfers from the US government to European governments for war reconstruction and recovery.[9] Money was spent, inter alia, on rebuilding critical infrastructure like roads, power plants, and housing projects. In addition to government-to-government aid, the United States also used third parties, primarily US-based nonprofits, to ship food commodities to recovering nations.[10] In 1950 alone, the United States sent the equivalent of $195 million in food to 36 countries. By 1955, this number reached $1.3 billion.[11] Most of the nonprofits serving as conduits for food delivery were faith-based, including Catholic Relief Services, Hadassah, Lutheran World Relief, Church World Service, American Friends Service Committee, and the American Jewish Joint Distribution Committee.[12]

Atop the undercurrent of American food shipments, the surface waters of American aid began to shift from war relief to economic development. This change followed the new world order following World War II. The war had left the world with two superpowers, the United States and the Soviet Union, each of which extolled a different political and economic ideology and vied for global preeminence. Much of the so-called third world had yet to pick a side.[13] America thus began to see aid as a means to both mitigate poverty and quell the threat of Communism. Truman explained that the goal was to "help the free peoples of the world, through their own efforts, to produce more food, more clothing, more materials for housing, and more mechanical power to lighten their burdens."[14] By helping developing nations help themselves, Truman said, "more and more nations [will] come to know the benefits of democracy and to participate in growing abundance."[15] For its part, America would provide the necessary technical assistance and funds for capital projects.[16]

The president initially carried his vision out through the Mutual Security Administration (MSA), the Foreign Operations Administration (FOA), and the International Cooperation Administration (ICA) in successive order.[17] Later, in 1961, President John F. Kennedy consolidated these efforts by establishing USAID. USAID took up the mantel of providing humanitarian assistance and promoting economic development, and it increasingly elicited the support of private partners in both endeavors. In so doing, it continued to rely on many of its former faith-based partners but also welcomed the support of a growing number of secular organizations.[18] Soon, these smaller secular NGOs (sometimes referred to as "volagencies") vastly outnumbered USAID's faith-based partners.[19]

The numeric discrepancy between USAID's secular and faith-based partners became even more pronounced in the so-called golden age of grants, ushered in by the 1973 Foreign Assistance Act. Congress wanted USAID to rely more heavily on NGOs to carry out its humanitarian and development work, yet also wanted to ensure these organizations were up to the task. The 1973 Foreign Assistance Act, also known as "New Directions," allowed USAID to give funds directly to NGOs to increase their capacity to serve as proxies in areas where USAID lacked missions. Congress also intended the legislation to help organizations shift from myopic aid toward long-term projects aimed at economic development. In 1981, in an amendment to the Foreign Assistance Act, Congress required 12%–16% of USAID's development and disaster funds go through NGOs.[20] Figure 3.1 illustrates USAID funding to NGOs from 1948 to 2005, including the proportion allocated to FBOs.

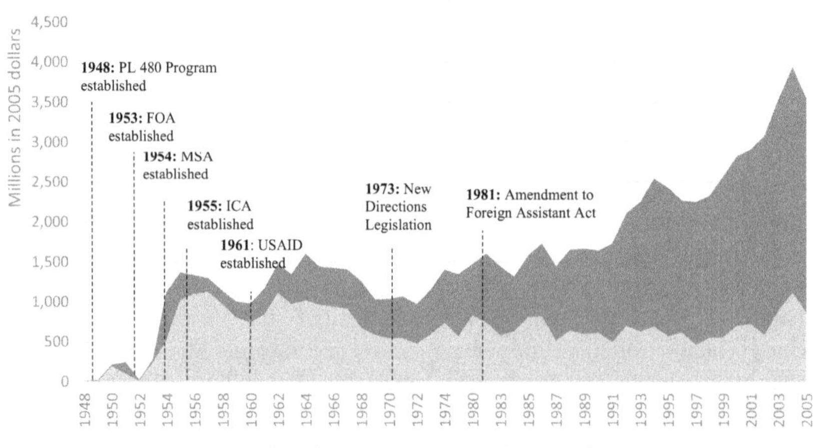

Figure 3.1 US Foreign Aid Funds to NGOs and FBOs, 1948–2005.

Note: Dataset excludes years 1975–1977, 1979, and 1982.

Source: McCleary and Barro (2011).

Two factors largely account for the increased number of USAID's secular NGO partners in its first 40 years. First, the development zeitgeist led to a steady supply of secular, technical NGOs that USAID officials often perceived were more agile and better equipped to address specific development challenges than larger, older humanitarian FBOs.[21] Second, several US Supreme Court rulings were seen by USAID to implicate the agency's funding of FBOs, and the agency shaped its rules accordingly.[22] These rules generally precluded "pervasively sectarian organization" from receiving funds.[23] The effect was that the FBOs most eligible for government funds were those that mirrored secular development organizations in their operations and hiring processes. This changed at the turn of the century with the Faith-Based Initiative.

The Faith-Based Initiative

President George W. Bush disapproved of the paucity of faith-based partners at USAID. He wanted FBOs to be more prominently represented among the government's funded organizations. The Faith-Based Initiative, launched in 2001, was his solution to the problem. Yet the Initiative was bigger than USAID. And it was bigger than President Bush. Instead, the Initiative grew to encompass over a dozen executive entities. And the story of faith-based funding began before Bush and continued after him.

The direct antecedent to the Faith-Based Initiative was the Charitable Choice provision of the 1996 Welfare Reform Bill.[24] Buried amidst the bill's nearly 800 pages, the provision allowed the privatization of previously state-run welfare programs and included religious groups among the service providers eligible to receive government grants. Most legislators were either unaware or relatively insouciant toward the provision when it was first introduced, but a few were genuinely enthused.[25] These advocates considered the Charitable Choice provision evidence, however inchoate, of the government's increasing accommodation toward religion.[26] One of the provision's more ardent supporters was Texas Governor George W. Bush.[27]

When running for president, Governor Bush pushed to extend Charitable Choice across federal programs. He also wanted to see a more comprehensive and coordinated federal effort in reaching out to FBOs, or as he called them, "little armies of compassion" to fight against social ills such as poverty.[28] His political palliative was to provide greater legal clearance, at all levels, for FBOs to apply for government grants. He was able to realize his desires when he assumed the Oval Office.

The objective of the Faith-Based Initiative, according to Bush's first executive order, was to use government resources to "enlist, equip, enable, [and] empower" FBOs and community organizations to continue serving the nation's (and the world's) most vulnerable.[29] The requisite institutional infrastructure included a special office in the White House and implementing offices across the executive branch. The president rolled out his plan in several installments across his two terms. By the time he left office, eleven federal agencies had a "Center for Faith-Based and Community Initiatives."[30] Other centers were later added, bringing the total number of participating executive entities to 13. Figure 3.2 illustrates the expansive political infrastructure of the Faith-Based Initiative.

Under President Bush, the Centers for Faith-Based and Community Initiatives were tasked with auditing current funding practices, issuing clarifying regulations, and ensuring uniform standards for FBOs and secular NGOs in the application for federal funding.[31] The centers were also responsible for educating FBOs about their eligibility for grants and providing FBOs with the necessary resources and training to make them more competitive grant applicants.

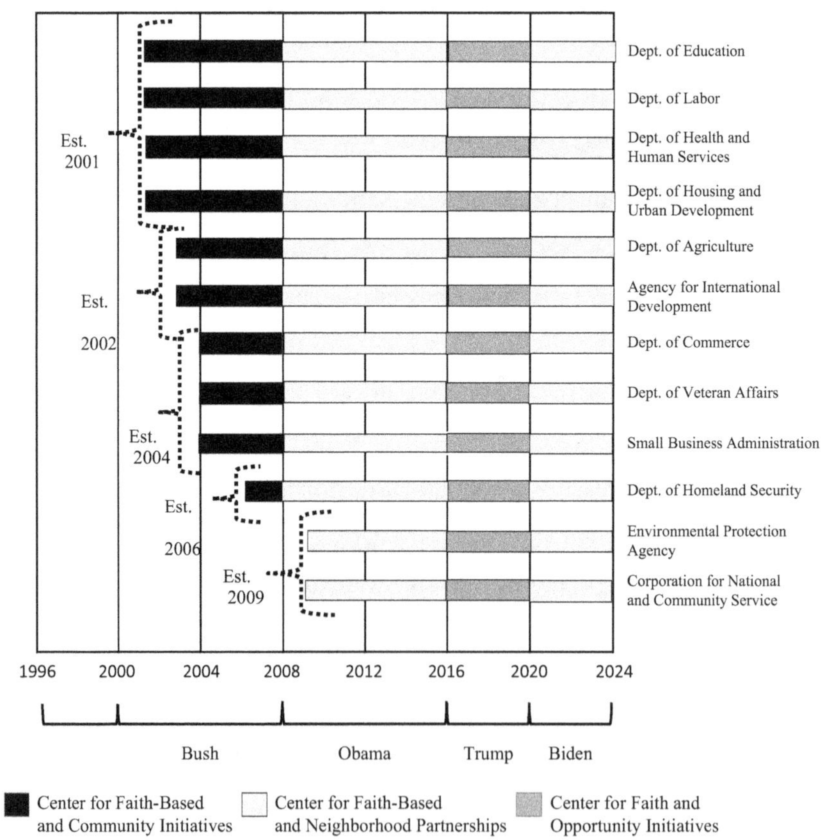

Figure 3.2 Participating Agencies and Departments in the Faith-Based Initiative, 2008–2024.

While the Charitable Choice provision laid the legal groundwork for the Faith-Based Initiative, the latter was *sui generis* in many ways. The primary difference between Charitable Choice and the Faith-Based Initiative lies in the latter's scope and method of implementation. The Charitable Choice provision allowed *states* to provide money to FBOs, while the Faith-Based Initiative primarily focused on federal agencies.[32] Moreover, while Congress passed Charitable Choice, Bush's Faith-Based Initiative went into effect without the imprimatur of the legislative branch through a series of executive orders.[33] It was the president who took the lead and who fast-tracked the initiative, not Congress. The result was a robust network of offices spanning horizontally across executive agencies and vertically down to state and local governments.[34]

Many assumed Bush's successor, Barack Obama, would dismantle the Faith-Based Initiative's institutional apparatus or, at least, disassociate himself from the initiative. Instead, shortly after taking office, Obama issued Executive Order 13498, maintaining but renaming the White House Office of Faith-Based and Community Initiatives (OFBCI).[35] He also added to the sinews of the initiative two additional faith-based centers in the Environmental Protection Agency and the Corporation for National and Community Service. One of the most meaningful actions Obama undertook was to form a special Advisory Council on faith. Comprised of 25 religious and community leaders representing varying faiths, the president intended for the Council to provide guidance on how the federal government could best partner with religious actors.[36] The Council's efforts resulted, inter alia, in the 2013 National Strategy on Religious Leader and Faith Community Engagement and in the implementing office of Religion and Global Affairs at the State Department. Obama's efforts led some to claim he had ushered in "Faith-Based Initiative 2.0."[37]

Obama's version of the Faith-Based Initiative was followed by another iteration under President Donald J. Trump.[38] Trump replaced the White House Office with a White House Advisor within the Office of Public Liaison and dissolved the State Department's Office on Religion and Global Affairs. He also requested that all executive departments and agencies lacking a faith-based center designate a liaison to interface with the White House Advisor. In addition to these institutional and bureaucratic changes, President Trump issued several executive orders on religious freedom.[39] One of the primary effects of these orders was to codify further the protections of FBOs receiving federal funds. Trump made clear, for instance, that FBO awardees could maintain their religious expression and prefer co-religionists in their hiring and firing decisions without facing legal recourse.[40] He also abrogated the requirement, implemented under Obama, that federally funded FBOs make beneficiaries aware of similar secular services.[41] The president's orders were published as rules in the federal register a month before his successor, Joe Biden, took office.

As of 2022, Biden had not yet rescinded these actions, but he did revert the name of the White House Office to the name it assumed under Obama.[42] He also selected the same director for the office who had been in place during Obama's second term. In describing the scope and purpose of the office in his executive order, Biden lifted language almost verbatim from George W. Bush's original order but made it more inclusive. In describing the purpose of the White House Office, he said it would assist in "the Federal Government's comprehensive effort to enlist, equip, empower, and expand the work of community-serving organizations, both faith-based and secular ... ."[43] One of the ways Biden distinguished the direction of his administration's office was in the factsheet accompanying his executive order. This factsheet specified that Biden's White House Office would include international development and global humanitarian work among its top priorities. USAID later published a press release explaining how its "faith-based approach" fulfilled the president's vision.[44]

The Rule

Though seemingly a top priority under Biden, USAID was not among the first agencies incorporated into President Bush's Faith-Based Initiative. President Bush established the CFBCI at USAID in December 2002—nearly two years after he announced the initiative and established centers at five other federal agencies.[45] Pursuant to the president's directive, USAID issued the 2004 USAID Ruling "Participation by Religious Orders in USAID Programs," commonly referred to as "The Rule." The Rule revised existing USAID regulations to remove any "unwarranted barriers to the equal participation of faith-based organizations."[46] Though other agency and department regulations relating to FBOs have changed under different presidential administrations, The Rule has remained relatively unchanged for the past 20 years. Its purpose is to outline what is permitted and prohibited for USAID mission officers in awarding funds and to delineate the same for USAID's FBO award recipients.

The Rule first makes clear that an organization is not to be denied funds due to its religious character, religious exercise, or religious affiliation.[47] USAID also cannot ask an organization to change its religious character as a condition of receiving funds. Essentially, The Rule draws a red line around FBO names, mission statements, board composition, hiring practices, and imagery. FBOs with explicitly religious names and mission statements and those that prefer co-religionists in hiring and selecting board members are not required to change practices. This means a Catholic hospital can prominently display a cross on its walls; a Jewish orphanage can display the Star of David; and a Muslim organization can have a logo that incorporates the star and crescent and can display its logo on all its material—including items given to beneficiaries. These organizations can also hire only individuals who profess the organization's faith, or they can require all employees to sign a statement of faith. They can have a similar requirement for their board. President

Bush considered this provision especially critical to facilitating greater FBO–government collaboration. "Why would I want to access federal money if the federal government ... tries to take away my mission, to take the cross ... or the Star of David off the wall?" asked Bush in one of his earlier speeches. Why collaborate if it means "you are forced to change your calling?"[48]

The Rule protects FBOs from making this kind of trade-off, but it doesn't allow for the unfettered use of federal funds. There are lines that FBOs also cannot cross. Part 205 of The Rule originally articulated that USAID award recipients could not use funds to support "inherently religious activities, such as worship, religious instruction, and proselytization." The Rule also specified that while organizations could not use funds to construct or rehabilitate buildings solely or predominately used for religious purposes, they could fund the construction or repair of dual-use buildings. For example, building or reconstructing a church or mosque would be prohibited, while constructing a soup kitchen attached to a place of religious instruction would be permissible. [49]

The Obama administration provided further guidance. Under 80 FR 47237, "inherently religious activities" was replaced with "explicitly religious activities," and more examples of acceptable and unacceptable activities were provided. Secular services like feeding the hungry, for instance, are authorized no matter who the provider is, while areas like education and counseling prove more delicate. The amendment specifies that an organization can use a grant to "study religion as a historical or cultural reality" but not pay for devotional guides or other religious content. The amendment also prohibits recipients from using award money to pay for worship services and proselytization, and it requires that all publicly funded activities be separate in time and space from such activities.[50] Similarly, if a USAID award pays for counseling, the amendment bars the counselors in the funded program from introducing religious content. Only if a beneficiary begins a conversation about religion can providers engage accordingly. They are not obligated to cease or redirect the conversation. Another amendment passed under Obama (81 FR 42245) clarified that USAID was not barred from funding the acquisition, construction, and rehabilitation of structures that housed religious instruction or served primarily as houses of worship in situations where such buildings were similarly situated to others in need of assistance (for instance, in the wake of a natural disaster).

In addition to clarifying grant eligibility and conditions of use, The Rule also lessens the grant application requirements of FBOs.[51] Before The Rule, FBOs applying for a USAID grant or contract generally had to submit additional documentation ensuring they would not use the funds for religious purposes. They would be asked to create a separate memorandum, code of conduct, or written assurance. The Rule eliminates this requirement, exemplifying the dictum *abusus non tollit usum*—possible abuse does not preclude all use. In other words, the agency accepts that while an FBO *could* divert public funds for religious purposes, it does not assume such malfeasance and use this to preclude FBOs from receiving agency awards or as a justification for greater FBO oversight.

The Rule's publication had a Janus-like effect. It assuaged the anxiety of some (encouraging new FBOs to apply for funds) while simultaneously inciting the anger of others (inviting lawsuits and public backlash). Those most critical of The Rule had three primary complaints, saying it violated the US Constitution, it represented a political mirage, and it harmed America's interests and image abroad.

The Constitutional Controversy

To some, the coupling of "faith" and "foreign aid" counters the long-standing legal tradition in the United States concerning the separation of church and state.[52] This doctrine derives from the Establishment Clause of the First Amendment of the US Constitution, which states that "Congress shall make no law respecting an establishment of religion." The most obvious reading of this clause prohibits the US federal government from establishing a national church or religion, but the US Supreme Court previously assumed a broader interpretation. Most famously, in *Everson v. Board of Education* (1947), the Court borrowed the metaphor of Thomas Jefferson to explain that the Establishment Clause required a wall between church and state.[53] According to Justice Hugo Black, this meant, at minimum, that "No tax in any amount, large or small should ... be levied to support any religious activities or institutions."[54]

For four decades, strict separatism was the doctrine du jour, but this changed at the turn of the century when the Court began to emphasize religious neutrality and even religious accommodation. The Faith-Based Initiative and USAID's implementation of The Rule were one of many programs and policies enacted just as the jurisprudential sands were shifting. Their constitutionality was thus an open question. In fact, the direct federal funding of FBOs presented several questions ripe for judicial review, including whether providing money to FBOs led to the advancement of religion or government entanglement with religion, whether federally funded FBOs could legally adopt religious hiring criteria, and whether the government favored religious organizations or funded religious activities in its implementation of the Faith-Based Initiative.

Advancement and Entanglement

The primary question surrounding The Rule (and the Faith-Based Initiative generally) is whether direct government funding of sectarian institutions too closely aligns the US government with the interests and aims of religious entities. In 1973, the Court clarified the conditions under which government funding crossed this line. According to the Court, the Constitution prohibits the government from funding religious entities if such funds (1) support non-secular purposes, (2) have the effect of either advancing or inhibiting religion, or (3) foster excessive entanglement between the state and religion.[55] Most scholars agreed that the Faith-Based Initiative and The Rule likely cleared the first hurdle: the purpose of the program and regulation appeared generally secular.[56] However, scholars disagreed on whether offering government largesse to FBOs, especially those engaged in religious activities, had the likely effect of advancing religion. There was also considerable debate surrounding whether the government, in an effort *not* to advance religion, would need to expend extra resources and energy to ensure compliance from FBOs, thereby becoming impermissibly entangled with the operations of the religious entities it funded. These questions fueled significant debate among legal scholars, politicians, and political commentators, not least due to the Court's seemingly equivocal stance on the matter.[57] Over time, however, the Court came to effectively supply an answer.

For three decades following the *Everson* case, the US Supreme Court seemed to prioritize maintaining a "high and impregnable" wall between church and state. It did so by striking down a multitude of laws on the grounds that they impermissibly advanced religion or fostered excessive state entanglement. This included laws subsidizing student tuition, teacher salaries, remedial instruction, and instructional material at sectarian schools.[58] The wall seemed sacrosanct. This began to change in the mid-1980s.

The first brick fell when the Court allowed states to fund vocational programs at parochial schools.[59] Washington state passed legislation to advance the career prospects of visually impaired people. This included paying for their education. Larry Witters attended a Bible school in the state and applied for funds through the program. Though otherwise eligible, Witters was denied funds due to his pursuit of pastoral studies at a religious institution. The state reasoned that extending government beneficence to Witters represented an unconstitutional breach between the separation of church and state and was prohibited by the Establishment Clause. The Supreme Court disagreed. In a unanimous decision, it ruled that the barrier between church and state need not fully exclude religious entities from government funds. Instead, while the Establishment Clause barred the government from *directly* handing funds to religious entities, it did not prohibit individuals from serving as intermediaries, with funds passing from the government's hands to an individual, who, in turn, chose to spend these funds at a religious institution.

One of the key points in *Witters* was the attenuated link between the state and the religious entity and the consequent rationale that the program in question could not be taken to endorse or advance religion broadly. The Court extended this logic in *Bowen v. Kendrick* two years later. Like *Witters*, *Bowen* also evaluated the structural integrity of the proverbial wall, this time in light of a federal program promoting abstinence until marriage (AUM).[60] The law sponsored sex education programs provided by both public and private organizations and included religious entities among those eligible for federal grants. Though, in this case, funds went directly to religious entities, the Court nonetheless found the program aligned with the Establishment Clause because it did not have the effect of advancing religion.[61] The Court further distinguished the program's religious grant recipients from "pervasively sectarian" institutions like parochial schools and thus argued the program avoided aggressive oversight of fund administration (excessive entanglement).[62]

The "pervasively sectarian doctrine," as applied in *Bowen*, allowed funds to go directly to entities associated with religious denominations but still barred government funds from going to institutions whose primary purpose was the inculcation of religious values. This distinction, which guided the Court's decision in several other cases in the latter half of the 20th century, was less relevant in the Court's decision in *Mitchell v. Helms* in 2000, where the Court sustained aid to parochial secondary schools by emphasizing the principle of neutrality. "If the religious, irreligious, and areligious are all alike eligible for governmental aid," opined the Court, "no one would conclude that any indoctrination that any particular recipient conducts has been done at the behest of the government."[63]

The cumulative effect of the Court's Establishment Clause jurisprudence in the latter half of the 20th century was a noticeable shift away from the strict separation of church and state toward a more capacious interpretation of church–state relations. This provided enough legal ambiguity for President Bush to enact the Faith-Based Initiative in 2001. In fact, in the final 2008 report summarizing the effects of the Faith-Based Initiative, the Bush administration explained that it not only had the legal *clearance* to enact the initiative, per the *Witters*, *Bowen*, and *Mitchell* decisions, but actually that it had a legal *imperative* to do so—taking the neutrality principle recognized by the Court and deeply embedding it federal and state government.[64] This was the position taken by the Court much later in *Trinity v. Lutheran* (2017).

Trinity involved a church preschool that had been denied state funds to resurface its playground. The state argued that its denial complied with previous Court precedent and that its prohibition against such funding aligned with the Establishment Clause.[65] The Court, however, took a different position and ruled that not only does the Establishment Clause *permit* government funds to go to religious entities for secular purposes, but the First Amendment's Exercise Clause *requires* religious entities to be made eligible for such funds. Religious organizations wishing to apply for state funds, the Court reasoned, should not have their access to funds dependent upon the revocation of their religious commitment and convictions. The majority explained: "The express discrimination against religious exercise here is not the denial of the grant, but rather the refusal to allow the Church—solely because it is a church—to compete with secular organizations for a grant."[66] While not ruling on the Faith-Based Initiative directly, *Trinity* nonetheless seemed to settle the issue in favor of the Initiative's constitutionality.

Hiring

The *Trinity* ruling and subsequent cases further entrenched the so-called nondiscrimination principle of the Exercise Clause.[67] However, another question regarding discrimination remains unanswered. If the First Amendment prohibits the government from discriminating against FBOs in funding, does it allow US-funded FBOs to discriminate in hiring? Can organizations that accept funding from the US government adopt religious criteria for their employees? The Rule and other regulations implemented under the Faith-Based Initiative allowed organizations to employ such preferential hiring practices, but whether the Constitution allowed this was another question and one that engendered separate controversy.

US law allows religious organizations to be exempt from certain federal and state laws if they are deemed to unduly burden religious practice.[68] One of the most notable exemptions carved out for religious organizations is to permit discrimination based upon hiring, which typically would violate Title VII of the Civil Rights Act.[69] This exemption allows religious organizations to hire (or fire) individuals based on their religion (or lack thereof). This exception has been scrutinized by the Court and found consistent with the First Amendment's Free Exercise Clause.[70] The extension of this exception to federally funded organizations is more controversial.[71] Part 205.1(g) of The Rule specifies that religious organizations funded by USAID may continue to include religious beliefs among their hiring criteria. For instance, a Catholic organization may decide only to hire Catholics, or an Islamic organization may choose to hire only Muslims. What these organizations *cannot* do is discriminate against a *beneficiary*'s religion. In other words, while an FBO may be selective in who provides the service or good, it cannot be selective regarding who it gives it to.

To some, this distinction matters little. The front-end discrimination, they argue, when effectively funded by the US government, amounts to "institutionalized religious bias" in violation of the First Amendment's Establishment Clause. Others use stronger words. "It would be bitter irony, indeed," says Paul Weber, "if legislation touted as creating a level playing field provided a wedge to reintroduce discrimination."[72] Under The Rule, an FBO accepting USAID funds can require its employees to sign statements of faith and attend religious services.[73] In some cases, the employer might provide religious services to its employees. This, says Lupu and Tuttle, could be perceived as tantamount to the religious inculcation the First Amendment prohibits.

Advocates of the provision counter that exemptions to Title VII of the Civil Rights Act are not necessarily exclusive to religious organizations and thus can equally apply to secular organizations. Planned Parenthood, for example, can refuse to hire an evangelical Christian due to their religious conviction that life begins at conception and consequent disagreement with abortion services. Likewise, the Human Rights Campaign can deny employment to a Muslim based on their religious belief that homosexuality is a sin when the group advocates for LGBTQ+ equality and inclusion. Under this logic, Part 205.1(g) is less a government endorsement of religious discrimination and more an extension and protection of an exemption previously afforded equally to non-funded religious and secular groups.[74]

The Court's quiescence in this area and the continuation of the policy by all four presidential administrations demonstrates a general presumption of the provision's constitutionality. Additionally, while the Supreme Court has not ruled directly on the issue, its recent decisions in related cases suggest that if it chose to hear a case on the matter, it would likely condone providing exceptions to federally funded religious organizations in employment discrimination under the rationale that such exceptions are obligated by the First Amendment Exercise Clause.[75]

Implementation

In addition to challenges regarding the *de jure* constitutionality of the Faith-Based Initiative, others question the *de facto* constitutionality of the initiative and the funding of FBOs. In other words, while the Faith-Based Initiative may be constitutional in concept or as a matter of written law, the initiative's implementation is a separate question. Debate on this issue embroiled both the Faith-Based Initiative generally and USAID's Rule specifically.

Most legal scholars debating the constitutionality of the Faith-Based Initiative focused on the effect of FBO funding. However, another issue more particular to the Bush administration was how FBOs were informed of their eligibility for government funds. Part of the president's initiative involved executive officials holding conferences and information sessions for faith-based groups to inform them of the changed legal requirements surrounding federal aid. These meetings were quickly subject to legal challenges. Petitioners argued that in conferences promoting the Faith-Based Initiative, President Bush and the Secretary of Education used "religious imagery" and hortative language to directly encourage the participation of religious entities in the program. These actions, they averred, violated the neutrality principle of the Establishment Clause because they evinced a distinct preference for religious entities over secular ones. The Supreme Court reviewed these claims in *Hein v. Freedom from Religion Foundation* in 2007 but ultimately side-stepped the issue. Rather than rule on the merits, the Court ruled that the taxpayers lacked standing to challenge an executive program—a decision that effectively immunized the initiative from further legal challenge.

After *Hein*, the constitutionality of the Faith-Based Initiative was relatively settled, though one could argue that The Rule at USAID warranted special review. This is because, unlike other executive agencies, USAID funds organizations for work they do abroad, and thus there is a greater geographic expanse separating the agency and its implementing partners. To date, The

Rule has not been reviewed separately by the Courts, but its implementation has been scrutinized by USAID's Office of the Inspector General (OIG).[76]

The same executive order that Obama used to establish the White House Office of Faith-Based and Neighborhood Partnerships also inter alia sought a review of faith-based funding within specified executive agencies. According to the president's directive, the OIG at USAID began reviewing how The Rule was carried out under the Bush administration at USAID. It issued its final report in July 2009.[77] While the OIG did not find direct instances of government funds going toward proselytization or the purchasing or distributing of overt religious material, its investigation revealed several legally suspect cases. These included instances where FBOs used USAID grant money to reconstruct mosques in Iraq and to prevent HIV/AIDS in Africa with scripture-laced educational material. In both cases, the OIG report suggests the actions likely derived from the agency's equivocal guidance and not a group's intent to circumvent the rules. According to the report, even USAID's legal officers were reluctant to judge whether these examples abrogated the First Amendment in light of the Supreme Court's deferential position in foreign policy and the domestic focus of the Court's Establishment Clause jurisprudence.[78] This is further exemplified by the repeated requests USAID sent to the Department of Justice requesting review and additional guidance—all of which went unanswered.[79]

Ultimately, the president and the faith-based entities interviewed for the OIG report were absolved of any illegal activity, and The Rule and the larger Faith-Based Initiative from which it derives survived four presidential administrations. In effect, the metaphor of a "high and impregnable" wall between church and state has become increasingly anachronistic.[80] A more apt description, notes Michael McGinnis, accounts for the dynamism in church–state relations across different policy areas. In some areas, says McGinnis, the church and state may be separated by "a fence, across which neighbors can freely communicate, or a gate, which allows both sides easy egress to the other." In others, it can form a "well-worn path" or even an "expressway."[81]

McGinnis likens state–church relations in foreign aid to an expressway. Others agree, but for different reasons. Rather than a unidirectional transfer of funds, they contend that the initiative creates a dynamic where funds and favors flow both ways. Even if the initiative survived judicial scrutiny regarding the separation of church and state, they argue, its political motivations warrant closer examination.

The Political Controversy

The Faith-Based Initiative received a vitriolic reception from many politicians and advocacy groups upon implementation.[82] In addition to arguments involving the initiative's perceived unconstitutionality, many impugned what they perceived to be the initiative's political motives.[83] Rather than poverty reduction, they argued, Bush's true intention in establishing the initiative was to secure political dividends. The advantages, claimed critics, were two-fold: conceptually, the initiative capitalized upon the growing number of religious voters; practically, it freed up funds to buy or reward religious interest groups for their political loyalty.[84] The press peddled both theories, though at different times. The overarching theme was that the president was using the initiative for political capital, either for the presidential election or the midterms (where he used it to advance Republican Congressional races). The idea of the initiative providing "kickbacks" to specific groups was also a prominent critique of the Faith-Based Initiative's extension to foreign aid.

President Bush was vocal during his presidential campaign about his Christian faith. His campaign platform also included socially conservative policies generally endorsed by Christian evangelicals. Such positioning made the president a natural favorite among the Religious Right, but he needed the support of moderate voters to secure electoral victory. The religious resurgence had led to a "renegotiated ... relationship between religion and public life," with more people thinking favorably toward faith and faith-based entities.[85] The Faith-Based Initiative, it was argued, was a part of Bush's larger electoral strategy, engineered by political strategist Karl Rove, to tap into this growing constituency of voters—both for the benefit of securing the executive office and (later) maintaining congressional control.[86] Critics claimed the president was particularly interested in attracting Catholics and African Americans.[87]

A similar critique followed Obama when, as a presidential candidate, he promised to expand the Faith-Based Initiative. In the case of Obama, though, the claim was that he used the initiative as political bait to entice evangelical voters to switch sides.[88] According to the *New York Times*, this strategy was particularly prudent because "While evangelical voters, a sizable minority, generally vote strongly Republican, McCain [Obama's Republican counterpart] ... had a shaky relationship with the group."[89] Since neither Trump nor Biden announced their intent to continue the OFBCI on the campaign trail, critics could not make the same claim in their cases. However, all four administrations were subject to claims that the initiative may be a political feint, allowing them the means to ingratiate themselves with key interest groups.[90] Funds flowing to international FBOs through USAID became a particular focal point.

When Bush first instituted the CFBCI at USAID, the primary question concerning critics was who would benefit most from the changed regulations. Many opponents suggested that the biggest beneficiaries would likely be the organizations closest to the president—in terms of connections and ideology. One group accused the president of using AIDS relief, in particular, "as a political payout to faith-based supporters of administration policies."[91] Others cast the blame on FBOs. A representative from a large secular NGO explained the dynamic by saying: "There was ... a lot of pressure, from the Religious Right feeling that they supported Bush ... and they wanted to get paid their dues, they wanted a piece of the pie in terms of foreign assistance."[92] Tom Hart, president of the ONE campaign and former government relations director for the Episcopal Church, echoed this sentiment. Hart noted that USAID's CFBCI was evidence that "Evangelicals were capable of using their political voice to get greater access to foreign aid."[93]

A 2006 investigative report by the *Boston Globe* was more specific in its critique. According to the report, the most significant "winners" in USAID's pivot to FBOs had close ties to the Bush administration. World Vision, Food for the Hungry, and Samaritan's Purse received millions of dollars from USAID under the Bush initiative. They also all seemingly had direct connections to the president. Bush's USAID director, Andrew Natsios, previously worked for World Vision. Contemporaneously, the president of Food for the Hungry, Benjamin Homan, was appointed by the president as Chair of USAID's advisory board. The report also claims the president had a personal connection to Samaritan's Purse since the father of the organization's president, Billy Graham, was pivotal in the president's spiritual renewal.[94]

Speculation surrounding the general quid-pro-quo nature of the Faith-Based Initiative largely subsided once Bush left office, though specific accusations resurfaced under President Trump.[95] In a report by ProPublica in 2020, the administration, and in particular Vice President Mike Pence, was accused of "meddling" in USAID's grant decisions to advantage Christian FBOs. "Decisions about U.S. aid are often no longer being governed by career professionals applying a rigorous review of applicants and their capabilities," the report said, but "political pressure, particularly from the office of Vice President Mike Pence, had seeped into aid deliberations and convinced key decision-makers that unless they fell in line, their jobs could be at stake."[96] The result? Two Christian organizations working in Iraq that had previously been denied USAID funds received awards under Trump. The report tied the administration's Christian preference in USAID's FBO funding with its broader push to support Christian minorities in Iraq and Syria. Both moves, it claims, were primarily political. Channeling funds to Christian minorities in the Middle East, says the report, sent the right message to Christian conservatives in the run-up to the 2020 presidential election. The question of what kind of message this sends globally is the subject of another debate.

The Foreign Affairs Controversy

President Bush established the CFBCI at USAID in December 2002, 14 months after the terrorist attacks of September 11. America's War on Terror was well underway at this point, and the president's speeches had assumed a "messianic and crusading tone."[97] While the president took care not to vilify Islam, his rhetoric and policies were still suffused with religious undertones. The 2002 National Security Strategy, for example, explained that America's objective was to rid the Middle East of the "evil" evinced by the "radical ideology" of terrorists.[98] Stripped of its euphemistic veneer, the administration's view of global affairs looked a lot like the prophesied world of Samuel Huntington—one torn apart by religious allegiances.[99] Given the global context, critics argued that America's use of FBOs to deliver foreign aid risked reifying civilizational constructs. The problem, they claim, involves both the *optics* of the United States portraying itself as a Christian nation and the *reality*, in some cases, of the US government funding Christian FBOs engaged in proselytization or fashioned to advance Christian principles.

Over 80% of the FBOs USAID funds are Christian. Many of these have overt Christian symbology and messaging protected by The Rule. The effect is that a Christian organization may prominently display a crucifix on a building adjacent to the requisite signage saying "From the American people."[100] Critics suggest this positioning inadvertently signals to people of other countries that America is a "Christian nation," in contrast to its claims of secularism. Others suggest it can amount to America "exporting" the Christian faith—especially when proselytization is part of a funded organization's operations.[101] At best, opponents suggest this signals a "Christian soft spot" in US foreign policy, and at worst, it gives the impression that the United States may have an "anti-Islam agenda."[102] In areas where most beneficiaries are Christian, this may matter less. However, in areas where an organization's Christian message stands in juxtaposition to the beliefs of beneficiaries, it could potentially erode the legitimacy and credibility of US aid and even "inflame religious tensions."[103]

In addition to the problematic *perception* of Christian bias, critics also point to the problematic *practice* of the United States funding Christian FBOs—especially to serve in areas where Christianity is not the dominant religion. One argument involves FBO staffing. For example, If USAID funds a Christian FBO to work in a Muslim or Buddhist-majority country, and the FBO requires its staff to share its faith—which it is legally entitled to do—then might it not staff more expatriates than locals? Critics suggest that such organizations might fail to consider and account for cultural norms when providing service.[104] Even if the staff isn't required to adhere to the faith of an organization, if the organization's programs are designed around its faith, critics argue this can also lead to ineffectual aid.

The United States' use of Christian organizations to combat the HIV/AIDS epidemic is often seen to exemplify this dynamic. In 2003, President Bush instituted the President's Emergency Plan for AIDS Relief, or PEPFAR, which focused on reducing both the incidents of HIV and the deaths associated with AIDS. In 2004, Bush allocated 20% of all PEPFAR funds to prevention programs. The sexual transmissibility of HIV led the administration to prioritize programs aimed at changing individual sexual behavior. More specifically, the administration encouraged PEPFAR-funded organizations to adopt the "ABC" approach to prevention, promoting *Abstain*ing from sex until marriage, *Being* faithful while in marriage, and using *Condoms* when engaged in sex outside of marriage. While the program emphasizes all three approaches to prevention, implementing organizations are not required to promote all three methods. Under Bush, implementing organizations could promote abstinence and faithfulness *or* teach about condom use. Under subsequent administrations, organizations applying for funding were assumed to incorporate all three prevention methods into their programming, but organizations having moral or religious objections to one of the three prevention methods (such as those that perceive condom distribution as conflicting with the Biblical injunctive against premarital sex) could invoke the "Conscience Clause" before applying for an award and still be considered eligible for funding.[105]

Critics suggest FBOs taking this approach lessen the overall effectiveness of PEPFAR in mitigating the spread of HIV. They argue that a singular focus on AUM fails to consider the risks of individual noncompliance, a risk they say is especially high among adolescents.[106] Moreover, critics suggest that teaching only abstinence stigmatizes those who *are* sexually active—even if those individuals are taking the necessary precautions.[107] Additionally, groups such as Human Rights Watch, the American Academy of Pediatrics, and the American Public Health Association argue that AUM programs are in jeopardy of human rights violations. Presenting abstinence as the only option, they argue, further reifies sexist and racist stereotypes and may alienate members of the lesbian, gay, bisexual, transgender, and questioning (LGBTQ) community.[108] Ultimately, the critique is that FBOs are choosing a strategy based on faith over science, and the US government is doing the same by funding such entities.

Those defending FBOs' promotion of AUM argue that in many of the areas where HIV/AIDS is most prevalent, religion is also prevalent. Nearly 90% of people living in sub-Saharan subscribe to either the Muslim or Christian faith.[109] Since both these faiths condemn sex before and outside of marriage, the argument follows that FBOs emphasizing abstinence before marriage and faithfulness in marriage are not introducing religious ideas in contradiction to the cultural context but reinforcing community values.[110] Alternatively, organizations emphasizing condom use can be perceived as alienating religious individuals and communities.[111] A secondary strength of this approach, emphasized by some, is its individual efficacy rate. Condom use is not 100% effective in preventing the sexual transmission of HIV/AIDS. However, if one abstains from sex altogether, they can be sure not to contract the disease from intercourse.[112] Less evidence is available for the collective success of AUM and faithfulness over condom use in reducing the spread of HIV/AIDS, yet the dramatic decline of the disease in Uganda stands as one example.[113]

A final consideration concerns the religious freedoms of funded FBOs—specifically, the freedom *not* to engage in activities that are deemed against one's religious beliefs. If the government required organizations receiving PEPFAR funds to distribute condoms, some FBOs would consider this tantamount to the promotion of sin, and the Court's recent jurisprudence could suggest it would implicate the Exercise Clause. Obama attempted to thread the needle in this debate. Under his administration, FBOs wishing to promote abstinence exclusively to prevent HIV transmission remained eligible for

PEPFAR funding but no longer benefited from earmarked funds.[114] President Trump took another approach. Rather than focus on the method of prevention, he appealed directly to FBOs by introducing the PEPFAR Faith-Based and Community Initiative in 2018 and contributing an additional $100 million specifically to FBOs.[115]

PEPFAR is a poignant example of how political forces can shape aid policy. But do these decisions have any effect on actual FBO funding? One can ask this question of USAID funds more broadly. If faith-based funding serves as a kind of political currency, as critics have claimed, wouldn't we expect FBO funding to fluctuate under different administrations? More to the point, might we expect more FBOs to be funded or for FBOs to receive more funds under Republican administrations? Did FBO funding surge under Bush, wane under Obama, and then spike again under Trump? If it isn't the president who is directly involved in fund distribution or "meddling" in aid, then do presidential policies relating to aid, like those involving HIV/AIDS and AUM, have the effect of either attracting or deterring a large number of FBOs from applying for funds? Chapter 4 explores these questions in more detail by looking at existing FBO funding data and introducing new funding data for 2008–2021.

Notes

1 "Religion and Politics: The Ambivalent Majority," *Pew Research Center*, September 20, 2000, www.pewresearch.org/politics/2000/09/20/religion-and-politics-the-ambivalent-majority/

2 Dennis R. Hoover, "Charitable Choice and the New Religious Center," *Religion in the News* 3, no. 1 (Spring 2000), www3.trincoll.edu/csrpl/RINVol3No1/charitable_choice_2000.htm

3 Bill Clinton, "Remarks by the President at a Breakfast with Religious Leaders," (speech, Washington, DC, White House State Dining Room, September 28, 1999), https://clintonwhitehouse3.archives.gov/WH/New/html/19990928.html

4 Jim Wallis, "A Seat at the Table," *Washington Post*, July 11, 1999, www.washingtonpost.com/archive/opinions/1999/06/11/a-seat-at-the-table/09c6f4be-3505-4f0a-9aee-d3632453307d/; "Excerpts from Bush's Speeches on Goals," *New York Times*, July 23, 1999, https://archive.nytimes.com/www.nytimes.com/library/politics/camp/072399wh-gop-bush-text.html

5 Hoover, "Charitable Choice and the New Religious Center."

6 George Walker Bush, Jr. "Bush President Bush Implements Key Elements of his Faith-Based Initiative" (speech, Philadelphia, PA: Downtown Marriott Hotel). https://georgewbush-whitehouse.archives.gov/news/releases/2002/12/20021212-3.html

7 Ibid.

8 Congress authorized this money in 1948 under the European Recovery Program, informally known as the Marshall Plan, after Secretary of State George C. Marshall. The Economic Cooperation Administration dispersed it across 16 European countries. While one may be tempted to frame the Marshall Plan as an act of pure benevolence, British historian Norman Davies more aptly described the plan as "an act of the most enlightened self-interest in history." Jones, *The Marshall Plan and the Shaping of American Strategy*, 2.

9 Such transfers comprised over 90% of all aid provided. United States Library of Congress, Congressional Research Service, *The Marshall Plan*, 3.
10 The US government incentivized the involvement of the private sector by providing surplus commodities and freight reimbursements with the Agricultural Trade and Development Act of 1954. The PL 480 food program, as it is more commonly known, allowed humanitarian nonprofits to distribute or monetize surplus agricultural commodities for overseas relief work. PL 480 authorized organizations receiving commodities under the program to sell these in exchange for local currency in the country of service (Title I), to donate them to people in need (Title II), or to exchange them for strategic materials (Title III). Most organizations at the start of the program engaged in Title I transfers. Epstein, *Primer on PL 480.*
11 McCleary, *Global Compassion*, 75.
12 These organizations comprised seven of the top eight funded organizations. McCleary, *Global Compassion*, 76.
13 The term was first used to identify nonaligned countries. Wolf-Phillips, "Why 'Third World'?"
14 Harry S. Truman, "Inaugural Address of Harry S. Truman" (speech, Washington, DC, January 20, 1949), The Avalon Project, https://avalon.law.yale.edu/20th_century/truman.asp
15 This was President Truman's so-called Point Four Program (the name derived from the fact that it was the fourth point Truman made in his 1949 inaugural address).
16 The United States also provided technical assistance during the Marshall Plan but to a much smaller degree (accounting for less than one-half a percent of all aid allocated). United States Library of Congress, Congressional Research Service, *The Marshall Plan*, 12.
17 The Mutual Security Agency (MSA) was an independent agency created by the Mutual Security Act of 1951. Congress dissolved it in 1953 by creating the Foreign Operations Administration (FOA) under *Reorganization Plan No. 7 of 1953 (67 Stat. 639)*. A year later, Executive Order 0610 transitioned US foreign assistance operations from the FOA to the newly established International Cooperation Administration (ICA).
18 USAID continued to fund Catholic Relief Services, Lutheran World Relief, Church World Services, the Adventist Development and Relief Agency (ADRA), and the United Jewish Appeal, among others. It also added a select few evangelical organizations to its partner list, including Feed the Children and World Vision in the 1980s.
19 McCleary, *Global Compassion,* 84.
20 Ibid., 124.
21 Ibid., 84.
22 USAID rules prohibited grant recipients from proselytizing and merging grant money with private money spent on religious activities. They also barred award recipients from choosing personnel based on religious belief. As a result, the FBOs most eligible for government funds during this time were those that most mirrored secular development organizations, meaning they had obtained 501c(3) status and hired without regard to religion.
23 In fact, the constitutionality of USAID funding FBOs remained an open question since the Supreme Court was effectively silent on the applicability of the Establishment Clause to the federal funding of organizations operating in foreign

environments. Lupu and Tuttle, "The Faith-Based Initiative and the Constitution," 94–95. These rulings are discussed in more detail later in the chapter. For USAID's interpretation of these rulings, see McCleary, *Global Compassion*, 84.

24 The bill was officially entitled "The Personal Responsibility and Work Opportunity Reconciliation Act." (PL 104–193) HR 3734]) [Welfare Reform Act].

25 Formicola and Segers, "The Bush Faith-Based Initiative," 694.

26 Between 1996 and 2001, Congress passed two other laws with Charitable Choice provisions, including the Community Service Block Grants Act (Section 201 of PL 105–285) and the Public Health Service Act (Titles V and XIX—Section 3305 of PL 106–310 and Section 1 of PL 106–554.) Congress also attempted but failed to insert Charitable Choice language in the Workforce Investment Act, the Older Americans Act, and the Head Start Law.

27 As governor of Texas, Bush established an Advisory Task Force on Faith-Based Community Service Groups, which produced the "Faith in Action" plan, the impetus and bedrock of later state legislation expanding Charitable Choice Legislation in Texas (Texas HB 21; HB 2481; HB 2482, and SCR 44).

28 This phrase was first coined by Marvin Olasky. See Olasky, *Compassionate Conservatism*, 2010; Dan Balz, "Armies of Compassion' in Bush's Plans," *Washington Post*, April 25, 1999, A1, www.washingtonpost.com/wp-srv/politics/campaigns/wh2000/stories/bush042599.htm

29 Executive Order 13199, 66 FR 8499 (January 29, 2001).

30 These include the Department of Labor, Department of Education, Department of Agriculture, Department of Justice, Department of Health and Human Services, Department of Housing and Urban Development, Agency for International Development, Small Business Administration, Department of Commerce, Department of Veterans Affairs, and Department of Homeland Security.

31 See Executive Order 13198, 66 FR 8497 (January 31, 2001) and Executive Order 13279, 67 FR 77141 (December 16, 2002).

32 The Charitable Choice provision provided funds to states as a capped block grant under Temporary Assistance to Needy Families (TANF). States could spend these funds hiring private service providers or allowing beneficiaries to choose their services by providing service vouchers.

33 President Bush candidly acknowledged that "Congress would not act" on the Faith-Based Initiative, so he decided to do it "on [his] own" through executive order. See Farris, Nathan, and Wright, *The Expanding Administrative Presidency*, 4.

34 At the end of Bush's tenure, 35 states had established Faith-Based and Community Initiative offices or liaisons. The same was true for over 100 US cities. The White House, *The Quiet Revolution*, 95.

35 Executive Order 13498, 74 FR 6533 (February 5, 2009) changed the White House Office of Faith-Based and Community Initiatives to the White House Office of Faith-Based and Neighborhood Partnerships (OFBNP). Though the order did not explicitly rename the associated centers, most centers went by the new acronym (CFBNP) following the White House lead.

36 The formal name of the Advisory Council was the President's Advisory Council on Faith-Based and Neighborhood Partnerships.

37 Bettiza, *Finding Faith in Foreign Policy*, 115.

38 Trump changed the name of the White House OFBNP to the White House Faith and Opportunity Initiative. Trump also changed the names of subsidiary centers

to match the White House Office. See Executive Order 13831, 83 FR 20715 (May 3, 2018).

39 See Executive Order 13798, 82 FR 21675 (May 4, 2017) and Executive Order 13926, 85 FR 34951 (June 2, 2020).

40 Executive Order 11246, issued under President Lyndon B. Johnson, prohibits organizations and businesses accepting federal funds from discriminating based on race, color, religion, sex, sexual orientation, gender identity, or national origin. However, it permits an exemption for religious organizations to hire individuals based on religion. Executive Order 13771, 82 FR 9339 (January 30, 2017), issued by Trump, reiterates this exemption.

41 In Executive Order 13559, 75 FR 71319 (November 17, 2010), Obama required participating federal agencies to include a provision in their regulations requiring FBO fund recipients to provide beneficiaries with notice of secular alternatives. (USAID was exempt from this requirement.) Trump eliminated this requirement with Executive Order 13771, 85 FR 82037, issued on January 30, 2017 (Reducing Regulation and Controlling Regulatory Costs).

42 Executive Order 14015, February 14, 2021 (Establishment of the White House OFBNP).

43 Ibid.

44 United States Agency for International Development Office of Press Relations, "Administrator Power's Meeting on Faith-Based Engagement, Human Rights, and International Religious Freedom," May 10, 2021, www.usaid.gov/news-information/press-releases/may-10-2021-administrator-power-meetings-faith-based-engagement-human-rights

45 Bush established the White House OFBCI in January 2001 and established corresponding centers to implement his Initiative at the Department of Justice, Departments of Labor, Health and Human Services, Education, and Housing and Urban Development. Executive Order 13280, issued in December 2002, established centers in USAID and the Department of Agriculture.

46 *69 FR 61715*. The Rule revised 22 CFR part 205, "Payments to and on Behalf of Participants in Nonmilitary Economic Development Training Programs."

47 The original wording of The Rule used the term "religious character," while the Trump administration changed this to "religious exercise and affiliation" in 2020 with 85 FR 2916.

48 Bush, "Remarks to Leaders of Hispanic Faith-Based Organizations," 562.

49 The caveat to dual-use buildings is that USAID cannot directly fund any part of a building primarily used for sectarian purposes.

50 205.1(b). The Rule's stipulation specifically states that if a funded organization is engaged in "inherently religious activities, such as worship, religious instruction, or proselytization," then these activities "must be offered separately, in time or location, from the programs or services funded with direct financial assistance from USAID, and participation must be voluntary for beneficiaries of the programs or services funded with such assistance." The Rule exempts prisons, detention facilities, or community correction centers from this requirement.

51 Under The Rule, FBOs and secular organizations follow identical procedures when applying for USAID funds. Under Obama, however, FBOs were required to complete an extra step after receiving funds. Executive Order 13559 necessitated agencies and departments amend existing regulations relating to faith-based organizations to require FBOs to notify all beneficiaries that their involvement

in any religious activity was voluntary and that they had a right to an alternate provider. FBOs further had to inform beneficiaries of the conditions of the organization's funding, namely, the prohibition against discriminating among beneficiaries. They also had to notify beneficiaries of their funding conditions, including their restriction to secular goods and activities. FBOs were further required to provide beneficiaries with information on reporting violations. USAID was exempt from the order mandates, explaining the 2016 Final Joint Rule. President Trump again eliminated the notice-and-referral requirements from all regulations.

52 Such concerns were expressed amply by the press and members of the public in the period of public comment before The Rule's final publication. The Federal Register (69 FR 61715) published a summary of the comments received and USAID's responses on October 20, 2004.

53 Jefferson first used the phrase on January 1, 1802, in his written response to a letter sent by the Danbury (Conn.) Baptist Association congratulating him upon winning the presidency.

54 *Everson v. Board of Education*, 330 US 1 (1947).

55 *Lemon v. Kurtzman*, 403 US 602, (1971). *Agostini v. Felton*, 521 US 203, (1997) amended this test to consist of only two prongs, purpose and effect, but the more robust Lemon test was used more frequently in subsequent cases. The Lemon test was abandoned in Kennedy v Bremerton School Dist. 597 US__(2022).

56 The presumption in evaluating the FBCI (and other government actions and statutes) is that the government's stated aim is genuine and to consider the primary purpose and not an unstated secondary or tertiary purpose that might be non-secular.

57 Scholars raising exploring the topic include Lin, Michaels, Nayak, Newberger, Shanbhag, and Sullivan, "Faith in the Courts?" 183–225; Goldenziel, "Administratively Quirky, Constitutionally Murky," 372–373; Boden, "Compassion Inaction," 991–1030; Cole, "Faith and Funding," 559–604; Lupu and Tuttle, "The Faith-Based Initiative and the Constitution," 274–292; Fitzgerald, "The Expansion of Charitable Choice," 211–236.

58 See *Lemon v. Kurtzman*, 403 US 602, (1971); *Committee for Public Education v. Nyquist*, 413 US 756, (1973); *Meek v. Pittenger* 421 US 349, (1975); *Levitt v. Committee for Public Education*, 413 US 472, (1973); and *Aguilar v. Felton*, 473 US 402 (1985).

59 See *Witters v. Washington Department of Services for the Blind*, 474 US 481, (1986).

60 Adolescent Family Life Act (AFLA), 42 U.S.C. §300z et seq. (1981).

61 In both *Witters* and *Bowen*, the Court applied the so-called Lemon Test, established in *Lemon v. Kurtzman*, 403 US 602, (1971), which asks if the government act or program in question has (1) a valid secular purpose, (2) a primary effect of either advancing or inhibiting religion, or if it (3) effectively entangles the government with religion. In both cases, the Court ruled the laws did not violate any of the three prongs of the test.

62 The "pervasively sectarian doctrine" applied in *Bowen* was first established in *Roemer v. Maryland Public Works Board*, 426 US 736 (1976) and applied by the Court in *Tilton v. Richardson*, 403 US 672 (1971), *Hunt v. McNair*, 413 US 734 (1973), and *Agostini v. Felton*, 521 US 203 (1997).

63 *Mitchell v. Helms*, 530 US 793 (2000).

64 The 2008 report also cited *Zelman v. Simmons-Harris*, 536 US 639, (2002), which, though decided after the initiation of the Faith-Based Initiative, further reified the neutrality principle.

65 The state's denial of funds was based upon its constitution, which stated in Article I, Section 7, that "no money shall ever be taken from the public treasury, directly or indirectly, in aid of any church, section or denomination of religion."

66 *Trinity Lutheran Church of Columbia, Inc. v. Comer*, 582 US, 449 (2017). *Trinity* serves as a strong precedent in support of the constitutionality of the Faith-Based Initiative but could also be construed as not reaching that far since the case deals with state funding and not federal funding. The Court's previous position has been that states have more leeway to "experiment with involvement [in religion] on a neutral basis than the federal government." See *Walz v. Tax Comm'n of City of New York*, 397 US 664, (1970) and Thomas's concurrence in *Zelman v. Simmons-Harris*, 536 US 639, (2002). Moreover, four justices in *Trinity* signed onto a footnote (footnote 3) limiting the case's scope, saying: "This case involves express discrimination based on religious identity with respect to playground resurfacing. We do not address religious uses of funding or other forms of discrimination."

67 See *Espinoza v. Montana Department of Revenue*, 591 US___ (2020), and *Carson v. Makin*, 596 US___(2022).

68 See the Religious Freedom Restoration Act of 1993 (L. 103–141, §1, November 16, 1993, 107 Stat. 1488).

69 Title VII of the Civil Rights Act prohibits employers from discriminating based on race, color, religion, sex, and national origin but provides an explicit for religious organizations wanting to hire co-religionists.

70 *Corporation of Presiding Bishop v. Amos, 483* US 327 (1987).

71 This was done through a 2007 Memo issued by the Department of Justice, which remains in effect.

72 Segers, "The Bad in the Faith Based Initiative," 77.

73 Lupu and Tuttle, "The Faith-Based Initiative and the Constitution," 103–104.

74 John Dilulio, the original White House Director of the Office for Faith Based and Community Initiatives, espoused this position. Formicola, "The Good in the Faith-Based Initiative," 43.

75 A series of cases have held that religious institutions are exempt from the nondiscrimination requirements of Title VII of the Civil Rights Act when hiring individuals who serve a ministerial role. These cases do not address whether or in what way federal funding alters the constitutional analysis. See *Hosanna-Tabor Evangelical Lutheran Church and School v. EEOC*, 565 US 171 (2012); *Our Lady of Guadalupe School v. Morrissey-Berru*, 591 US, 140 (2020).

76 The final report drew upon survey answers from 31 USAID regional legal advisors and nine of the ten FBOs that received the most USAID funding.

77 The report also addressed whether USAID officers complied with Bush's executive order in awarding funds to FBOs and community organizations.

78 US Agency for International Development. Office of the Inspector General. *Audit of USAID's Faith-Based and Community Initiatives*. Audit Report No. 9-000-09-009-P. Washington, DC, 2009, https://oig.usaid.gov/sites/default/files/2018-06/9-000-09-009-p.pdf

79 US Agency for International Development OIG, Audit, 7.

80 In her dissent in *Trinity Lutheran*, Justice Ruth Bader Ginsburg remarked that the majority opinion resulted in the separation of church and state being "a constitutional slogan not a constitutional commitment."
81 Michael M. McGinnis, "Religion Policy and the Faith-Based Initiative: Navigating the Shifting Boundaries Between Church and State" (presentation, 2011 Annual Meeting of ASREC, Association for the Study of Religion, Economics and Culture, Washington, DC, April 7–10, 2011), 27.
82 "Media Coverage of the Faith-Based Initiative in the First Six Months of 2001 and 2009," *Pew Research Center* (Washington, DC: Pew Research Center, 2009), www.pewforum.org/2009/08/12/the-starting-line/
83 Even the president of the Interfaith Alliance, Dr. C. Welton Caddy, testified before Congress that he believed "the Faith-Based Initiative is about something other than charity and religion." See Testimony of Congressman Dr. Caddy Welton, House Committee on Government Reform, Subcommittee on Criminal Justice, Drug Policy, and Human Resources Hearing, "*Authorizing Presidential Vision: Making Permanent the Efforts of the Faith-Based and Community Initiative*," 19th Congress, June 21, 2005.
84 Michael Kranish, "Religious Right Wields Clout: Secular Groups Losing Funding Amid Pressure," *Boston Globe*, October 9, 2006; Daly and Dinerman, "Faith in the Faith-Based Initiative?" 409.
85 Dionne, E.J. Jr., "A Shift Looms." *The Washington Post,* October 3, 1999; Page B01. www.washingtonpost.com/wp-srv/WPcap/1999-10/03/061r-100399-idx.html.
86 Bettiza, *Finding Faith in Foreign Policy*, 104.
87 James Gerstenang, "Some on Right Miffed as Bush Courts Catholics," *Los Angeles Times*, March 23, 2001, www.latimes.com/archives/la-xpm-2001-mar-23-mn-41705-story.html, "Bush Targets Support of Blacks," Mary Leonard, *Boston Globe*, March 11, 2001; Robert A. Jordan, "Bush Looking for Black Votes, But Not Earning Them," *Boston Globe*, April 1, 2001; "Faith-Based-Flim-Flam," *Church & State*, October 2002, www.au.org/church-state/october-2002-church-state/featured/faith-based-flim-flam. David Kuo, the first Deputy Director of the White House Office of Faith-Based and Community Initiatives (OFBCI), confirmed these allegations in his 2006 memoir. According to Kuo, *he* was the one who suggested holding OFBCI events in areas with close Congressional races to rally religious voters. The Bush White House denied these claims. Kuo, *Tempting Faith*, 2007.
88 Jane Lampman, "Obama Would Overhaul Bush's Faith-Based Initiative," *The Christian Science Monitor*, July 2, 2008, www.csmonitor.com/USA/Politics/2008/0702/p25s10-uspo.html
89 Jeff Zeleny and Brian Knowlton, "Obama Borrows a Bush Policy to Court Evangelical Voters," *New York Times*, July 1, 2008, www.nytimes.com/2008/07/01/world/americas/01iht-campaign.4.14141355.html
90 Thomas Edsall, "Grants Flow to Bush Allies on Social Issues," *Washington Post*, March 22, 2006, www.washingtonpost.com/wp-dyn/content/article/2006/03/21/AR2006032101723.html
91 Michael Kranish, "Religious Right Wields Clout: Secular Groups Losing Funding Amid Pressure," *Boston Globe* (October 9, 2006), www.boston.com/news/nation/articles/2006/10/09/religious_right_wields_clout/

92 Alejandra Fernández Morera, "Cooperative Assistance and Relief Everywhere, Inc. (CARE)," *The Center for Public Integrity*, December 13, 2006, https://publicintegrity.org/health/cooperative-for-assistance-and-relief-everywhere-inc-care/
93 Bettiza, *Finding Faith in Foreign Policy*, 110.
94 Farah Stockman, "Christian Lobbying Finds Success," *Boston Globe*, October 14, 2004, http://archive.boston.com/news/nation/articles/2004/10/14/christian_lobbying_finds_success/
95 The Trump administration, specifically, faced such criticism. See Adam Taylor, "How Trump's Foreign Policy Mixes Religion with Money," *Washington Post*, November 7, 2019, www.washingtonpost.com/world/2019/11/07/how-trumps-foreign-policy-mixes-religion-with-money/
96 Yeganeh Torbati, "How Mike Pence's Office Meddled in Foreign Aid to Reroute Money to Favored Christian Groups," *ProPublica*, November 6, 2019, www.propublica.org/article/how-mike-pences-office-meddled-in-foreign-aid-to-reroute-money-to-favored-christian-groups
97 Turek, "Religious Rhetoric and the Evolution," 975–998.
98 White House, 2002. *National Security Strategy of the United States of America*. Washington, DC: White House, 31, https://georgewbush-whitehouse.archives.gov/nsc/nss/2002/
99 Huntington, "The Clash of Civilizations?"
100 The US Foreign Assistance Act of 1961 requires USAID-funded programs and program assets to mark their aid products with the USAID logo, which includes the seal, the brand name (USAID), and the tagline "From the American People." Per ADS section 320.3.2.4, this information must be included on all agency-funded vehicles and program sites as well as in communication about the funded project.
101 "Bush Brings Faith to Foreign Aid," *Boston Globe*, October 8, 2006, https://archive.boston.com/news/nation/articles/2006/10/08/bush_brings_faith_to_foreign_aid/
102 Bettiza, *Finding Faith in Foreign Policy*, 214; Susan Milligan, "Together But Worlds Apart," *Boston Globe*, October 10, 2006, https://wwrn.org/articles/23008/
103 Marsden, "Bush, Obama and a Faith-Based US Foreign Policy," 974.
104 Ferris, "Faith Based and Secular Humanitarian Organizations," 318–319.
105 The "Conscience Clause" is located in Section 301(d) of the Leadership Act and states:

> An organization, including a faith-based organization, that is otherwise eligible to receive funds for HIV and AIDS prevention, treatment, or care—1) Shall not be required, as a condition of receiving such assistance—(i) to endorse or utilize a multisectoral or comprehensive approach to combating HIV and AIDS; or (ii) to endorse, utilize, make a referral to, become integrated with, or otherwise participate in any program or activity to which the organization has a religious or moral objection; and 2) Shall not be discriminated against in the solicitation or issuance of grants, contracts, or cooperative agreements for refusing to meet any requirement described in (1) above.

This language is also included in the Acquisition & Assistance Policy Directive 14-04.

106 Santelli et al., "Abstinence-Only-Until-Marriage," 273–280.
107 Santelli, Speizer, and Edelstein "Abstinence Promotion Under PEPFAR," 5.
108 Ibid., 4.
109 Zurlo, "A Demographic Profile of Christianity," 3.
110 Kavinya, "Opinions on the Church's Stand," 33.
111 Follér and Vembane, "Muslim Community-Based Organisations," 166.
112 The CDC reports the efficacy rate of condoms at 98%, though this is under controlled conditions, and some reports specific to condom use in Africa suggest much lower protection. Still, the claim made by some that condoms are largely *ineffective* at preventing the spread of HIV/AIDS is patently false. Rigillo, "Faith in God, But Not in Condoms," 55.
113 Setswe, "Abstinence and Faithfulness Programmes," 11.
114 Bush reserved 33% of all prevention funds under PEPFAR for organizations advocating only abstinence and faithfulness.
115 While Trump was critical of foreign aid, he generally expressed unequivocal support for PEPFAR, stating in 2015 that he "strongly" believed in the program and would support its expansion. See Donald J. Trump, "Trump's PEPFAR Commitment" (comments, No Labels Convention, October 2, 2015), www.c-span.org/video/?c4555530/user-clip-trumps-pepfar-commitment. President Trump selected ten FBOs to receive funding for the PEPFAR Faith and Community Initiative (FCI) in Country Operational Plan (COP) 2019, including Botswana, Eswatini, Haiti, Kenya, Lesotho, Malawi, Tanzania, Uganda, Zambia, and Zimbabwe. Adva Salvinger, "What Happened with PEPFAR's Faith-Based Initiative?" *Inside Development*, October 14, 2020, www.devex.com/news/what-happened-with-pepfar-s-faith-based-initiative-98295

Bibliography

Bettiza, Gregorio. *Finding Faith in Foreign Policy: Religion and American Diplomacy in a Postsecular World* (Oxford: Oxford University Press, 2019).

Boden, Martha A. "Compassion Inaction: Why President Bush's Faith-Based Initiatives Violate the Establishment Clause." *Seattle Law Review* 29 (2006): 991–1030.

Bush, George Walker. "Remarks to Leaders of Hispanic Faith-Based Organizations." In *George W. Bush*, vol 1 (Washington, DC: U.S. Government Printing Office, 2003): 561–563.

Cole, David. "Faith and Funding: Toward an Expressivist Model of the Establishment Clause." *Southern California Law Review* 75 (2002): 559–604.

Daly, Alfrieda and Miriam Dinerman. Faith in the Faith-Based Initiative? *Affilia* 16, no. 4 (2001): 405–410. https://doi.org/10.1177/08861090122094334

Farris, Anne, Richard P. Nathan, and David J. Wright. *The Expanding Administrative Presidency: George W. Bush and the Faith-Based Initiative.* The Roundtable on Religion and Social Welfare Policy, Rockefeller Institute of Government, 2004. https://rockinst.org/wp-content/uploads/2018/02/2004-08-the_expanding_administrative_presidency_george_w_bush_and_the_faith-based_initiative.pdf

Ferris, Elizabeth. "Faith Based and Secular Humanitarian Organizations." *International Review of the Red Cross* 87, no. 858 (2005): 311–325.

Fitzgerald, Steven. "The Expansion of Charitable Choice, the Faith-Based Initiative, and the Supreme Court's Establishment Clause Jurisprudence." *The Catholic Lawyer* 2, no. 42 (2002): 211–236.

Follér, Maj-Lis and João Vembane, "Muslim Community-Based Organisations in Mozambique: Exclusion or Inclusion in Development Aids Projects." In *Faith in Civil Society: Religious Actors as Drivers of Change*, edited by Heidi Moksnes and Mia Melin (Uppsala: Uppsala Centre for Sustainable Development, 2013): 164–171.

Formicola, Jo Renee. "The Good in the Faith-Based Initiative." In *The Good the Bad and the Ugly: Faith-Based Initiatives and the Bush Administration*, edited by Jo Renee Formicola, Mary C. Segers, and Paul J. Weber (Lanham, MD: Rowman & Littlefield Publishers, 2003): 25–62.

Formicola, Jo Renee and Mary Segers. "The Ugly Politics of the Faith-Based Initiative." In *The Good the Bad and the Ugly: Faith-Based Initiatives and the Bush Administration*, edited by Jo Renee Formicola, Mary C. Segers, and Paul J. Weber (Lanham, MD: Rowman & Littlefield Publishers, 2003): 115–160.

Goldenziel, Jill. "Administratively Quirky, Constitutionally Murky: The Bush Faith-Based Initiative." *Legislation and Public Policy* 8 (2005): 359–388.

Huntington, Samuel P. "The Clash of Civilizations?" *Foreign Affairs* 72, no. 3 (Summer 1993): 22–49.

Jones, Bruce D., ed. *The Marshall Plan and the Shaping of American Strategy* (Washington, DC: Brookings Institution Press, 2017).

Kavinya, Thengo. "Opinions on the Church's Stand against Condom Use by the Youth." *Malawi Medical Journal* 21, no. 1 (2009): 33. PMID: 19780477

Kuo, David. *Tempting Faith: An Inside Story of Political Seduction* (New York: Free Press, 2007).

Lin, Elbert, Jon D. Michaels, Rajesh Nayak, Katherine Tang Newberger, Nikhil Shanbhag, and Jake Sullivan. "Faith in the Courts? The Legal and Political Future of Federally-Funded Faith-Based Initiatives." *Yale Law & Policy Review* 20, no. 1 (2002): 183–225.

Lupu, Ira C. and Tuttle, Robert W. "The Faith-Based Initiative and the Constitution." *DePaul Law Review* 55, no. 1 (2005): 201–318.

Marsden, Lee. "Bush, Obama and a Faith-Based US Foreign Policy." *International Affairs (Royal Institute of International Affairs 1944–)* 88, no. 5 (2012): 953–974. ISSN 0020-5850

McCleary, Rachel. *Global Compassion: Private Voluntary Organizations and U.S. Foreign Policy Since 1939* (New York: Oxford University Press, 2009).

McCleary, Rachel and Robert Barro. "Replication Data for: Private Voluntary Organizations Engaged in International Assistance, 1939–2004," 2011. https://doi.org/10.7910/DVN/T0PJVX, Harvard Dataverse, V2, UNF:5:CDCNGIiDcwyKXA4tW6FwMQ== [fileUNF]

Olasky, Marvin. *Compassionate Conservatism: What It Is, What It Does, and How It Can Transform America* (New York: Free Press, 2000). ISBN 978-0-7432-0131-5

Pallios, Andrea. "Should We Have Faith in the Faith-Based Initiative: A Constitutional Analysis of President Bush's Charitable Choice Plan." *Hastings Constitutional Law Quarterly* 30, no. 1 (2002): 131–172.

Rigillo, Nicole. "Faith in God, But Not in Condoms: Churches and Competing Visions of HIV Prevention in Namibia." *Canadian Journal of African Studies/ Revue Canadienne Des Études Africaines* 43, no. 1 (2009): 34–59. https://doi.org/ 10.1080/00083968.2010.9707582

Santelli, John S., Ilene S. Speizer, and Zoe R. Edelstein. "Abstinence Promotion Under PEPFAR: The Shifting Focus of HIV Prevention for Youth." *Global Public Health* 8, no. 1 (2013): 1–12.

Santelli, John S., Leslie M. Kantor, Stephanie A. Grilo, Ilene S. Speizer, Larua D. Lindberg, Jennifer Heitel, Amy T Schalet, Maureen E Lyon, Amanda J. Mason-Jones, Terry McGovern, Craig J. Heck, Jennifer Rogers, and Mary A Ott. "Abstinence-Only-Until-Marriage: An Updated Review of U.S. Policies and Programs and Their Impact." *Journal of Adolescent Health* 61, no. 3 (2017): 273–280. https://doi.org/10.1016/j.jadohealth.2017.05.031. PMID: 28842065.

Segers, Paul. "The Bad in the Faith-Based Initiative." In *Faith Based Initiatives: The Good, the Bad, and the Ugly*, edited by Jo Renee Formicola, Mary C. Segers, and Paul J. Weber (Lanham, MD: Rowman & Littlefield Publishers, 2003): 63–114.

Setswe, G. (2007) "Abstinence and Faithfulness Programmes for Prevention of HIV/AIDS Among Young People: What Are the Current Debates?" *South African Family Practice* 49, no. 8 (2007): 5–10. https://doi.org/10.1080/20786204.2007.10873610

The White House. Office of the Press Secretary. *The Quiet Revolution: A Seven Year Progress Report* (Washington, DC: U.S. Government Printing Office, 2008).

Turek, Lauren Frances. "Religious Rhetoric and the Evolution of George W. Bush's Political Philosophy." *Journal of American Studies* 48, no. 4 (2014): 975–988.

United States Library of Congress, Congressional Research Service. *The Marshall Plan: Design, Accomplishments, and Significance*. R45079. 2018. https://crsreports.congress.gov/product/pdf/R/R45079/3

Wolf-Phillips, Leslie. "Why 'Third World'?" *Third World Quarterly* 1, no. 1 (1979): 105–115.

Zurlo, Gina A. "A Demographic Profile of Christianity in Sub-Saharan Africa." In *Christianity in Sub-Saharan Africa*, edited by Kenneth R. Ross, J. Kwabena Asamoah-Gyadu, and Todd M. Johnson, 1 (Edinburgh, UK: Edinburgh University Press, 2017): 3–18.

4 Trends in Faith-Based Funding

Introduction

The United States Agency for International Development (USAID) held its first Evidence Summit on Strategic Religious Engagement in 2020. The conference signaled a significant transition in development thinking. The skepticism of policymakers, practitioners, and academics regarding the role of religion in development had worn thin, and the conference foregrounded the present consensus regarding the overall value of faith-based organizations (FBOs) in providing humanitarian and development services overseas. The predominant question was thus no longer whether the government *should* cooperate with faith-based development organizations but *how* it could collaborate with such organizations more effectively.[1] More specifically, USAID asked how it could more *strategically* engage FBOs in aid delivery.

The idea of moving beyond mere "engagement" with FBOs to something more intentional was generally welcomed, yet it also posed several important questions, such as whether there was any real data on USAID's prior FBO engagement efforts. Several scholars highlighted the paucity of this data in a written review after the Summit. Despite nearly 20 years of the international aid regime endeavoring to "engage" with FBOs, they explained, there remains no aggregate statistics on faith-based financing—at USAID or elsewhere. "Better statistics in this area," they argued, "is of paramount interest to all parties."[2]

This chapter fills this lacuna by gathering existing data on USAID's faith-based funding under the Bush administration and introducing an original dataset on FBO USAID nonprofit grant recipients from 2008 to 2021.[3] The dataset includes how many total FBOs and new FBOs were funded each year, how many grants they were provided, and how much each organization received in assistance. It also identifies the faith of each FBO and details each FBO's primary place of operations. Taken together, these numbers provide an interesting snapshot of how the Faith-Based Initiative has played out at USAID. Further analysis reveals the extent to which there are patterns in FBO funding over time and across administrations.

DOI: 10.4324/9781003456704-4

In the following section, I outline the existing numerical data on the Faith-Based Initiative pertaining to USAID. This includes information provided by the government as well as outside sources. I then provide descriptive statistics for the information in the Faith-Based Organizations Receiving Foreign Aid (FORFA) dataset. The subsequent section looks at the story these numbers tell longitudinally, answering questions relating to the overall growth of USAID's FBO partner base over time. This information is followed by a statistical analysis that tests whether FBO funding varies depending upon the party of the president. The chapter's conclusion explains the relevance of this data to USAID's present endeavors and ends with remaining questions.

Existing Data

USAID, like other Western donors, has never routinely collected or published data relating to FBO funding.[4] In fact, before 2008, it did not publish any information relating to its awards to nongovernmental organizations (NGOs). This does not mean, however, that such information did not exist. Several sources were able to obtain and publish parts of this information, including the Government Accountability Office (GAO), the Bush White House, the *Boston Globe*, Harvard scholar Rachel McCleary, and the President's Emergency Fund for Aids Relief.

The GAO produced a report detailing USAID's funded FBOs in 2002.[5] This report was the result of Congressional concern over the opacity of USAID's NGO-funding procedures. At the time, information was available on the broad contours of US foreign aid, but granular data concerning the *types* of USAID-funded organizations was conspicuously absent. As a result, to satisfy Congress's request for recipient funding data, the GAO reviewed all USAID fund recipients for FY2001 and employed its own methodology for classifying funded organizations. The GAO's final report reveals that 439 NGOs were registered with USAID in 2001. Twenty-six percent of these were faith-based.[6]

One of the suggestions provided by the GAO at the end of its report was that USAID needed a way to produce "more reliable" data on its NGO award recipients. USAID responded by adopting a new information system, which allowed for more detailed and coherent data collection. Nevertheless, it chose not to track the faith status of its award recipients going forward.[7] Instead, this information was only collected upon request using ex-post surveys.[8] The primary requesting entity was the Bush White House.

The Office of Faith-Based and Community Initiatives (OFBCI) under the Bush administration produced five public reports on the outcomes of the Faith-Based Initiative, including annual reports for FY2004–2007 and a comprehensive report in 2008. The annual and final reports aimed to track the progress of the Faith-Based Initiative across implementing executive agencies as measured by FBO funding.[9] The final report reveals that the federal government allocated $2.18 billion in competitive awards to FBOs

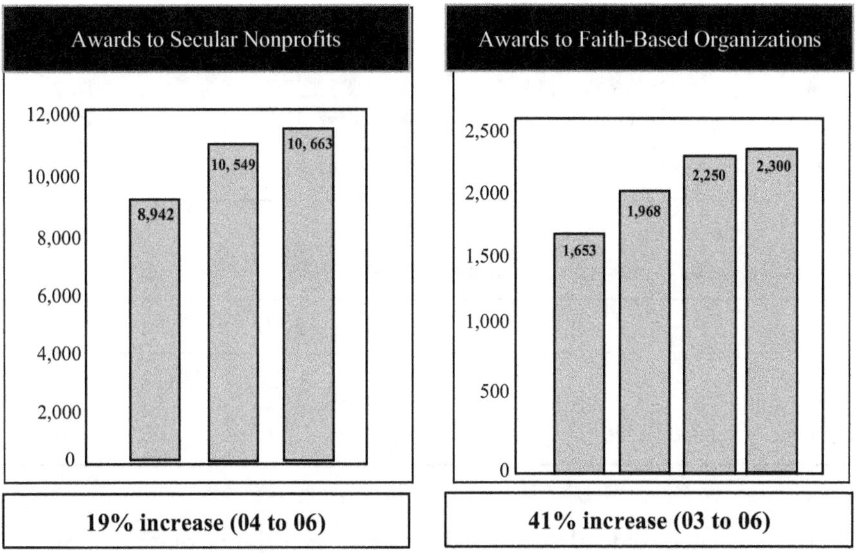

Figure 4.1 Accompanying Graphic in White House Report on the Faith-Based Initiative Outlining Grants Given to Secular and Faith-Based Organizations, 2003–2006.

over five years.[10] It also highlights that the number of awards allocated to FBOs increased from 1,634 in 2003 to 2,300 in 2006.[11] Figure 4.1 shows the graphic displayed in the final White House report.

The White House report indicates FBOs experienced a 41% increase in federal awards from 2003 to 2006, compared to a 19% increase in federal awards to secular NGOs from 2004 to 2006. While this information is technically accurate, the way it was displayed suggests that the Initiative specifically advantaged FBOs. However, while FBOs received more grants between 2004 and 2006, secular organizations also received more grants at this time at a similar rate. This means that rather than FBOs receiving a larger piece of the pie, the pie itself became larger, and the proportion of federal awards allocated to FBOs remained relatively constant at 20%. A similar trend is seen in the monetary amount allocated to FBOs during this time, with FBOs consistently being awarded an average of 10% of funds across all reporting years. At USAID, this number was slightly higher at 14%. The data in the White House report specific to USAID appears in Table 4.1.

The White House report claims that the Faith-Based Initiative led to "an expansion of partnerships of all kinds," yet the data presented in the report doesn't automatically support this conclusion.[12] For one, more grants do not necessarily mean more partnerships. It is possible—and perhaps likely—that

Table 4.1 USAID Funds Allocated to FBOs, 2004–2007

Fiscal year	*Available funding*	*Funds allocated to FBOs*	%
2004	$3,686,179,114	$521,872,579	14.2
2005	$4,152,560,232	$591,047,452	14.2
2006	$3,884,458,053	$552,363, 250	14.2
2007	$4,333,719,700	$585,281,010	13.5

Table 4.2 USAID Funds Allocated to FBOs, 2001–2005

	2001	*2002*	*2003*	*2004*	*2005*
FBO funds (in US millions)	$247	$260	$420	$419	$375
Number of funded FBOs	81	86	95	98	103

USAID and other federal agencies dispersed the majority of "new" money to many of the same organizations that had previously received funds.[13] Thus a better proxy measure for expanding secular and faith-based NGO partnerships would be the number of organizations funded. Additionally, to truly know the effect of the Initiative, one would need to have data on FBO funding *before* the Initiative took effect, yet the report does not include this information.

An investigative piece published by the *Boston Globe* in 2006 appears prima facie to address both issues. The report identifies 149 FBOs that received approximately 52,000 USAID grants, cooperative agreements, and contracts from 2001 to 2005.[14] It includes both detailed financial information and partner information for these fiscal years. The data shows that USAID provided FBOs with a total of $1.7 billion between 2001 and 2005. In addition, the Globe reports that more than 20 new FBOs received USAID funds during this time. Table 4.2 summarizes this data.

The *Boston Globe* published a complete list of humanitarian FBOs funded by USAID between 2001 and 2005.[15] Its analysis of this information led it to conclude that the establishment of the Faith-Based Initiative caused an increase in the absolute number of USAID's faith-based partners and the proportion of such organizations among USAID's partner base. The investigative article accompanying the data, for example, suggests that the proportion of funding provided to FBOs nearly doubled during this time, with FBOs receiving 10.5% of all USAID funding in 2001 and 19.9% of funding in 2005.[16] This statistic continues to circulate in the religions and development literature.[17] However, one should have more than two data points to measure America's faith-based engagement in foreign aid. The usefulness of the data is further limited by the lack of information on the total number of NGOs funded or the total amount of funding provided for all NGOs each year under investigation.

Fortunately, data collected by Harvard scholar Rachel McCleary provides additional information. In her book *Global Compassion*, McCleary presents an original dataset of all registered US-based private voluntary organizations (PVOs) engaged in humanitarian assistance and international development from 1939 to 2005.[18] Her dataset includes information on each organization's faith affiliation and revenue contributions. Information for organizations receiving USAID grants begins in 1988.[19] Table 4.3 includes data from McCleary's dataset on the amount of funding USAID allocated to FBOs and the number of FBOs USAID funded from 1989 to 2005.

The McCleary dataset ends in 2005, only one year after USAID changed its regulations regarding the eligibility of FBOs for funding. In contrast to the *Boston Globe* report, McCleary's research suggests that the FBO gains in USAID funds under President Bush immediately following the implementation of the Faith-Based Initiative were relatively minimal. FBOs received approximately 16% of all USAID grants in 2001 and approximately 18% of all USAID grants in 2005 following The Rule's implementation. Additionally, according to the McCleary data, the proportion of USAID grant recipients that were faith-based changed only slightly from 2001 to 2005, with FBOs comprising approximately 29% of all recipients in 2001 and 33% in 2005. This information leads McCleary to the circumspect conclusion that Bush's Faith-Based Initiative "has been succeeding to some extent" at achieving Bush's objective of attracting new FBO partners to deliver US aid.[20]

One of the programs primarily excluded from the *Boston Globe* analysis and the McCleary dataset is the President's Emergency Plan for AIDS Relief (PEPFAR), introduced by President Bush in 2003. Over the past 20 years, PEPFAR has allocated millions of dollars to organizations combating HIV and AIDS. Evidence indicates Bush intentionally established PEPFAR outside of USAID to "bypass existing funding mechanisms."[21] The organization continues today under the State Department, with the Office of the US Global AIDS Coordinator managing the organization's collaboration with donors and partner nations. USAID is only one of several implementing agencies.[22]

President Bush considered PEPFAR "among the best successes" of the Faith-Based Initiative due to the many FBOs funded through the plan.[23] USAID has also lauded PEPFAR as one of the "most impactful" examples of effective religious engagement.[24] Some even cite FBO participation as critical to PEPFAR's success.[25] PEPFAR funding for FBOs for 2005–2020 appears in Table 4.4.

The PEPFAR data suggests a relative "surge" in FBO funding upon the establishment of the program, followed by a stabilization in funding in subsequent years. Throughout the program's existence, however, the proportion of funding going to FBOs has remained relatively minimal. It is unclear from existing data whether USAID's total FBO funding follows a similar pattern. The United States is recognized as having "engaged" FBOs in foreign aid delivery

Table 4.3 USAID Grants Allocated to FBOs, 1989–2005

Fiscal Year	*FBO funds*	*Total funds*	%	*Total no. of funded FBOs*	*Total no. of funded NGOs*	%
1989	$80,257,101	$381,102,707	21.06%	82	246	33.33%
1990	$86,232,730	$382,332,452	22.55%	81	275	29.45%
1991	$56,787,987	$426,377,127	13.32%	93	335	27.76%
1992	$63,041,758	$572,913,029	11.00%	104	393	26.46%
1993	$78,365,950	$645,931,235	12.13%	114	418	27.27%
1994	$98,287,564	$772,157,875	12.73%	132	506	26.01%
1995	$96,698,247	$802,736,732	12.05%	126	481	26.20%
1996	$104,311,272	$766,862,969	13.60%	134	480	27.92%
1997	$93,136,414	$807,052,310	11.54%	129	464	27.80%
1998	$130,597,785	$852,807,575	15.31%	137	471	29.10%
1999	$128,398,849	$911,199,778	14.09%	141	479	29.44%
2000	$171,787,156	$1,034,097,315	16.61%	139	486	28.60%
2001	$180,114,987	$1,118,008,879	16.11%	150	509	29.47%
2002	$180,024,069	$1,343,344,689	13.40%	175	539	32.47%
2003	216345321	$1,497,536,796	14.45%	180	581	30.98%
2004	302551956	$1,796,802,420	16.84%	187	567	32.98%
2005	313405287	$1,735,622,709	18.06%	179	543	32.97%

Source: McCleary and Barro (2011).

Table 4.4 PEPFAR Allocations to FBOs, 2005–2020

Fiscal year	*Funding allocated to FBOs*	*Percentage of total*
2005	$84,975,336	7.05
2006	$109,387,290	6.42
2007	$250,171,114	8.75
2008	$286,070,958	7.21
2009	$243,676,191	6.24
2010	$170,453,188	4.15
2011	$175,834,536	4.18
2012	$140,935,220	3.94
2013	$141,433,553	3.86
2014	$127,474,928	3.73
2015	$141,100,577	3.75
2016	$94,326,348	2.67
2017	$101,018,136	2.77
2018	$96,553,288	2.47
2019	$165,160,196	4.07
2020	$128,584,149	3.04

Source: amfAR PEPFAR Country/Regional Operational Plans database.

for the past 20 years, yet nowhere is there supporting longitudinal quantitative funding and partner information equivalent to what is released by PEPFAR. We have only partial information.[26] More complete and updated information needs to be available. The remainder of this chapter provides a comprehensive look at USAID's funding of FBOs since the Bush administration.

Original Data

While the PEPFAR data is continuous from 2005 to the present, the data presented by the OFBCI, *Boston Globe*, and McCleary is now at least 15 years old. Little to no information exists on USAID's FBO funding after Bush left office. The FORFA dataset, introduced here for the first time, fills this gap. This data reveals that USAID awarded over 9,000 grants to nonprofit organizations between 2008 and 2021, amounting to nearly $85 billion.[27] Less than 10% of this went to FBOs, and these organizations comprised 13% of all USAID nonprofit prime grant recipients.[28] A detailed examination of the full population of the FBOs receiving USAID assistance reveals several additional observations relating to the faith profile, size, and geographic locale of funded FBOs.

First, the data reveals what many know to be true: the United States channels most of its foreign aid through a relatively small number of large implementing organizations.[29] This "aid cartel," as some have called it, has a relatively long history.[30] In 1992, two-thirds of all USAID assistance went to only 20 organizations.[31] This same dynamic held in 2021. More than half of all USAID's nonprofit assistance funding went to only five organizations.

Table 4.5 Top Ten Nonprofit USAID Fund Recipients, 2008–2021

Rank	*Organization*	*Total grant funding (in US billions)*	*NGO type*
1	United Nations	10.07	Secular
2	Family Health International	3.77	Secular
3	Catholic Relief Services	3.32	Christian
4	Consortium for Elections and Political Process	3.06	Secular
5	Save the Children	1.95	Secular
6	Jhpiego Corporation	1.64	Secular
7	Mercy Corps	1.63	Secular
8	JSI Research and Training Institute, Inc.	1.59	Secular
9	Research Triangle Institute	1.44	Secular
10	World Vision	1.34	Christian

Note: Family Health International assumed the abbreviated label of FHI 360 after acquiring AED in mid-2011.

The top ten organizations received 70% of all allocated assistance. Table 4.5 lists the top ten USAID-funded nonprofits from 2008 to 2021 and the total amount they received in USAID assistance during these years.

The "top heavy" arrangement of USAID nonprofit implementers is mirrored by USAID's FBO partners. Five FBOs are among USAID's top 100 prime partners, including Catholic Relief Services (CRS), World Vision (WV), Food for the Hungry, Adventist Development and Relief Agency (ADRA), and Interchurch Medical Assistance (IMA World Health). These five organizations received the lion's share (76%) of all prime funds allocated to FBOs in 2021. Notably, four of these organizations (WV, CRS, ADRA, and Food for the Hungry) received USAID funding *before* USAID changed its regulations. CRS alone received approximately 40% of all USAID assistance to FBOs in 2021 and nearly 47% of all FBO funding between 2008 and 2021.[32] Table 4.6 shows the top ten USAID FBO awardees between 2008 and 2021.

A second observation concerns the faith diversity, or lack thereof, among USAID-funded FBOs. When the *Boston Globe* first reported on USAID's partnerships with FBOs, it claimed Christian organizations had a near monopoly on the funds provided to FBOs. Its analysis showed that between 2001 and 2005, 98.3% of the grants and contracts USAID awarded to FBOs went to Christian organizations. It also revealed that among the 149 FBOs USAID had funded during those years, 142, or 95.3%, were Christian. Updated information reveals only slightly more diversification. Evaluating the 264 FBOs that received funding between 2001 and 2021, we see Christian organizations continued to receive precisely 98% of all FBO funding, yet their representation among all USAID-funded FBOs dropped to 87.5%.[33] More specifically,

Table 4.6 Top Ten FBO USAID Fund Recipients, 2008–2021

Rank	*Organization*	*Total grant funding*	*NGO type*
1.	Catholic Relief Services (CRS)	$3.32 billion	Christian
2.	World Vision	$1.34 billion	Christian
3.	Food for the Hungry	$387.92 million	Christian
4.	Adventist Development and Relief Agency (ADRA)	$366.91 million	Christian
5.	Samaritan's Purse	$236 million	Christian
6.	Interchurch Medical Assistance (IMA)	$229.96 million	Christian
7.	Medair	$147.74 million	Christian
8.	Caris Foundation	$143.32 million	Christian
9.	Tearfund	$83.41 million	Christian
10.	World Relief	$81.47 million	Christian

Table 4.7 Top Non-Christian FBOs Receiving USAID Funds, 2008–2021

	Organization	*Faith*	*Number of received grants*	*Total USAID funding, 2008–2021 (in millions)*
1.	Aga Khan Foundation of the USA	Islamic	15	$58,820
2.	Dhaka Ahsania Mission	Islamic	1	$18,068
3.	Buddhist Digital Resource Center, Inc.	Buddhist	1	$11,801
4.	American Committee for Shaare Zedek Hospital in Jerusalem, Inc.	Jewish	21	$8,706
5.	Hadassah	Jewish	16	$10,470
6.	Aga Khan University	Islamic	2	$6,187
7.	Lanka Jathika Sarvodaya Shramadana Sangamaya	Buddhist	5	$4,038
8.	Public Foundation Mountain Societies Development Support Program Kyrgyzstan (A branch of the Aga Khan Development Network)	Islamic	1	$3,305
9.	Lembaga Kesehatan Nahdlatul Ulama (LKNU)	Islamic	1	$3,021
10.	The Hebrew Immigrant Aid Society (HIAS) Inc.	Jewish	1	$1,000,000

of the total 264 USAID-funded FBOs between 2001 and 2021, 229 are Christian (86.74%), 12 are Muslim (4.95%), 10 are multireligious (3.78%), 8 are Jewish (3%), 3 are spiritually ambiguous/indigenous (1.1%), and 2 are Buddhist (<1%).[34] Table 4.7 lists the ten top-funded non-Christian FBOs and the number of grants and amount of assistance they received.[35]

A third related but distinct observation from organization faith affiliation is how faith is exhibited in an organization's operations. At the fulcrum of the debate over the Faith-Based Initiative under Bush was the dubious constitutionality of the government funding so-called pervasively sectarian institutions. Organizations engaged in proselytization were seen as particularly suspect, and many assumed the majority of funded FBOs engaged in such activity.[36] Lee Marsden, for example, argued in his book that "Much of the money ... has gone to evangelical organizations, which combine their assistance work with a strong proselytizing emphasis."[37] The *Boston Globe* was even more incriminatory. According to the report, the changed regulations at USAID "helped change the message American aid workers bring to many corners of the world, from emphasizing religious neutrality to touting the healing powers of the Christian God."[38] Fast forward 15 years, and the refrain continues. A 2021 Devex report lists this as one of the primary "myths" impeding the work of FBOs in development.[39]

While the number of proselytizing organizations has increased globally, most FBOs in the humanitarian space do not engage in strategic proselytization, and the same is true among USAID-funded FBOs. Of the FBOs that received USAID awards between 2001 and 2021, approximately 22% explicitly include proselytization among their mission objectives. Most of these organizations would best be characterized as "faith saturated" FBOs per Sider and Uruh's typology, meaning that religion is suffused throughout nearly all the organization's operations. Funded entities range from church associations or collectives to missionary societies to individual churches to broader parachurch organizations. Notably, most of these organizations received in-kind grants in the form of food to feed the hungry.[40] In contrast to these organizations, 4% of USAID-funded FBOs state explicitly on their website that they do *not* proselytize, potentially as a way of combatting the negative perception surrounding proselytization and humanitarian aid.[41]

A fourth observation involves the geographic locale of USAID's funded FBOs. The vast majority of organizations funded by USAID are based in the United States. USAID, along with most Western donors, has acknowledged this presents a problem, in large part because it reinforces the power asymmetry between donor countries and beneficiary communities. The accepted solution called for by most of the foreign aid regime is to champion "locally led development," which prioritizes, in part, seeking to empower and partner with more local organizations and increasing the funding going toward such organizations.[42] The localization agenda and the prioritization of strategic religious engagement intersect in important ways, not least because many of the local actors donors could empower and partner with are faith-based.[43] Yet, as some suggest, such "Local Faith Actors," or LFAs, often suffer from a double penalty because "they are local in an internationally dominated sector and (...) they are faith-based in a secularized system."[44] This is supported by the data. LFAs comprised only a third of all USAID-funded FBOs between

2001 and 2021.[45] Most recently, in 2020 and 2021, when additional aid funding was available to combat the COVID-19 pandemic, USAID funded only 14 and 19 LFAs, respectively. By contrast, USAID reported that for those same years, it funded 1,532 and 1,473 local partners.[46]

A final observation surrounds the primary funding channels for FBOs. Organizations seeking to secure funds from USAID generally apply under a specific program. Two programs with significant FBO recipient representation are the Food for Peace (FFP) program and the American Schools and Hospitals Abroad (ASHA) program, both of which began before USAID was established.

The FFP program began in 1954 with the express purpose of sending America's surplus agricultural commodities overseas to those in need.[47] What began as a temporary program soon became a mainstay of American foreign policy. Today, the program operates under the aegis of USAID, and its programmatic ambit has substantially increased.[48] The amount of funds has also increased, with congressional allocations more than tripling between 2001 and 2017.[49] The evolution and expansion of the program have led to an increased number of implementing partners, with FBOs heavily represented. In 2021, for example, FBOs comprised nearly 39% of the implementing partners for USAID's food assistance programs. The FBOs represented include large organizations like CRS, which has a staff exceeding 5,000, and smaller organizations like Evangelistic International Missions (EIM), which has a staff of six. As a large implementing partner of FFP, CRS provides emergency food relief to a large number of countries and also uses food aid for non-emergent food programs like Feed the Future, which funds farmer training to advance the agricultural output and economic development of beneficiary countries.[50] In the case of EIM and similar, smaller FBOs, the most likely avenue for their participation is the International Food Relief Partnership (IFRP) program, which typically provides grants under $200,000 for food distribution in a single country. In 2021, most of the IFRP program award recipients were faith-based.[51] These organizations received shelf-stable food to distribute in institutional settings like schools and hospitals.

Another program where one sees FBOs heavily represented among implementing organizations is USAID's ASHA program. Established in 1947, ASHA provides funds to US organizations that support education and health institutes overseas. FBOs are heavily represented among ASHA award recipients. An illustrative example is the Shaare Zedek Medical Center in Jerusalem. Established under the Ottoman Empire, Shaare Zedek is the oldest medical institution in Jerusalem and is also among ASHA's oldest partners. ASHA funds have helped the Jewish institution grow from 20 beds to 1,000 and have further furnished it with advanced medical equipment, including, most recently, a Da Vinci Robotic Surgical System. The hospital is estimated to treat 600,000 people annually.

Longitudinal Trends

The American Committee for Shaare Zedek Hospital in Jerusalem is a long-standing partner of USAID, and it began receiving funds well before the establishment of the Faith-Based Initiative and the agency's changed regulations relating to FBOs.[52] This is true of many of the faith-based partners involved in the FFP and ASHA programs. In fact, some of USAID's modern faith-based partners first received USAID funding over five decades ago, including WV, ADRA, Church World Service, the Salvation Army, Lutheran World Relief, the American ORT Foundation, the Domestic and Foreign Missionary Society of the Episcopal Church, the American Friends of Kiryat Sanz Laniado Hospital, the Hebrew Immigrant Aid Society, the Paul Carlson Medical Program, and World Renew.[53] Others, like Aga Khan, Bethany Christian Services, Christian Relief Services, Food for the Hungry, and American Leprosy Missions, were funded in the 1990s.[54]

So, how many new faith-based partners did the Faith-Based Initiative bring to USAID? The data suggests that 40% of all USAID's FBO partners, 102 total, began their relationship with USAID after the agency established its faith-based center and changed its regulations, with the agency funding an average of eight new FBOs per year.[55] Yet the data also shows that most of these organizations, approximately 82%, were only one-time partners. This means that the number of FBOs USAID has funded annually has changed fairly little over time.

When recoding the Boston Globe FBO data, it appears that in 2001, before USAID changed its regulations relating to FBOs, USAID funded 55 FBOs. This number dropped to 51 in 2002 and rose to 60 in 2003 and 2004. By 2005, one year after the changed regulations at USAID went into effect, the agency had funded 63 FBOs.[56] This was the highest number of USAID-funded FBOs on record. Data on FBO funding for subsequent years shows the annual number fluctuating between 34 and 58, with no significant pattern of increase. Figure 4.2 shows the numbers and percentage of FBOs USAID funded from 2008 to 2021.

The number of FBOs funded by USAID is one indicator used to measure the agency's faith-based engagement. Another is the amount of funding allocated to FBOs. The longitudinal data suggests a slight increase in the assistance provided to FBOs from 2008 to 2021 as a proportion of overall funding and in absolute dollars, though this trend is not uniform across all years. As a proportion of total funding, FBOs received between 5.9% and 19.1% of the assistance allocated to nonprofits in the years investigated, with FBOs receiving an average of approximately 10% of all funds. The greatest percentage of USAID-funded FBOs relative to all nonprofit awardees occurred in 2020 and 2021. These years also saw more absolute dollars given to FBOs than previous years. In 2021, in particular, the amount of grants

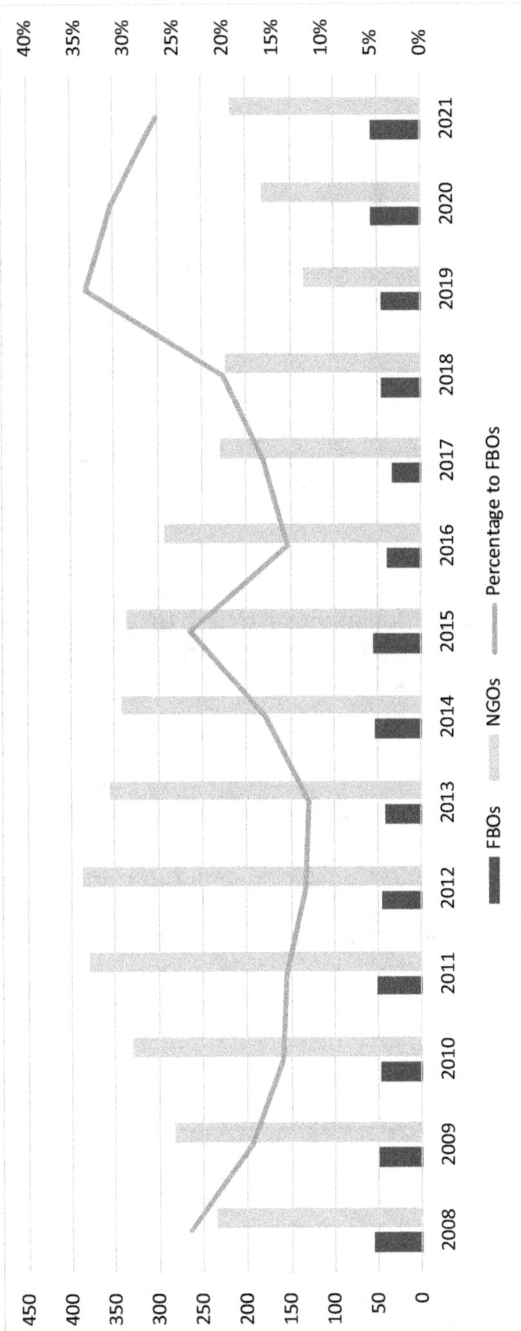

Figure 4.2 Number of Secular NGOs and FBOs Funded by USAID, 2008–2021.

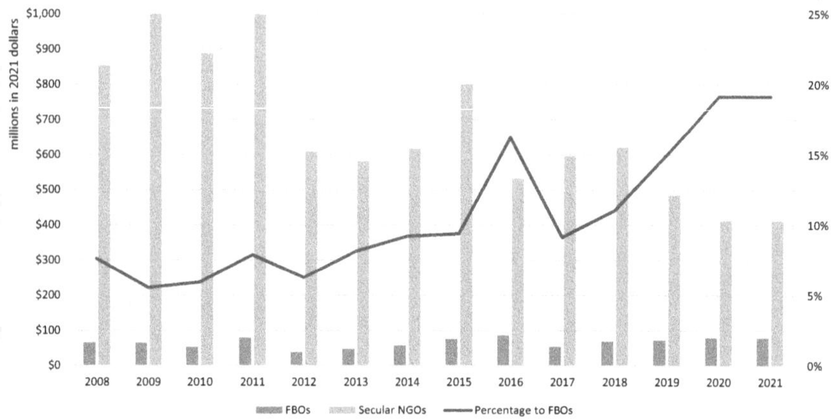

Figure 4.3 USAID FBO Funding, 2008–2021 in 2021 Millions.

and cooperative agreements provided to FBOs was nearly double the amount provided in 2013 after adjusting for inflation. Figure 4.3 illustrates this data.

One can see from the longitudinal trends that the long-term effects of the Faith-Based Initiative do not support earlier predictions of cataclysmic change. Contrary to the claims of some, the Faith-Based Initiative did not introduce a deluge of funds to FBOs relative to secular NGOs in foreign aid.[57] It also did not result in a boom of new FBO partners. Instead, the data suggest that, as a result of the Initiative, the funding stream to FBOs has widened slightly, as has the door allowing more FBOs access to federal funding. At the same time, these increases are not uniform, and many partners do not seem to sustain their relationship with the agency. Funding levels also appear to fluctuate. The next section examines what, if anything, contributes to this observed difference.

Statistical Analysis

The data presented from the FORFA dataset allows researchers, for the first time, to test some of the claims made surrounding the Faith-Based Initiative. One hypothesis tested by researchers in other cases is that FBO funding depends primarily upon whether a conservative occupies the executive office.[58] The early critics of the Faith-Based Initiative were not shy in insinuating that the Initiative had a distinctly Republican brand. The causal mechanism behind this assertion varied. In some cases, critics charged that the funds were part of a quid-pro-quo on the part of Republicans, who benefited from connecting with well-funded and recognized religious organizations.[59] Others widened the aperture of their critique to suggest that Republicans implemented specific policies that directly favored FBOs. Much of the attention focused on the earmarked PEPFAR funds promoting Abstinence Until Marriage programs discussed in Chapter 3, yet the Republican policy of denying funds to abortion-providing/promoting organizations was also hypothesized to appeal to and potentially favor FBOs.[60] Gregorio Bettiza explains the effect of the policy by saying, "In certain circumstances, the playing field was not leveled but tilted in favor of religious organizations."[61] Bettiza mentions several secular organizations disadvantaged by the policy, including Planned Parenthood, Marie Scopes International, Population Services International, and Cooperative Assistance and Relief Everywhere (CARE). He also explains which FBOs benefited from the policy, naming WV, Samaritan's Purse, and Food for the Hungry. But did these organizations represent a more significant funding trend? More to the point, do we see more FBOs funded or more allocated dollars to FBOs under Republican administrations?

A *T*-test of the funds allocated to FBOs in 2021 dollars by Republican and Democratic presidents reveals no significant difference between the two, $t(17) = .2109$, $p = .3156$.[62] A simple linear regression further shows that a Republican presidential administration does not significantly predict increased FBO spending, $R^2 = .0003$, $F(1{,}800) = .27$, $p = .6003$.[63] While the number of total observations is fewer due to incomplete data, the available numbers suggest that this also holds when testing the difference between the number of funded FBOs generally and newly funded FBOs.[64] USAID funds a relatively similar number of FBOs each year whether a Republican president is in office ($M = 50.6$, SD = 10.25) or whether a Democratic President is in office ($M = 45.11$, SD = 6.85).[65] An independent samples *T*-test also reveals that there is not a statistically significant difference in the number of new FBOs funded under Republican and Democratic administrations, $t(15) = 2.13$, $p = .47$.[66] Instead, the average number of FBOs that are first-time USAID fund recipients remains relatively unchanged regardless of whether a Republican ($M = 9.25$, SD = 4.17) or Democrat ($M = 10.89$, SD = 4.91) occupies the Oval Office. Table 4.8 provides the figures used to reach these conclusions, though funding dollars appear in real dollars and were adjusted for the above calculations.

Conclusion

The GAO report found that 26% of all USAID-registered NGOs in 2001 were faith-based. McCleary's data on funded NGOs for the same year. According to her data, in 2005, one year after USAID changed its regulations on FBOs, the percentage of funded FBOs increased slightly to 33%. The FORFA data reveals that while USAID maintained a faith-based center in the ensuing years, the number of funded FBOs relative to secular NGOs remains relatively low. While the funding data certainly shows that FBOs are not "forgotten" at USAID, it also doesn't demonstrate a definitive "turn

Table 4.8 FBO Funding and Partisanship, 2001–2021

Year	*President*	*President's party*	*No. of FBOs funded*	*Assistance allocated to FBOs*	*No. of new FBO awardees*
2001	George W. Bush	Republican Party	55	$211,835,281	–
2002	George W. Bush	Republican Party	51	$202,192,773	10
2003	George W. Bush	Republican Party	60	$368,501,701	9
2004	George W. Bush	Republican Party	60	$344,711,003	7
2005	George W. Bush	Republican Party	63	$292,492,554	2
2008	George W. Bush	Republican Party	51	$413,684,108	20*
2009	Barack Obama	Democratic Party	43	$513,607,415	7
2010	Barack Obama	Democratic Party	43	$514,352,444	10
2011	Barack Obama	Democratic Party	48	$436,515,958	4
2012	Barack Obama	Democratic Party	41	$665,810,880	7
2013	Barack Obama	Democratic Party	37	$327,122,329	15
2014	Barack Obama	Democratic Party	49	$412,417,332	14
2015	Barack Obama	Democratic Party	55	$496,033,266	14
2016	Barack Obama	Democratic Party	36	$664,526,159	3
2017	Donald Trump	Republican Party	30	$781,870,426	6
2018	Donald Trump	Republican Party	41	$504,568,498	6
2019	Donald Trump	Republican Party	42	$646,867,844	6
2020	Donald Trump	Republican Party	53	$694,734,993	13
2021	Joe Biden	Democratic Party	54	$791,007,620	13

Data unavailable for FY2006 and FY2007.
* Artificially inflated due to the exclusion of FY2006 and FY2007.

to religion," as some have surmised. The number of USAID's faith-based partners did not precipitously increase following the implementation of the Faith-Based Initiative. They also did not receive a surge of funding relative to secular NGOs.

The data does not demonstrate a "religious resurgence" at USAID, nor does it demonstrate what some have called "post-secular rapprochement." In other words, it does not appear that a significant number of FBOs are now more likely to deliberately enter into a partnership with an organization that does not share their faith tradition.[67] Nor does it necessarily appear that USAID seeks to engage *all* faith-based actors. Instead, to use the words of Emma Tomalin, the data shows a kind of "selective," rather than strategic, engagement.[68]

What does selective engagement look like? First, it is clear from the data that the Faith-Based Initiative's implementation at USAID succeeded in forging new partnerships between the US government and religious actors involved in humanitarian work overseas. This means both development FBOs and the government, generally, have become more willing to traverse the theological-secular divide for the sake of a common humanitarian purpose. Engagement is happening, but not with all, or even a majority, of FBOs. Instead, while religious organizations make up nearly two-third percent of all international humanitarian organizations in the United States, they comprised 13% of USAID's nonprofit awardees between 2008 and 2021. My research indicates neither the number of FBOs funded nor their funding level varies when there is a change in the oval office. Chapter 5 explores this dynamic in more detail. In particular, I explore whether the relatively small number of USAID-funded FBOs is a consequence of the US government selectively supplying FBOs with development funds or whether fewer FBOs are selectively demanding (applying for) these funds.

Notes

1 Mandaville, "Right-Sizing Religion and Religious Engagement," 93.
2 Marshall, Roy, Seiple, and Slim, "Intrinsic and Strategic Leverage of Religion," 32.
3 The full Faith-Based Organizations Receiving Foreign Aid (FORFA) dataset is openly available in Lipscomb University's Carolyn Wilson Digital Collections at https://digitalcollections.lipscomb.edu/hpp_fac/1/
4 The reasons for this are likely manifold, but one can isolate at least three: First, there is a methodological issue. As discussed in Chapter 1, there is no legal definition in the United States for a "faith-based organization," nor is there an academic consensus on the term. As a result, any attempt to measure FBO engagement will likely require contested identification procedures. Second, the collection of quantitative data may be stymied by concerns that numbers are likely to tell only part of the story. A complete assessment of USAID's efforts at religious engagement would rely on both quantitative and qualitative data and measure the depth and scope of the government's partnerships with FBOs. Another reason could be that the numbers may not tell the "right" story, as perceived by the

entities involved. This is the reason suggested by Marshall, Roy, Seiple, and Slim, "Intrinsic and Strategic Leverage of Religion," 32. This point is reiterated in Marshall, "Impressions & Indications of Religious Engagement, 20.

5 The Government Accountability Office, "Foreign Assistance: USAID Relied Heavily on Non-governmental Organizations, But Better Data Needed to Evaluate Approaches," GAO-02-471, April 25, 2002, www.gao.gov/products/gao-02-471

6 The Government Accountability Office, "Foreign Assistance," 29.

7 The six years following the GAO report saw the creation and implementation of USAID's Executive Information System. This system rectified many outstanding issues in agency reporting and added greater coherence to the agency's overall data collection efforts.

8 Notes provided for the 2004, 2005, and 2006 White House reports indicate that all participating agencies made "good-faith efforts" to provide FBO-funding data, relying primarily on SF-424 application cover sheets and an optional survey distributed with grant applications. Additional means of collecting this information included phone calls and internet searches.

9 The report clarifies that the White House Office of Faith-Based and Community Initiatives relied upon the various implementing agencies for the report numbers, and its staff was not responsible for directly collecting the data.

10 The White House. Office of the Press Secretary, *The Quiet Revolution*, 87.

11 The full report reviewed 134 programs and 35 program areas at 11 federal agencies. The data in Figure 4.1 represents only five agencies, including the US Department of Housing and Urban Development (HUD), the US Department of Health and Human Services (HHS), the US Department of Justice (DOJ), the US Department of Interior, and the US Department of Education (ED).

12 The White House. Office of the Press Secretary, *The Quiet Revolution*, 86.

13 This trend would run contrary to Bush's stated objective of identifying and building relationships with *new* private organizations. See McCleary, *Global Compassion*, 157.

14 *Boston Globe*, "USAID Contracts with Faith-Based Organizations," October 8, 2006, http://archive.boston.com/news/special/faith_based/faith_based_organizations.htm

15 "USAID Contracts with Faith-Based Organizations."

16 Farah Stockman, Michael Kranish, and Peter S. Canellos, "Bush Brings Faith to Foreign Aid," *Boston Globe*, October 8, 2006, https://web.archive.org/web/20061026112537/https://www.boston.com/news/nation/articles/2006/10/08/bush_brings_faith_to_foreign_aid/

17 Deacon and Tomalin, "A History of Faith-Based Aid and Development," 69; Volberg, *The Politicization of Humanitarian Aid*, 32; Tomalin, "Thinking About Faith-Based Organisations in Development," 690; Bettiza, *Finding Faith in Foreign Policy*, 112; Cooper, "Faith-Based Organisations and Current Development Debates," 2; Marshall, Roy, Seiple, and Slim, "Intrinsic and Strategic Leverage of Religion," 33.

18 McCleary, *Global Compassion.*

19 The McCleary data only reports USAID grants to PVOs after this time, but USAID's relationship with PVOs began earlier. The agency's first shift in this direction occurred with the 1973 "New Directions" legislation, which ushered in the "human needs approach" to development. USAID established the Office of Private and Voluntary Cooperation the following year to facilitate PVO–USAID

relations. The 1982 President's Private Sector Survey on Cost Control (established under Executive Order 12369) further encouraged the agency to allocate funds through PVOs. Congress also contributed to the conversation with the proposal of HR 1675 to amend the Foreign Assistance Act of 1961, which would have required USAID "… to increase the involvement in assistance programs of such private nonprofit channels for the delivery of assistance." Though Congress did not pass the bill, USAID began to allot most of its funding through grants instead of the previous precedent of direct wires or loans.

20 McCleary, *Global Compassion*, 159.

21 McCleary mentions the program but notes it "largely bypassed the existing funding mechanisms for aid delivery that existed within USAID." *Global Compassion*, 152.

22 PEPFAR's primary implementing agencies are the Peace Corps, USAID, Department of Commerce, Department of Defense, Department of Health and Human Services, Department of Labor, and Department of the State.

23 The White House. Office of the Press Secretary, *The Quiet Revolution*, vii.

24 United States Agency for International Development (USAID), "Building Bridges in Development," 5.

25 Blevins, Jalloh, and Robinson, "Faith and Global Health Practice."

26 One could also make the case that various parties interpret this information to advance a specific position. (The White House used the data to highlight the program's success, while the *Boston Globe* used the data to critique the administration's efforts.)

27 The total number USAID-funded nonprofits is based upon Unique Entity IDs (UEIs) retrieved from USASpending.gov and thus does not account for instances where organizations' identities are not disclosed.

28 Here forward, I use the term "grants" to refer to both forms of USAID assistance: grants and cooperative agreements.

29 Present USAID administrator Samantha Power has also acknowledged this as a problem. See Samantha Power, "A New Vision for Global Development" (speech, Washington, DC: Georgetown University, November 4, 2021), www.usaid.gov/news-information/speeches/nov-4-2021-administrator-samantha-power-new-vision-global-development

30 Hopgood and Vinjamuri, "Faith in Markets," 50.

31 Government Accountability Office, "Foreign Assistance," Chapter 0.4.3.

32 CRS's heavy reliance on government funding predates the establishment of USAID. The FBO received more than half of all food aid (under PL 480) from 1953 to 1963. See McCleary, *Global Compassion*, 79.

33 This does not include organizations coded as "ambiguous or spiritual" (code 45) or those coded as multifaith (code 47).

34 Looking exclusively at the FORFA data only minimally changes the numbers. Reviewing all funded prime FBOs between 2008 and 2021, excluding data for 2006 and 2007, we find 148 of the 179 FBOs are Christian (82.68%), 13 Muslim (7.26%), 16 multireligious (3.35%), 7 Jewish (3%), 3 spiritually ambiguous/indigenous (<1%), and 2 Buddhist (<1%).

35 Since all the interfaith or multireligious organizations USAID funded include Christian partners, this list excludes such organizations.

36 For an excellent overview of how scholars have openly disparaged religious proselytization in the humanitarian space and "the proselytization problem"

(erroneously) assumed to apply to most development FBOs, see Lynch and Schwarz, "Humanitarianism's Proselytism Problem."

37 Marsden, *For God's Sake*, 127.

38 Stockman, Kranish, and Canellos, "Bush Brings Faith to Foreign Aid."

39 Rebecca L. Root, "4 Myths Affecting Faith Actors' Role in Development," *Inside Development*, Devex, May 12, 2021, www.devex.com/news/4-myths-affecting-faith-actors-role-in-development-98884

40 This finding supports the finding of others that evangelical FBOs are more likely to engage in humanitarian relief because the "barriers to entry are lower and the need to engage with governments and their complex agendas more limited." See Hopgood and Vinjamuri, "Faith in Markets," 45.

41 Bush, "What Is a Religious NGO?" 265.

42 USAID's localization agenda was most prominently articulated by USAID Administrator Samantha Power in November 2021, when she announced the agency's intent to allocate at least 25% of its funds to local organizations by the end of FY2025 and amplify the voices of local actors and organizations by letting them take the lead on at least half of the agency's projects by 2025. The focus on the number of local partners, while not stated as an official target, is included in USAID's first localization progress report. United States Agency for International Development, "Moving Toward a Model of Locally Led Development," 6.

43 Wilkinson et al., "Faith in Localisation?"

44 Joint Learning Initiative on Faith and Local Communities, "Local Faith Communities and the Promotion of Resilience in Humanitarian Situations," 9.

45 Researchers coded FBOs as local using USAID-determined criteria; namely, an organization must be (1) a prime recipient of USAID funds, (2) legally recognized/registered in a developing country, and (3) be serving in that same country.

46 United States Agency for International Development, "Moving Toward a Model of Locally Led Development," 6. The number of LFAs identified in the author's dataset may be lower than the total number of LFAs funded by USAID during these years since it is limited to nonprofit organizations receiving USAID assistance and excludes for-profit entities or nonprofit entities receiving only contracts.

47 The program was also meant to be a solution for excess US crop production caused by federal subsidies. The authorizing legislation was the Agricultural Trade Development and Assistance Act of 1954 (PL 83–480).

48 In 2021, for example, USAID sent 1.7 million metric tons of US food commodities to 35 countries. In addition to in-kind aid, which has been the historic hallmark of the FFP program, USAID also began in 2010 relying upon market-based assistance, purchasing more food from the country or region where it will be distributed. United States Agency for International Development, "International Food Assistance Report," 1.

49 FFP allocations in 2001 were slightly less than 1 billion, compared to approximately 3.6 billion in 2018. This includes Title II Emergency and Nonemergency funds, Community Development Funds, and funding from the Annual Emergency Food Security Program. Morgenstern, "International Food Assistance," 10.

50 Morgenstern, "International Food Assistance," 4.

51 Appendix H in the International Food Assistance Report for FY 2021 Report to Congress (26) explains that IFRP grants are "predominately" provided to FBOs. A precise figure is not provided because the implementing partners in Somalia and Sudan were omitted due to security concerns.

52 A 1995 Congressional report includes the American Committee for Shaare Zedek Hospital in Jerusalem among the 1982 USAID grant recipients. Government Accountability Office, "Foreign Assistance," Appendix II.

53 Note World Renew changed its name from Christian Reformed World Relief Committee in 2012. Government Accountability Office, "Foreign Assistance," Appendix II.

54 Government Accountability Office, "Foreign Assistance," Appendix II.

55 This number is calculated by determining the first year of funding for the 264 FBOs that are identified in the FORFA dataset and included in the *Boston Globe* analysis for 2001–2005. It omits new entrants for 2006 and 2007 since data from these years is unavailable. It also excludes 2008 since the number of new entrants for this year is artificially inflated due to missing data from the two prior years. While USAID longitudinal partner information is not publicly available before 2001, a 1995 GAO report helped identify partners from 1982 to 1992.

56 The *Boston Globe* reports the number of FBOs funded during these years as 81, 85, 95, 98, and 103, respectively. However, the Globe's coding of FBOs includes what we classify as "secular with religious roots," as well as secular organizations with religious programming. The lower numbers reflect our attempt to vet the Globe FBO list using our coding criteria. These numbers are not presented in Figure 4.2, because the *Boston Globe* did not report total funded NGOs for these years.

57 Lee Marsden is among the most vocal scholars taking this position. According to Marsden, President Bush's Faith-Based Initiative ushered in the beginning of the United States "faith-based foreign policy," where "faith-based approaches are seen as the solution to all of America's and, by extension, the international community's problems." "In this discourse," says Marsden, "'big government' is no longer seen as the answer to welfare and humanitarian problems, and secular organizations with strong records of accomplishment in service delivery are increasingly marginalized or less highly regarded than their religious counterparts." The result, says Marsden, is "a significant shift in resources from secular NGOs to FBOs" in US foreign aid. According to Marsden, this shift toward FBOs continued under Obama and "there seems little prospect of change" under future administrations. See Marsden, *For God's Sake*, 956, 972.

58 Francois Audet et al. found a significant increase in Canada's funding of FBOs when the prime minister (and government) were conservative. Ray Vander Zaag later challenged this finding by conducting a similar analysis using a different dataset and methodology. Audet, Paquette, and Bergeron, "Religious Non-governmental Organisations and Canadian International Aid, 2001–2010"; Vander Zaag, "Trends in CIDA Funding to Canadian Religious Development NGOs."

59 Zehavi, "The Faith-Based Initiative in Comparative Perspective"; Stockman, Kranish, and Canellos "Bush Brings Faith to Foreign Aid."

60 This is sometimes referred to as the "Mexico City Policy," so named because it was originally articulated by President Reagan at the Second Session of the UN International Conference on Population held in Mexico City on August 13–16, 1984. The policy has been in effect under every Republican administration since Reagan, earning, from those on the left, the pejorative moniker of the "Global Gag Rule." Reagan's articulation of the policy seemingly encompassed both US and foreign NGO activity, but the policy's primary aim is to restrict *foreign* NGOs' activities. Thus US NGOs receiving USAID family planning funds, though

not directly restricted from providing or promoting abortion, are prohibited by the policy from subcontracting with organizations in foreign countries that do so. The nature and scope of the policy have remained consistent under Republican presidents except for President Trump, who expanded the scope to include all global assistance and contracts and expanded the policy to cover other executive agencies. See USAID, "Protecting Life in Global Health Assistance Frequently Asked Questions and Answers," October 2019, www.usaid.gov/sites/default/files/documents/1864/FINAL_Protecting_Life_in_Global_Health_Assistance_FAQs_Oct_2019_USAID.pdf and www.uib.no/sites/w3.uib.no/files/attachments/mexico_city_policy_1984.pdf

61 Bettiza, *Finding Faith in Foreign Policy*, 114.

62 All values were adjusted for inflation and entered in 2021 dollars. The observation years include the funding amounts for 2001–2005, calculated by recoding the FBO list published by the *Boston Globe* for those years.

63 The linear regression model does not control for secular NGO funding since this data was not provided in the *Boston Globe* dataset for 2002–2004.

64 I could not use regression to test the relationship between the party of the president and the number of funded FBOs, because the *Boston Globe* list does not include the total number of NGOs funded.

65 The number of total observations for the proportion of funded FBOs is less than the number of total observations for FBO funding because there is no data on the total number of NGOs funded for 2001–2005.

66 The observation years in this test exclude 2001 since there is no data from previous years to determine newly funded organizations. Data for FY2008 is also omitted from this analysis since data is unavailable for FY2006 and FY2007, leading to an artificially high number of "newly funded FBOs" for 2008.

67 Cloke and Beaumont, "Geographies of Postsecular Rapprochement in the City," 11.

68 Tomalin, "Global Aid and Faith Actors."

Bibliography

amfAR, the Foundation for AIDS Research. PEPFAR Country/Regional Operational Plans (COPs/ROPs) Database. Available from: https://copsdata.amfar.org/

Audet, François, Francis Paquette, and Stéfanie Bergeron. "Religious Non-governmental Organisations and Canadian International Aid, 2001–2010: A Preliminary Study." *Canadian Journal of Development Studies/Revue Canadienne D'études du Développement* 34, no. 2 (2013): 291–320. DOI:10.1080/02255189.2013.794721

Bettiza, Gregorio. *Finding Faith in Foreign Policy: Religion and American Diplomacy in a Postsecular World* (New York: Oxford University Press, 2019).

Blevins, John B., Mohamed F. Jalloh, and David A. Robinson. "Faith and Global Health Practice in Ebola and HIV Emergencies." *American Journal of Public Health* 109 (2019): 379–384. DOI:10.2105/AJPH.2018.304870

Bush, Evelyn. "What Is a Religious NGO? Conceptual and Classificatory Challenges in Research on Transnational Religion." In *Faithful Measures: New Methods in the Measurement of Religion*, edited by Christopher Bader and Roger Finke (New York: New York University Press, 2017):260–286.

Cloke, Paul and Justin Beaumont. "Geographies of Postsecular Rapprochement in the City." *Progress in Human Geography* 37, no. 1 (2012): 27–51. DOI:10.1177/030913251244020

Cooper, Rachel. "Faith-Based Organisations and Current Development Debates," K4D Helpdesk Report 624 (Brighton, UK: Institute of Development Studies, 2019).

Deacon, Gregory and Emma Tomalin. "A History of Faith-Based Aid and Development." In *The Routledge Handbook of Religions and Global Development* edited by Emma Tomalin (Routledge, 2015): 68–79.

Government Accountability Office. *Foreign Assistance: Private Voluntary Organizations' Contributions and Limitations* (Chapter Report, December 15, 1995, GAO/NSIAD-96-34). www.govinfo.gov/content/pkg/GAOREPORTS-NSIAD-96-34/html/GAOREPORTS-NSIAD-96-34.htm

Hopgood, Stephen and Leslie Vinjamuri. "Faith in Markets." In *Sacred Aid: Faith and Humanitarianism*, edited by Michael Barnett and Janice Gross Stein (New York: Oxford University Press, 2012): 37–64.

Joint Learning Initiative on Faith and Local Communities. "Local Faith Communities and the Promotion of Resilience in Humanitarian Situations: A Scoping Study." In *RSC/JLI Working Paper* 90, edited by E. Fiddian-Qasmiyeh and A. Ager, 2013. www.rsc.ox.ac.uk/files/files-1/wp90-local-faith-communities-resilience-2013.pdf

Koehrsen, Jens and Andreas Heuser. "Beyond Established Boundaries: FBOs as Developmental Entrepreneurs." In *Faith-Based Organizations in Development Discourses and Practices*, edited by Jeffrey Haynes. Routledge Studies in Religion and Politics (New York: Routledge, 2020): 10.

Lynch, Ceclia and Tanya B. Schwarz. "Humanitarianism's Proselytism Problem." *International Studies Quarterly* 60, no. 4 (December 2016): 636–646. https://doi.org/10.1093/isq/sqw024

Mandaville, Peter. "Right-Sizing Religion and Religious Engagement in Diplomacy and Development." *The Review of Faith & International Affairs* 19, sup1 (2021): 92–97. DOI:10.1080/15570274.2021.1983345

Marsden, Lee. "Bush, Obama and a Faith-Based US Foreign Policy." *International Affairs (Royal Institute of International Affairs 1944–)* 88, no. 5 (2012): 953–974. ISSN 0020-5850

Marsden, Lee. *For God's Sake: The Christian Right and US Foreign Policy* (New York: Zed Books, 2010).

Marshall, Katherine. "Impressions & Indications of Religious Engagement in Development." *The Review of Faith & International Affairs* 19, no 1 (2021): 12–30. DOI:10.1080/15570274.2021.1983358

Marshall, Katherine, Sudipta Roy, Chris Seiple, and Hugo Slim. "Intrinsic and Strategic Leverage of Religion in Development." *The Review of Faith & International Affairs* 19, sup1 (2021): 31–41. DOI:10.1080/15570274.2021.1983356

McCleary, Rachel. *Global Compassion: Private Voluntary Organizations and U.S. Foreign Policy Since 1939* (New York: Oxford University Press, 2009).

McCleary, Rachel and Robert Barro. "Replication Data for: Private Voluntary Organizations Engaged in International Assistance, 1939–2004," 2011. https://doi.org/10.7910/DVN/T0PJVX, Harvard Dataverse, V2, UNF:5:CDCNGIiDcwyKXA4tW6FwMQ== [fileUNF]

Morgenstern, Emily M. "International Food Assistance: Food for Peace Nonemergency Programs." *Congressional Research Service R45879*, August 21, 2019, Washington, DC. https://crsreports.congress.gov/product/pdf/R/R45879/2

The White House. Office of the Press Secretary. *The Quiet Revolution: A Seven Year Progress Report* (Washington, DC: U.S. Government Printing Office, 2008).

Tomalin, Emma. "Global Aid and Faith Actors: The Case for an Actor-Orientated Approach to the 'Turn to Religion'." *International Affairs* 96, no. 2 (March 2020): 323–342. DOI:10.1093/ia/iiaa006

Tomalin, Emma. "Thinking About Faith-Based Organisations in Development: Where Have We Got to and What Next?" *Development in Practice* 22, no. 5/6 (2012): 689–703. www.jstor.org/stable/41723132

United States Agency for International Development. "Building Bridges in Development: USAID's Strategic Religious Engagement Policy." September 2023. www.usaid.gov/sites/default/files/2023-09/USAID-Strategic-Religious-Engagement-Policy-9-6-23_1.pdf

United States Agency for International Development. "International Food Assistance Report: Fiscal Year 2021 Report to Congress." April 2022. www.usaid.gov/sites/default/files/2022-06/USAID_-_FY21_International_Food_Assistance_Report.pdf

United States Agency for International Development. "Moving Toward a Model of Locally Led Development: FY2022 Localization Progress Report." June 2023. www.usaid.gov/sites/default/files/2023-06/FY%202022%20Localization%20Progress%20Report-June-12-23_vFINAL_1.pdf

Vander Zaag, Ray. "Trends in CIDA Funding to Canadian Religious Development NGOs: Analysing Conflicting Studies." *Canadian Journal of Development Studies/Revue Canadienne D'études du Développement* 35, no. 3 (2014): 458–474. DOI:10.1080/02255189.2014.937405

Volberg, Thorsten. "The Politicization of Humanitarian Aid and Its Effect on the Principles of Humanity, Impartiality and Neutrality." Master's Thesis, Ruhr-University of Bochum, 2006. www.grin.com/document/67908

Wilkinson, Olivia, Kuyang Harriet Logo, Emma Tomalin, Wani Laki Anthony, Florine De Wolf, and Asha Kurien. "Faith in Localisation? The Experiences of Local Faith Actors Engaging with the International Humanitarian System in South Sudan." *International Journal of Humanitarian Action* 7, no. 4 (2022):2–15. https://doi.org/10.1186/s41018-021-00113-8

Zehavi, Amos. "The Faith-Based Initiative in Comparative Perspective: Making Use of Religious Providers in Britain and the United States." *Comparative Politics* 40, no. 3 (2008): 331–351. https://doi.org/10.2307/20434085

5 Faith-Based Organizations Opting Out

Introduction

President George W. Bush wanted the United States Agency for International Development (USAID) to develop a robust network of faith-based partners to help carry out its work. The evidence indicates his vision did not come to fruition. Instead, while USAID changed its regulations to increase the funding eligibility of faith-based organizations (FBOs) and continued to rhetorically support religious engagement, the number of FBOs it funded remained relatively low. The agency's newest administrator, Samantha Power, is attempting to rectify this situation. In September 2023, Power announced the agency's first Strategic Religious Engagement (SRE) Policy. According to Power, USAID's mission officers had previously pursued the president's vision of religious engagement with varying degrees of fidelity. This was partially due, she explained, to a kind of institutional malaise surrounding the federal financing of FBOs. "… there are genuine constraints in our own constitution," she said, and "Sometimes, instead of reckoning with this history, facing it squarely and coming up with a strategy to overcome these challenges … we refrain from engaging with religious leaders who might be able to further our goals."[1] USAID's new SRE Policy intends to eliminate any lingering legal ambiguity. The assumption is that the agency can advance and deepen its relations with FBOs by empowering USAID officials with clear guidance. Noticeably absent from the conversation is whether FBOs might have their own reservations.

FBOs account for 59% of all US-based nongovernment organizations (NGOs) providing humanitarian services overseas, yet comprised 13% of all USAID nonprofit award recipients between 2008 and 2021.[2] What accounts for this discrepancy? Power's account blames the lingering trepidation of US aid officials in FBO funding and tacitly assumes FBOs do not have trepidations of their own. But is this a safe assumption? In market terms, aid flows involve both supply *and* demand.[3] This means the underrepresentation of FBOs among USAID awardees relative to secular NGOs may very well be attributed to discrimination on the part of government aid officials (the side

DOI: 10.4324/9781003456704-5

supplying the funds), but it could also be due to discrimination on the part of FBOs (the side demanding the funds).

This chapter looks at both sides, relying upon data collected from 57 pilot phone interviews and an online survey of 405 US-based NGOs.[4] The following section provides descriptive statistics for the NGOs surveyed, including faith affiliation, issue area, staff size, countries served, and revenue. The survey answers these organizations provided inform the following sections. In the third section, I test the hypothesis inferred by Samantha Power regarding government discrimination against FBOs, asking whether the data reveals a *pattern* of such behavior. I then examine the related but separate question of whether FBOs are significantly less likely than their secular counterparts to apply for government funding. As the name of this chapter suggests, the data indicate that many development FBOs are opting out of government funding. The subsequent sections provide the reasons why, including the perceived barriers associated with applying for funds and those believed to come with receiving funds. The chapter concludes with a review of the additional questions the survey data presents and areas for future research.

Surveyed NGOs

Faith-based development organizations are the primary focus of this book, yet it is also important to collect information on secular development organizations to properly contextualize the experience and concerns of FBOs relative to their secular counterparts. Comparative data is especially critical to know whether the low number of funded FBOs at USAID is due to government discrimination. Ideally, this question would be approached by first examining USAID grant and contract applications from faith-based and secular organizations and determining if there is a significant difference in their acceptance rate. However, the absence of public applicant data makes this impossible. Without information on who has applied for USAID funds, I opted to contact organizations that *could* have applied for USAID funds, using a list of nonprofit organizations registered with the Internal Revenue Service whose records indicate they provide services abroad.[5] Over 2,500 organizations were contacted, with 405 completing the survey.

Of my 405 total survey responses, 40.4% identified as secular, 14.8% secular with religious roots, 36.5% faith based, 1.7% spiritual, 2.5% ethnic/cultural, and 4.1% other. Three organizations selected "other," and I reclassified these as "faith-based" upon further review of respondent remarks. Of the organizations that identified as "spiritual" or "ethnic/cultural," I recategorized one as an FBO after reviewing the organization's online mission statement. As expected, the vast majority of my respondents were Christian, followed by those who identified as either "multireligious" or "spiritual" (n = 13). Other religions represented included Judaism (n = 2), Hinduism (n = 2), and Buddhism (n = 1).

Organizations were also asked about the primary issue area(s) served by their organization. While all the organizations contacted were internationally focused, their specific service area(s) varied. The most prevalent service area among the organizations surveyed was education (n = 239), followed by children's issues (n = 167) and healthcare (n = 162). Other areas representing a sizable number of respondents include gender equality (n = 109), agriculture and food security (n = 96), and ministry (n = 96).[6] Most organizations selected more than one area of service.

In addition to asking about an organization's faith status and service area, the survey also asked questions relating to an organization's size, including the level of annual expenditures, number of paid staff, and areas/countries served.[7] A majority of the respondents (57.69%) were mid-size organizations with annual expenditures between $100,000 and $1,000,000. These were flanked by organizations representing the low and high tails of the distribution, including smaller organizations spending less than $100,000 (21.15%) and larger organizations spending over a million (21.15%).[8] Research shows that nonprofit organizations typically invest more in mission than overhead and thus are forced to do more with less, including less staff.[9] My sample supports this, showing that the vast majority of organizations surveyed (70%) had fewer than ten employees. In terms of geographic scope, nearly half of all surveyed organizations (48.62%) served only one country and 40.78% served between two and ten. Only a small proportion of the organizations surveyed (10.58%) served over ten countries. Table 5.1 shows the information specific to the FBOs and secular NGOs surveyed.

Table 5.1 Descriptive Statistics of Survey Respondents

	Secular NGOs *n (%)*	*FBOs* *n (%)*	*X^2 statistic* *p-value*
Annual Expenditures			
<$100,000	25 (19.1)	30 (23.26)	3.509
$100,000–$499,999	18 (13.74)	51 (39.53)	.479
$500,000–$999,999	58 (44.27)	23 (17.83)	
$1 million–$9,999,999	27 (20.61)	20 (15.5)	
Over $10 million	3 (2.29)	5 (3.88)	
Number of Paid Staff			
Zero	41 (31.78)	28 (23.73)	4.497
1–10	49 (37.98)	58 (49.15)	.349
11–49	29 (22.48)	21 (17.8)	
50–99	5 (3.88)	7 (5.93)	
>100	5 (3.88)	4 (3.39)	
Countries Served			
One	67 (51.94)	57 (45.23)	6.6878
2–9	54 (41.86)	50 (39.68)	.083
10–19	3 (2.33)	3 (2.38)	
>20	5 (3.86)	16 (12.7)	

While some of the largest and most well-known international development organizations are faith-based, including organizations like Catholic Relief Services and World Vision, these organizations are unlikely to represent the norm. Instead, the sample shows most development FBOs are small-to-mid-size organizations, with annual expenditures between \$100,000 and \$500,000 and a small paid staff. A large majority of FBOs are also fairly limited in their geographic scope, serving between one and ten countries. The secular NGOs we surveyed are fairly similar, though a greater proportion of these organizations could be classified as upper-mid-size organizations in terms of annual expenditures since they spend between \$500,000 and \$1,000,000 annually. Despite this difference, a chi-square test of independence shows no significant association between an organization's faith orientation and its level of expenditures, X^2 (4, n = 247) = 3.509, p = .476. There was also no association between the type of organization and its number of paid staff, X^2 (4, n = 247) = 4.497, p = .348556, nor was there an association between organization type and geographic reach, as measured by the number of countries served X^2 (43, n = 255) = 6.6878, p = .082542. These findings are important because they show that development FBOs, in general, are unlikely to have a structural disadvantage when applying for government funds. In other words, while research might suggest that smaller organizations are less likely to receive federal funding, my research indicates this is not a controlling factor for why development FBOs receive fewer USAID awards.[10] Other researchers have reached similar conclusions when examining US-based FBOs providing domestic services.[11]

Absent a distinction in size, it is reasonable to look for another explanation for why so few FBOs receive USAID funds. USAID Administrator Samantha Power admits that some US foreign aid officials have shown undue reticence in engaging with FBOs. If these were isolated instances, they'd unlikely influence the overall flow of agency funds to FBOs. However, if the bias against FBOs is more institutionalized, it could affect total FBO funding numbers. The next section explores this possibility.

Government Discrimination

When Senator Joseph Lieberman first sponsored the Charitable Choice Provision in the early 1990s, he claimed US government officials were "disqualify[ing] ... otherwise qualified faith-based group[s] just because they have a cross on their wall or a mezuzah on their door, or because they have a religious name in their title, or they have praise for God in their mission statement."[12] Ten years later, President Bush expressed similar concerns, saying that federal funding had been denied to organizations "just because they have a cross or a Star of David or a crescent on the wall."[13] Such "government discrimination," he attested, had no place in his administration.[14] However, in his 2006 testimony before the House Committee on International Relations, Ken Isaacs, who previously served as the director of the Office of Foreign Disaster Assistance at USAID, expressed that the agency likely continued to harbor "institutional bias" against FBOs. "I know first-hand," he said, "... the proposals [from faith-based organizations] didn't receive, let's say, as much review as they should have."[15] The president of Catholic Relief Services echoed his remarks when he said that FBOs often "use different language," wear "their motivations and inspirations ... right on their sleeves," and "talk about their beliefs, [and] there are some bureaucrats who are very uncomfortable with that." "That is the field we play on," he said.[16]

Several of the NGOs that were contacted for the pilot phase of the project expressed similar thoughts. Unlike Catholic Relief Services, however, they thought there was enough bias that they shouldn't bother applying. One respondent explained that he thought "many more grants [are] available for NGOs that are non-religiously oriented." The respondent further assessed that the label "Christian" "reduces one's chances [of grant acceptance] by 75–80%." A similar, though less specific, sentiment was shared by one of the *secular* NGOs interviewed. In regards to the discrepancy between FBO and nonreligious NGO aid applicants, the representative postulated:

> I would almost bet what I am going to say is true, that there is likely to be some degree of bias against [the government] giving faith-based organizations grants. There is probably at least some bias, whether it is really significant or extremely significant, that the people in USAID actually may favor other types of organizations.

Individual instances of discrimination against FBOs may exist, but the survey suggests the problem is unlikely to be systemic. A *Z* test of proportions of survey respondents showed that even though more FBOs (42%) than secular organizations (22%) reported having been denied government funding, there was no significant difference between the two, $Z = 1.67$; $p = .095$. This is due, in part, to the difference in the number of FBOs and secular organizations that reported having applied for a grant in the first place. A chi-square test of independence at the .01 level reveals that secular nonprofits were significantly more likely than FBOs to apply for USAID funds, X^2 $(1, n = 351) = 7.37$, $p = .006655$. Taken together, this suggests that the low number of FBO awardees is less likely due to the government purposely overlooking FBO applications and more likely the result of FBOs choosing not to apply.[17]

This finding is supported elsewhere in the literature. Though scholars have not specifically examined this dynamic at USAID or with development organizations, the research relating to other religious engagement programs in the United States suggests that many FBOs have reservations about accepting government money. For example, shortly after Congress passed the Charitable Choice Provision specifying that private FBOs could receive public funds to administer welfare services, a national survey revealed that only 36% of US congregations anticipated applying for such funds to support their secular programs.[18] Another smaller-scale study conducted after the initial implementation of the Faith-Based Initiative also suggested that many domestically focused FBOs were unlikely to take advantage of the Initiative's increased funding opportunities.[19] Additional research has provided further evidence, with scholars finding that religiosity is likely inversely correlated with government funding and collaboration.[20] In other words, these studies show that the more religious an organization is, the less likely it is to apply for government funding. If this is true, then the next question becomes *why*. Why are development FBOs generally more averse to pursuing public funds than their secular counterparts? The FBOs I surveyed provided a multitude of answers, but the most prominent were limited capacity, perceived government discrimination, the fear of mission drift, concerns of autonomy, and the potential for donor loss.

Limited Capacity

One of the most common answers provided by FBOs for why they chose not to apply for government funds, accounting for 45.63% of those surveyed, was that they generally lacked the time and resources to do so. Considering that over 60% of the FBOs I surveyed spent less than $500,000 annually, and nearly 23% spent less than $100,000, this is unsurprising. At these levels, one might expect an organization to employ less than five people. At best, one person may be dedicated to fundraising, though this task may also be shared among employees, board members, and volunteers. These individuals need to be strategic about where to seek funding. Rational actors operating in this environment will likely weigh the anticipated time and money associated with each income-generating activity with expected returns.

As discussed in Chapter 1, a partnership with the US government requires a significant time investment, and this begins at the application stage. While funding opportunities are likely to differ, the applications and accompanying guidelines for federal grants generally range between 20 and 30 pages long. The estimated time to complete these applications is anywhere from 80 to 200 hours.[21] Whether grant writing is done by someone on staff, by someone who is a friend of the organization, or is contracted out, an organization must have the capacity to absorb the cost if they want a chance of receiving an award. Organizations may also be asked, after applying, to complete additional interviews and to collect and provide further supplemental material. These steps are likely to cost the organization additional time. Most USAID grants also require the organization to share some of the cost of a proposed project. Organizations are typically asked to specify this amount at the outset.[22] In some circumstances, an organization may even be required to spend money before receiving an award, such as when the agency requests a pre-award financial audit.[23]

Taken together, as one interviewee explained, "there's a lot required to put together a grant, and an organization has to have the capacity to do it. It takes a lot of energy, and maybe some organizations ... think the juice isn't worth the squeeze." This may especially be the perception if an organization is applying for a smaller grant, like those provided by the American Schools and Hospitals Abroad program and the International Food Relief Partnership program. There is also always the possibility that an organization receives no "juice" at all—meaning they spend precious time and resources applying for a grant and then fail to secure the funds.

Relatedly, organizations may find award *administration* too costly and time-consuming. By law, all organizations receiving government awards must submit regular reports on project progress and outcomes.[24] Most are also required to submit annual financial audits.[25] The financial burden of these requirements can sometimes be offset by the award itself, but the organization nonetheless assumes some cost.[26] This presents yet another "squeeze" on organizations partnering with the government. It also represents an additional deterrent for FBOs seeking government funds, with 13.4% of the FBOs surveyed citing extensive post-award reporting as an additional deterrent to their pursuit of government funds.

Both the application for and the administration of government grants can be taxing on organizations with limited capacity. In these cases, while a reward may expand an organization's capacity, the upfront resources required are either too much or too much in light of what can seem like a small or uncertain return. Some also do not apply because they perceive the likelihood of an award not just to be uncertain, but to be especially unlikely.

Perceived Discrimination

In a Congressional hearing shortly after the establishment of USAID, one of America's longtime faith-based aid partners admitted that they were beginning to feel "pushed out" and marginalized due to their religious nature. USAID, they explained, seemed to prefer secular partners.[27] This sentiment continues to be shared today. 31.07% of the FBOs we surveyed that did not apply for government funds indicated that this decision was motivated by the belief that the government either *couldn't* fund their organization due to its religious status or likely *wouldn't* fund their organization for the same reason. Clearly, while the wall separating church and state has corroded in the courts, it remains erect in the minds of many.

During the course of the pilot interviews, one organization that was eligible for USAID funding explained: "I don't think we can [get USAID funding], at least not directly. There's the separation of church and state." Another simply responded, "We're religious. We can't," when asked why they had not sought federal funds. This same belief was reflected by 11.65% of the FBOs we surveyed who replied that they had not applied for federal grants because they believed it true that "The government is prohibited from funding faith-based organizations."

Another group, constituting approximately 20% of FBOs, acknowledged that while it was legal for the federal government to provide funds directly to FBOs, it was still unlikely due to the government's bias against FBOs. One organization chose to elaborate on the question's comments, saying that their belief of bias is informed by the government's "past history of negative treatment of conservative/Christian organizations."

This comment points to one of the issues generally left unaddressed by my research, namely, whether the organizations surveyed believed the government was likely to discriminate against *all* FBOs equally or whether they thought it was more likely to be biased against *specific* FBOs. The respondent cited above clearly thinks the government is prone to prefer more liberal, secular organizations, though it is unclear if they think the government may prefer a liberal Christian organization to a conservative one. One could also make the distinction that perhaps the government prefers "faith background" organizations or even "faith-centered" organizations to those that are "faith-saturated." If one thought in terms of the latter, then a faith-saturated FBO accepting the idea of government discrimination would feel their choice is between either not applying for funds or dialing back their religious expression. This kind of trade-off represents another distinct concern of the FBOs surveyed.

Mission Drift

One of the more popular critiques of the Faith-Based Initiative was its speculated effect on the FBOs that received federal funds. Critics suggested that accepting public funds could cause FBOs to abnegate their religious commitments over time, resulting in well-funded FBOs that had only a veneer of religious legitimacy. What is to stop public funding from turning FBOs into "government programs in clerical collars?" asked Michael Tanner.[28] FBOs today seem to have similar concerns. In fact, among the FBOs we surveyed, 11.65% chose not to apply for government aid because they believed doing so would likely lead their organization to compromise its religious mission and identity. This idea has theoretical support. Resource Dependency Theory states that financial donors have a significant influence on an organization's behavior and identity.[29] Nonprofit organizations, in particular, are often largely dependent upon external funding and are likely to make organizational and operational decisions with the interests of specific donors in mind. Sometimes, this can even cause an organization to change its identity and mission to align with donor wishes. Most often, this kind of change takes place gradually and without strategic intent. Organizations wanting to protect their missions from undue government influence thus may choose to limit the contributions they seek from the government or eschew government largesse altogether. Several well-known FBOs have chosen the latter.

HOPE International is an example of a faith-saturated FBO involved in international development that does not accept government funding. Their refusal is a strategic choice—one that is considerably influenced by the organization's conception of "mission drift." As explained by the organization's CEO and Vice President of Development in their book by that title, mission drift is when FBOs slowly succumb to the "gravitational pull of secularization" and shift away from their original religious purpose.[30] This is caused, they explain, by the accumulation of many small, incremental leadership decisions, including those relating to an organization's finances. As a particular example, the book warns that international religious organizations are often tempted to "tone down" their religious identity to attract or appease powerful secular donors. This includes the US government. CEO of Anglican Overseas Aid, Bob Mitchell, has also publicly taken this view.[31]

From this perspective, the culpability is primarily placed on FBO executives since they are the individuals seen as most responsible for safeguarding the organization's mission. "Mission Drift" suggests that these leaders lose their footing—lose sight of what their organization stands for to attract secular donors. More specifically, the claim is that FBOs circumscribe their religious expression and programming in pursuit of government dollars. Yet, change in an organization's behavior and identity can also be attributed to other causal mechanisms. Rather than voluntarily and somewhat unintentionally "drifting," an organization may be perceived as being *forced* to change and effectively secularize. In this scenario, the culpability is shared. Funds are seen as conditioned, and organizations accept these conditions, knowing their likely secularizing effects. Put differently; one could contend that government funding presents FBOs with a kind of Faustian bargain, with FBOs trading their religious identity and independence for government payouts.[32]

Loss of Autonomy

What does a partnership look like between the government and an FBO? Critics of the Faith-Based Initiative warned that it likely wouldn't look like a "partnership" at all. By accepting "government shekels," they warned, religious organizations were likely to be laden with "government shackles."[33] The president of the Interfaith Alliance spoke out against the possibility of such a "horrendous situation" in his testimony before Congress a year after the Faith-Based Initiative was in effect.[34] Twenty years later, others still express this fear.

Approximately 14.39% of the FBOs I surveyed expressed that they avoided government funds due to a perceived loss of autonomy. The thoughts on what was lost in the bargain for funds varied. Some believed the government would require the organization to change its religious operations, while others thought the government would require them to implement programs that went against their religious beliefs. Still others suggested that an organization risked losing its identity completely if it accepted public funds, with funds making it little more than the government's handmaid.[35]

One NGO I spoke to during the pilot phone interviews explained that when his organization last accepted government funds, he believed the government was using his organization for ends outside the organization's mission. For this reason, the organization representative explained he would no longer consider applying for government grants. Such anecdotal evidence, while compelling, has not seemed to influence most FBOs. While a sizable number of FBOs believe government funds likely lead to some loss of autonomy, far fewer (6.7%) believe that federal funding allows the government to effectively co-opt the organization. Whether this thought is pervasive among private donors, however, is a separate question.

Donor Exit

Some scholars have suggested that accepting government funds could place development FBOs in a precarious position vis-à-vis their private donors. Stephen Hopgood and Leslie Vinjamuri explain: By "secur[ing] public money … [a faith-based development organization] risks alienating more strongly religious supporters who may withdraw funding and instead shift their loyalty and financial support to a rival FBO with a strong commitment to faith identity."[36] They suggest this is likely the kind of trade-off Oxfam America would face if it began accepting money from the US government.[37] Those outside academia have reached similar conclusions, including many FBO leaders. In my conversations with organizations that had accepted USAID funds (explored more in Chapter 6), one FBO relayed that it had been asked whether the organization was now an "agent of the government" since accepting government funds. This person wanted to know who was in control of the organization's operations, and the FBO executive I interviewed felt he was obliged to provide a response. This exchange is the kind theorized in Greer and Horst's book *Mission Drift*. While an organization may choose to be financed by both "risky" secular donors and "safe" religious ones, they explain, FBO leaders should be particularly attentive to the concerns of their religious donors. It's these "mission-true" individuals, they claim, that can keep an FBO from drifting from its mission.

My research shows such individuals may also indirectly keep an organization from applying for government funds. One of the FBOs we spoke to during our pilot interviews mentioned it lost several key donors when it advertised that the organization had accepted government funds. The representative clarified that these individuals did not change their giving behavior because they believed their donations were no longer needed (an effect referred to as "crowding out"), but rather they stopped giving because they disagreed in principle with the organization accepting government aid. Ultimately, the representative explained that his FBO decided it would not apply for government funds if it meant it would damage the organization's reputation and relationship with individual donors. The survey suggests that some FBOs, though not going through the same experience, anticipate that they might face a similar situation, and thus, they preemptively foreclose this funding source as a possibility; however, this describes less than 5% of those surveyed.

Analysis

The development FBOs I surveyed relayed a multitude of reasons why they chose not to partner with the US government in delivering aid. Yet the reasons they provided are not necessarily unique to FBOs. Secular NGOs may also feel too constrained in terms of time and resources to apply for government aid. They may also feel that reporting requirements are too burdensome and beyond their present capacity. It is also possible that some secular development NGOs feel "pushed out" of the aid process and potentially discriminated against for various reasons. Additionally, Resource Dependency Theory equally applies to FBOs and secular NGOs, and both are subject to donor influence. Secular NGOs aware of this fact may thus be equally wary of accepting government largesse. Though it might not be for religious reasons, secular NGOs may fear that accepting government funds will lead to donor exodus or mission drift.

My survey shows that many secular NGOs are deterred from applying for government funds for the same reasons as FBOs. Both the secular and FBOs I surveyed, for instance, indicate that limited time and resources were one of the obstacles preventing them from applying for government aid, with 67.94% of NGOs citing this as a reason compared with 45.63% of FBOs. Similarly, the fear that government aid may lead an organization to compromise its mission was expressed by a relatively similar proportion of each group, with 14.1% of secular NGOs and 11.65% of FBOs supplying this answer. The two groups were also similar in the percentage that feared government funds came with a loss of autonomy, with only 14.10% and 14.39% of secular NGOs and FBOs, respectively, expressing this belief. The more extreme belief that accepting government funds led to the organization being effectively co-opted by the government was also not a distinguishing belief among secular NGOs and FBOs since less than 10% of both groups held this belief. The perception that an organization might lose donors after accepting government funds was also not a prevalent concern among the organizations surveyed, though, interestingly, a larger proportion of secular NGOs supplied this answer. In summary, for all the factors analyzed above, a chi-square test of independence reveals no significant difference between the two groups at the .01 level of significance. We thus cannot cite them as causal factors for the underrepresentation of FBOs among USAID grant applicants.

The only reason I tested that seemed to significantly influence more FBOs than secular NGOs was the perception of government discrimination. Among the survey respondents, 53.4% of FBOs and 23.08% of secular NGOs indicated that they did not apply for government aid because they believed the government was unlikely to fund the work they did. The secular organizations explained that they felt the government was more likely to reject grant applications from young organizations, organizations involved in specific types of work (i.e., family planning), and those operating in certain countries. The FBOs, by contrast, all perceived that the government would

Table 5.2 Reasons Surveyed Organizations Cited for Not Applying for Federal Funds

	Secular NGOs n (%)	*FBOs n (%)*	*X^2 statistic*	*p-Value*
Lack of time and resources to apply	53 (67.94)	47 (45.63)	5.9133	.015027
Acceptance of government funds likely to compromise the organization's independence	11 (14.10)	12 (11.65)	.0987	.753389
Accepting government funds allows the government to use our organization for its own ends	4 (4.9)	7 (6.7)	.2374[a]	
Government is unlikely to fund the work we do	18 (23.08)	55 (53.40)	15.7207	<.001***
Acceptance of funds likely to compromise the organization's reputation with donors	9 (11.54)	5 (4.85)	1.9211	.165738

Note: Chi-square test of independence with Yates correction. Percentages do not total 100 because respondents could select multiple answers.
*** Significant at .001 level of significance.
[a] Fisher's exact test was used due to the small number of respondents for this answer.

likely discriminate against their organization based on their faith status or faith programming. Table 5.2 provides this information in more detail.

Conclusion

Overall, the findings indicate that the most likely tested explanation for the difference between secular NGO and FBO aid applications in the United States is the belief by FBOs of government discrimination. A significant number of FBOs believe the government is biased against religious organizations. My analysis indicates that this belief is unlikely to be right in the aggregate, but this does not discount the possibility that individual instances of discrimination continue.[38] It remains unknown to what extent FBOs believe in government bias because they have had personal experiences that validate this belief or whether other organizations' stories with this experience shape this belief.

Another possibility is that this belief arises from the strong norm established in the United States regarding the separation of church and state and the previous interpretation of the Supreme Court that it is a constitutional requirement to withhold federal funds from religious institutions. While FBOs are now eligible for government money, they may believe that this history makes them unlikely to receive funds. Organizations could also draw conclusions from the numbers themselves, meaning that some FBOs might see the low number of FBO aid recipients as confirmation of government bias. Why FBOs perceive government discrimination is thus an area for future research.

Another opportunity for future research involves studying whether perceptions of governmental bias vary across different types of FBOs. The vast majority of FBO respondents for this study were Christian, and the minimum number of respondents representing other religions limits any inference about a particular subgroup. It thus remains an open question if Jewish or Muslim organizations, for instance, differ from Christian organizations in their application for and perception of government funds.

While these two questions remain for future research, Chapter 6 addresses the related question of whether the real experiences of USAID-funded FBOs either validate or disconfirm the beliefs expressed by our surveyed FBOs.

Notes

1 Samantha Power, "Administrator Samantha Power at the Launch of USAID's First-Ever Strategic Religious Engagement Policy," Transcript of Speech delivered at the United States Institute of Peace, Washington, DC: September 12, 2023, www.usaid.gov/news-information/speeches/sep-12-2023-administrator-samantha-power-launch-usaids-first-ever-strategic-religious-engagement-policy
2 Heist and Cnaan, "Faith-Based International Development," 19.
3 Kharas, *Trends and Issues in Development Aid*, 4.
4 Additional methodological information appears in Chapter 1.
5 See Chapter 1 for further details on the selection criterion for contacted organizations.
6 Though 96 organizations we surveyed included "ministry" among their issue areas, only 8 indicated their organization was exclusively involved in ministry. These organizations were not churches, nor did they file with the IRS under the NTEE code X to indicate they have a "religion-related" purpose.
7 We selected expenditures as an indicator of organizational size. Unlike gross receipts or net revenue, which are likely to oscillate depending upon an organization's capital and cash policies, expenditures are a relatively stable measure of an organization's work per annual cycle.
8 There is no standard categorization system for nonprofit size or breakpoints for nonprofit expenditures. The categories chosen here follow the National Center for Charitable Statistics.
9 Center on Nonprofits and Philanthropy, "Nonprofit Overhead Cost Project," *Facts and Perspectives Brief*, no. 3 (August 2004), www.urban.org/sites/default/files/publication/57731/311044-Getting-What-We-Pay-For.PDF; Gregory and Howard, "Nonprofit Starvation Cycle," 50.
10 Nunnenkamp, Öhler, Schwörer, "US-Based NGOs."

11 Park, "Comparing Faith-Based and Secular Community Service Corporations."
12 Chaves, "Debunking Charitable Choice."
13 George Walker Bush, "President Addresses Southern Baptist Convention Annual Meeting," Washington, DC, June 21, 2005, https://georgewbush-whitehouse.archives.gov/news/releases/2005/06/20050621-3.html
14 George W. Bush, "America's Compassion in Action," Remarks by the President at the First White House National Conference on Faith-Based and Community Initiatives, Washington Hilton and Towers, Washington, DC, June 1, 2004, https://georgewbush-whitehouse.archives.gov/news/releases/2004/06/20040601-10.html; George W. Bush, "President Highlights Faith-Based Initiative at Leadership Conference," Omni Shoreham Hotel, Washington, DC, March 1, 2005, https://georgewbush-whitehouse.archives.gov/news/releases/2005/03/text/20050301-4.html; Press Release, The White House, President's Remarks via Satellite to the Southern Baptist Convention, June 15, 2004, www.whitehouse.gov/news/releases/ 2004/06/20040615-9.html
15 U.S. Congress, House, Subcommittee, 100.
16 Ibid.
17 Since most of the FBOs surveyed indicate that the decision not to apply for federal funds was *not* the result of a board policy against the practice, the decision to "opt out" is assumed to come from executive leadership.
18 Chaves, "Religious Congregations and Welfare Reform," 839.
19 "Social Services in Faith-Based Organizations," *Tropman Report* 1, no. 7 (November 2002): 2–4, https://cdn-5f05fc84c1ac181b540e1330.closte.com/wp-content/uploads/2020/12/7SclSrsFaithBsdOrgs_TR02.pdf
20 Ebaugh, Chafetz, and Pipes, "Influence of Evangelicalism"; Altamuro, Bierstaker, Chen, and Harris, "Does It Pay to Pray?"; Fu, Cooper, and Shumate, "Do U.S. Faith-Based Social Service Organizations Resist Collaboration?"
21 Sarah Aswell, "34 Grant Statistics for 2020," https://blog.submittable.com/grant-statistics/
22 Though USAID generally expects recipients to share some costs in projects for which they receive agency awards, cost sharing is not a legal mandate, nor is there a set formula. If cost sharing is a decisive factor in an organization's application, USAID must disclose this in the specific funding announcement. ADS Chapter 303.3.10.1-2 specifies the agency's reliance on cost sharing and notes that while cost sharing is encouraged and can be required for given awards, "excessive reliance on cost sharing during the merit review may unfairly favor larger, better-funded organizations."
23 The possibility of USAID requesting a financial audit before award allocation is acknowledged on the Frequently Asked Questions page for organizations interested in USAID's Development Innovation Ventures (DIV) program. See www.usaid.gov/div/faq
24 CFR §200.329 requires grant recipients to submit quarterly financial reports and regular performance reports through the Office of Management and Budget during the performance period of a grant.
25 This is mandated by the Single Audit Act, which specifies that recipients of federal and state funding are required to submit annual financial and compliance audits.
26 To recover sunk costs or account for expected costs associated with grant administration, an organization must account for these in the grant budget, including it among its overhead or indirect per the audit requirements of 2 CFR, Part 200, Subpart F: §200.501.

27 Congressional Testimony of Edward M. Kinney, Director of Warehouse and Shipping at CRS: United States Congress House Committee on Foreign Affairs. Subcommittee on Africa, "Activities of Private United States Organizations in Africa" Hearings Before the Subcommittee on Africa of the Committee on Foreign Affairs, House of Representatives, 87th Congress, First Session, 1961, 147. The idea of institutionalized secular bias among development donors is well-researched. See Bartelink and Groeneweg, "Advocating the Value-Add of Faith," 5; Bompani, *Religion and Development*, 173; Clarke and Jennings, *Development, Civil Society*; Hovland, "Who's Afraid of Religion?"; Deneulin and Bano, *Religion in Development*; Paras, "CIDA's Secular Fiction," Carbonnier, "Religion and Development"; le Roux and Loots, "Unhealthy Divide."
28 Michael Tanner, "Obama's Faith-Based Boondoggle," The CATO Institute, January 28, 2010, www.cato.org/commentary/obamas-faith-based-boondoggle
29 Pfeffer and Salancik, *External Control of Organizations.*
30 Greer and Horst, *Mission Drift*, 2.
31 Mitchell, *Faith-Based Development*, 162.
32 Elliott, *Street Saints*, 251.
33 Kennedy and Bielefeld, "Government Shekels?"
34 Testimony of Congressman Dr. Caddy Welton, House Committee on Government Reform, Subcommittee on Criminal Justice, Drug Policy, and Human Resources Hearing, "*Authorizing Presidential Vision: Making Permanent the Efforts of the Faith-Based and Community Initiative*," 19th Congress, June 21, 2005.
35 Such fears could potentially be propagated by high-profile examples of the United States using international nonprofits to gather intelligence. For instance, in the US operation to find Osama bin Laden, the US government established a fake hepatitis B vaccination program to collect blood samples in a town suspected to have bin Laden. Though the program appeared to be an independent operation of the Central Intelligence Agency, Pakistan accused the nonprofit Save the Children of being involved and expelled six of the country's aid workers. Jon Boone, "Pakistan Orders Save the Children Foreign Workers to Leave," *The Guardian*, September 5, 2012, www.theguardian.com/uk/2012/sep/05/pakistan-voluntarysector
36 Hopgood and Vinjamuri, "Faith in Markets," 38.
37 Ibid., 51.
38 Patterson, *Politics in a Religious World*, 125–126; Marsden, "Bush, Obama."

Bibliography

Altamuro, Jennifer, James Bierstaker, Lucy Huajing Chen, and Erica Harris. "Does It Pay to Pray? Religious Nonprofits and Funding." *Journal of Accounting and Public Policy* 41, no. 4 (2022): 106858. https://doi.org/10.1016/j.jaccpubpol.2021.106858

Bartelink, Brenda E. and Ton Groeneweg. "Advocating the Value-Add of Faith in a Secular Context: The Case of the Knowledge Centre Religion and Development in the Netherlands." *HTS Teologiese Studies/Theological Studies* 75, no. 4 (2019): a5510. DOI:10.4102/hts.v75i4.5510

Bompani, Barbara. "Religion and Development: Tracing the Trajectories of an Evolving Sub-Discipline," *Progress in Development Studies,* 19, no. 3 (2019): 171–185. DOI: 10.1177/1464993419829598

Carbonnier, Gilles. "Religion and Development: Reconsidering Secularism as the Norm." *International Development Policy/Revue Internationale de Politique de Développement*, no. 4 (March 1, 2013): 1–5. DOI: 10.4000/ poldev.1351

Chaves, Mark. "Debunking Charitable Choice." *Stanford Social Innovation Review* 1, no. 2 (2003): 28–36. https://ssir.org/articles/entry/debunking_charitable_choice

Chaves, Mark. "Religious Congregations and Welfare Reform: Who Will Take Advantage of 'Charitable Choice'?" *American Sociological Review* 64 (1999): 836–846.

Clarke, Gerard and Michael Jennings. *Development, Civil Society, and Faith-Based Organizations: Bridging the Sacred and the Secular* (Basingstoke: Palgrave Macmillan, 2008).

Deneulin, Séverine and Masooda Bauno. *Religion in Development: Rewriting the Secular Script* (London: Zed Books, 2009).

Ebaugh, Helen R., Janet S. Chafetz, and Paula F. Pipes. "The Influence of Evangelicalism on Government Funding of Faith-Based Social Service Organizations." *Review of Religious Research* 47, no. 4 (2006): 380–392. www.jstor.org/stable/20058105

Elliott, Barbara J. *Street Saints: Renewing America's Cities* (Philadelphia, PA: Templeton Foundation Press, 2004).

Fu, Jiawei Sophia, Katherine. R. Cooper, and Michelle Shumate. "Do U.S. Faith-Based Social Service Organizations Resist Collaboration? Examining the Role of Religiosity and Operational Capacity in Interorganizational Partnerships." *Nonprofit and Voluntary Sector Quarterly* 50, no. 2 (2021): 241–261. https://doi.org/10.1177/0899764020952167

Goggins Gregory, Ann and Don Howard. "The Nonprofit Starvation Cycle." *Stanford Social Innovation Review* 7, no. 4 (Fall 2009): 49–53.

Greer, Peter and Chris Horst. *Mission Drift: The Unspoken Crisis Facing Leaders, Charities, and Churches* (Minneapolis, MN: Bethany House, 2014).

Heist, Dan and Ram A. Cnaan. "Faith-Based International Development Work: A Review." *Religions* 7, no. 3 (2016): 19. https://doi.org/10.3390/rel7030019

Hopgood, Stephen and Leslie Vinjamuri. "Faith in Markets." In *Sacred Aid: Faith and Humanitarianism*, edited by Michael Barnett and Janice Gross Stein (New York: Oxford University Press, 2012): 37–64.

Hovland, Ingie. "Who's Afraid of Religion? Tensions Between 'Mission' and 'Development' in the Norwegian Mission Society." In *Development, Civil Society and Faith-Based Organizations: Bridging the Sacred and the Secular*, edited by Gerard Clarke and Michael Jennings (Basingstoke: Palgrave Macmillan, 2008): 171–186.

Kennedy, Sheila Suess and Wolfgang Bielefeld. "Government Shekels without Government Shackles? The Administrative Challenges of Charitable Choice." *Public Administration Review* 62, no. 1 (2002): 4–11. www.jstor.org/stable/3110278

Kharas, Hami. *Trends and Issues in Development Aid.* Wolfensohn Center for Development Working Paper No. 1. (2007) Wolfensohn Center for Development. The Brookings Institution, Washington DC. Available at SSRN: http://ssrn.com/abstract=1080342

le Roux, Elisabet and Lizle Loots, "The Unhealthy Divide: How the Secular-Faith Binary Potentially Limits GBV Prevention and Response." *Development in Practice* 27, no. 5 (July 4, 2017): 733–744. DOI:10.1080/09614524.2017.1327023

Marsden, Lee. "Bush, Obama and a Faith-Based US Foreign Policy." *International Affairs (Royal Institute of International Affairs 1944–)* 88, no. 5 (2012): 953–974.

Mitchell, Bob. *Faith-Based Development: How Christian Organizations Can Make a Difference* (Maryknoll, NY: Orbis Books, 2017).

Nunnenkamp, Peter, Hannes Öhler, and Tillmann Schwörer, "US based NGOs in International Development: Financial and Economic Determinants of Survival." *World Development* 46 (2013): 45–65.

Paras, Andrea. "CIDA's Secular Fiction and Canadian Faith-Based Organizations." *Canadian Journal of Development Studies/Revue Canadienne d'études Du Développement* 33, no. 2 (2012): 231–49. DOI: 10.1080/02255189.2012.689253

Park, Chisung. "Comparing Faith-Based and Secular Community Service Corporations in Pittsburgh and Allegheny County, Pennsylvania." *Nonprofit and Voluntary Sector Quarterly* 34, no. 2 (2005): 206–223. DOI:10.1177/0899764004269306

Patterson, Eric. *Politics in a Religious World: Building a Religiously Informed U.S. Foreign Policy* (New York: Continuum International Publishing Group, 2011).

Pfeffer, Jeffrey and Gerald R. Salancik. *The External Control of Organizations: A Resource Dependence Perspective* (New York: Harper & Row, 1978).

U.S. Congress, House. Subcommittee on Africa, Global Human Rights, and International Operations of the Committee on International Relations. *The Role of Faith-Based Organizations in United States Programming in Africa,* 109th Congress, 2nd Session, 2006.

6 Faith-Based Organizations Opting In

Introduction

When Trump proposed significant cuts to American foreign aid in 2018, World Vision was among the most vocal critics. The organization's CEO, Rich Stearns, joined over 100 other Christian leaders in imploring Congress not to accept the president's proposal.[1] He also authored an independent statement inveighing the cuts, calling them "penny wise and pound foolish."[2] Cutting assistance, he argued, would have immediate deleterious effects on the world's poor and less conspicuous but no less consequential harm to American interests. Ultimately, Congress maintained the status quo in American aid, and World Vision received over $38 million in federal funds.[3]

Conversations surrounding the government's instrumentalization of faith-based organizations (FBOs) often neglect the agency and power of FBOs. Discussions about "Strategic Religious Engagement" can suffer from the same fallacy. The assumption is that FBOs are acted upon or engaged with, not the entities initiating or taking action. Olivia Wilkinson makes this point when she stresses that in addition to asking questions about Strategic Religious Engagement, we should also ask religious actors what "strategic *secular* engagement" looks like.[4] What does it look like from the perspective of the FBO to partner with the United States Agency for International Development (USAID)? Does it involve the kind of Faustian bargain that some FBOs fear? Does an organization's religious mission and identity necessarily diminish? Do private donors exit when FBOs gain access to public capital? What concessions, if any, are necessary?

World Vision's CEO has clarified that the organization would never accept federal funds if it meant it had to compromise its religious beliefs.[5] The implication is that World Vision values its Christian identity and mission over its relationship with the US government but has not felt pressured to choose between the two. Whether this describes the experience of other FBOs is an open question. This chapter looks at this issue and others in an attempt to more fully understand the experience of FBOs in partnering with USAID. The information provided is from interviews with 44 USAID-funded FBOs.

DOI: 10.4324/9781003456704-6

The chapter begins by providing details about the individuals interviewed and the organizations they represent. The subsequent section presents a brief but necessary digression to discuss the study's inclusion criteria and the opinions expressed by multiple participants regarding the terminology used. This is followed by an examination of some of the concerns expressed by non-funded FBOs included in Chapter 5, namely government discrimination, mission drift, and donor exit. The chapter closes by identifying areas of tension and foreseeable improvement in FBO–USAID relations.

Interviewed FBOs

Approximately 264 FBOs received USAID funding between 2001 and 2021.[6] Two student researchers and I reached out to 241 of these organizations.[7] Forty-four FBOs accepted our invitation to participate in an interview.[8] We did not specify who we wanted to speak to at each organization but, instead, informed each potential participant of the nature of our inquiry. This allowed the organization to select the most appropriate individual for the task. Most organizations connected us with someone in senior leadership. On several occasions, multiple individuals joined the conversation. On other occasions, we spoke with only one individual but the individual expressed that they had conducted several meetings before the call with various stakeholders who could inform their interview answers. (This was especially valuable in instances where the organization received a grant more than ten years ago, and the people most familiar with the grant no longer worked for the organization.)

The breakdown for all interview respondents is included in Table 6.1. We spoke to four organization presidents or CEOs and nine secretary generals or vice presidents. The most common participant was a senior-level director, followed by those directly involved in grant application or administration, such as a grant manager or development officer. On one occasion, a board member also joined the call.

In addition to information on the individuals interviewed, Table 6.1 includes organization characteristics like faith affiliation, service area and location, annual revenue, and grant frequency and history.[9] The vast majority of the organizations represented were Christian, reflecting the dynamics in the larger population.[10] Greater diversity was exhibited in organization issue area and primary place of performance. While all the organizations interviewed would classify themselves as development or humanitarian organizations (or both), many specialized in one or more subareas. The areas represented range from democracy promotion to agriculture, to migration and refugee services, to conflict restoration, among others.[11] The two service areas most prominently represented among those interviewed were education and health. This concentration reflects the dynamic explored earlier regarding two programs most associated with FBO funding: the American Schools and Hospitals Abroad program and the President's Emergency Program for AIDS Relief.

Table 6.1 Descriptive Statistics of FBO Interview Participants

Individual(s) Interviewed[a]	(4) President/CEO	(2) General Secretary	(7) Vice President	(20) Executive Director	(6) Director	(4) Manager	(3) Officer/ Coordinator	(1) Board Member
Faith	(35) Christian	(1) Jewish	(2) Islamic	(4) Interreligious	(0) Hindu	(2) Buddhist	(0) Druze	(0) Indigenous
Issue Area(s)[a]	(5) Agriculture	(6) Economic Development	(8) Relief	(14) Education	(16) Health	(2) Migration & Refugees	(5) Peace & Security	(2) Environment & Sustainability
Region(s) Served[a]	(27) Africa	(19) Asia	(6) Caribbean	(11) C. America	(6) Europe	(2) Oceania	(9) S. America	(2) Middle East
Annual Revenue[b]	(0) <$100K	(2) $101–$250K	(1) $251–$500K	(1) $501K–$1M	(6) $1–$5M	(7) $5,000,001–$10M	(12) $10,000,001–$100M	(4) <$100M
Grant Frequency[c]	(21) 1–2 grants	(10) 3–5 grants	(7) 6–10 grants	(2) 11–15 grants	(2) 16–20 grants	(2) 20–50 grants	(2) >50 grants	Over 100 grants
Last Grant Issued[c]	(13) Within the past two years	(11) 3–5 years ago	(15) 6–10 years ago	(3) 10–15 years ago	(2) 15–20 years ago			

[a] The row totals for rows one, three, and four exceed the total number of organizations surveyed. This is due, in row one, to the fact that, on numerous occasions, multiple individuals would represent one organization in an interview. The discrepancy in rows three and four is due to many organizations that serve multiple issue areas and regions.

[b] Data collected from Charity Navigator and public annual reports. Information not available for all participants.

[c] Data collected from USASpending.gov. Includes cooperative agreements.

The sample of interviewed organizations also reflects the prevalence of large organizations among USAID recipients since a majority of the FBOs interviewed made over $5 million annually. Lastly, most organizations we spoke to did *not* receive USAID grants regularly. Instead, the majority had received only one or two grants over the past 20 years. Additionally, half of the organizations we spoke to would be considered by USAID to be "underutilized partners," meaning they had not received a USAID grant in the past five years.

While the organizations interviewed varied in terms of their faith affiliation, size, issue area, and primary place of performance, they were all selected because they met two criteria: they were nonprofit organizations that had received a USAID grant or cooperative agreement in the past 20 years, and their online mission or values statement included overt religious language. As explained in Chapter 1, the latter was the methodology we used to classify FBOs. We opted to use the term "FBO," because it is a mainstay of the institutional lexicon at USAID and, in partial consequence, a prevalent term in the religions and development literature.[12] However, not every organization we spoke to appreciated the term or agreed that it applied to them.

Contesting Terms

Ronald Sider and Heidi Unruh's typology of FBOs, discussed in Chapter 1, is useful in disaggregating the term FBO and highlighting important distinctions among organizations in this category. Yet their typology, and those devised by others, still fails to reflect the full diversity of FBOs. One of its greatest shortcomings is its failure to distinguish between organizations with religious programs and those with religious motivations. Sider and Unruh measure an organization's faith as evidenced by its mission, staffing, and internal operations, and they assume that the more faith-forward an organization's mission and hiring practices, the more likely the organization is to exhibit "explicitly religious mandated content integrated into its programs."[13] Their typology does little to oblige organizations that exist in the in-between, such as those that may have more secular structures and staffing but offer services relating to religion. The most widely used definitions of FBOs suffer from the same shortcomings.[14] I attempted to account for this deficiency by adopting a more inclusive definition of FBOs, one that accommodates organizations with a faith component to their philosophy, membership, or programmatic.[15] However, I was still left to navigate the perceived narrowness of the concept. The three examples below demonstrate the inherent tension in the term. All three individuals represent organizations outside the Christian tradition.

One of the organizations I spoke to explained that she does not consider her organization to be "faith-based" but admits her organization likely "occupies a gray area" as far as this is concerned.[16] The ambiguity stemmed in part from whether or not the organization's work was *motivated* by faith when the organization's primary aim was to preserve texts associated with a specific religious tradition. In this case, the organization's name and mission statement reference a particular faith, and the organization's founder was a member of the same faith. Though the founder's motivations for establishing the organization appeared primarily academic, the interviewed representative explained that many, and perhaps most of the organization's donors, likely feel compelled to give to the organization for religious reasons. This also applied to many members of the board. These individuals, she explained, may see the organization's work as advancing the faith tradition by preserving and making available for dissemination religious texts they deem as sacred, but she and others saw the organization's work more in terms of cultural and historic preservation.

Another organization expressed somewhat similar views, though this individual *did* consider his organization an FBO. He explained that even though his organization hosted religious events, some might describe the organization in historical or cultural terms. He also clarified that the organization does not have any requirements for its board or staff to be members of a given faith and that, in fact, there is significant variance in this area. "Not all of our board members are members of our faith or even religious," he explained, "We have some who are agnostic, some who are atheist, and some who are religious but not terribly observant. We also have a [religious leader] on our board."[17] He expressed there was a similar diversity of beliefs among the organization's staff. "Some people make assumptions. They assume everyone is [religious,] but not everyone is."[18] He further explained that while he is a member of the faith associated with the organization, one of his coworkers is a member of another religion. He also explained that, while not everyone is aware, the person who designed the organization's logo (after winning a competition) was also a member of another faith. Despite this variance, the individual explained that the organization's funding comes almost entirely from one faith community. "Our donors are all generally [members of a specific faith]," he said, "I don't think we have had any funding from [anyone outside the faith]."[19]

Another organization, less focused on the faith of the organization's employees or board members, stressed that her organization's programs and mission could be seen to intersect or overlap with faith but weren't entirely about faith. "Whether or not we are faith-based," she explained, "is a question of perception."[20] In her view, focusing only or primarily on the faith aspect of the organization's work risked being reductionist, though she admitted that many might see her organization's work in this light, including those at USAID. She further emphasized that she would not typically characterize the organization's work as "interfaith," though "we might put a word like that in our proposal, to use their [USAID's] terminology."[21]

This person's perspective highlights the limitations of written text. I relied upon organization websites to determine whether an organization was faith-based or secular, and mission statements, in particular, are concise and lack considerable nuance. Put simply, you do not get the whole story from an organization's website. You are also unlikely to get the full picture from survey data. This is why I chose to conduct interviews.

Discrimination

The primary purpose of our interviews with USAID-funded FBOs was to test some of the assumptions expressed in our survey by non-funded FBOs. As Chapter 5 reveals, many FBOs eschewing federal funds do so because they perceive the government either *can't* fund religious organizations or *won't* fund such organizations. The Courts have refuted the former, and our survey data likely refutes the latter. We find, ceteris paribus, that qualified FBOs who apply for federal funding are equally likely to be accepted as their secular counterparts. However, it remains an open question whether we see discrimination manifest elsewhere. In other words, while the survey data seems to foreclose the possibility of systematic government discrimination against FBOs at the application stage, it does not speak to whether funded FBOs feel as though they are treated differently than secular organizations during the administration of their grants due to their faith status. This is a question we asked in our interviews. The response among all 44 of the FBOs surveyed was an unequivocal no. A few elaborated.

One organization provided their perspective: "I think if you were going to see discrimination, you'd see it in the details," they explained.[22] If a USAID mission officer was biased against religious organizations or skeptical of their value, they reasoned, one would expect this individual to impose stricter guidelines and be less accommodating when an organization requests exceptions or special considerations. If they want, "they can make life very difficult," the representative said. However, in this organization's experience, their contacts at USAID had always been reasonable, even when things did not go as planned. They provided a tangible example:

> There were some weather issues and issues of getting the containers to the ports. There were delays … and requests for delayed implementation for the grant. And those came back very promptly … they were very accommodating. If there was going to be a rub, that's where you'd see it.

Another organization expressed that they had anticipated they might be treated differently, especially when their primary point of contact at USAID changed, and they knew the replacement was a person who held religious beliefs that were different from the beliefs of the organization. However, the organization's relationship with this individual turned out to be very positive, and the interviewee expressed they still kept in contact even after the close of the contract.

Several other organizations we spoke to confirmed that they did not experience discrimination during the administration of their contracts but also went further to express that they believed FBOs occupied an advantageous position at USAID, especially as the agency had made concerted efforts to include FBOs as partners. Interestingly, some of these organizations mentioned the "Faith-Based Initiative at USAID" as a new phenomenon occurring in the past five years, while others recognized its duration across administrations.

Mission Impact

The conversation regarding discrimination centers around government action, whether it be in the application process or the administration of grants. Yet, as we learned in Chapter 5, some FBOs are deterred from applying for federal funds because they fear how their organization might act in response to federal funds. In particular, they feel government money might lead the organization down a slippery slope toward secularism, forcing the organization to compromise its religious mission and identity. When I asked USAID-funded FBOs if this had ever occurred, the consensus was no, though some acknowledged the presence of a "natural tension" between the perspectives and vernacular of secular and religious entities.[23] One representative provided their perspective, saying:

> The biggest challenge is discourse and language. In the early days, we communicated almost exclusively in spiritually-laden language in describing impact. It was a lot of "we are doing this, because it is a good thing to do," and we were not necessarily thinking about outputs, outcomes, impact, long-term sustainability, risk management. For me, as a kind of second-generation leader, I found all of it super interesting and dove in with a spirit of learning, but I also know others that did not apply for funding in the space that I work. And that's part of the reason they didn't. They felt like they would be forced to operate in a language and discourse, a framework that was foreign to them in a problematic way.[24]

As implied by the statement earlier, organizations may think differently about whether an FBO can effectively "shift registers" and engage in more secular discourse while remaining true to its religious mission and identity.[25] Among the organizations interviewed, however, none of them believed this practice jeopardized the organization's faith-based status.

Notably, the majority of the organizations we interviewed interpreted our question about whether USAID funds led them to compromise their religious mission or identity as one that implied that the organization provided religious services or engaged in proselytization. In these instances, many of the organizations said that since they do not proselytize or discriminate among beneficiaries based on faith, they saw no conflict with accepting USAID funds.[26]

Among the organizations that provided religious services or proselytized, the consensus remained that government funds did not jeopardize the organization's religious operations or mission. The organizations expressing this opinion explained that the rules on the use of US government funds were fairly explicit and unproblematic. One interviewee elaborated:

> We have been accepting government funds for years. Local, state, and federal ... the key is to present who you are. You are transparent and upfront about who you are, yet you also understand the rules—no proselytizing with federal funds ... when you sign the contract, you have to have integrity about how you operate that contract ... .We consider ourselves the hands and feet of Christ and we do it in deed and not word if that's what we need to do.[27]

Interestingly, the same organization that explained the rules were clear had once been penalized for not following the rules, though this was later judged to be a misunderstanding. "Only one time did we ever have the agency come back and tell us we violated our contract," they said. "In one of our classes, the teacher was using a coloring book with scripture references in it." This resulted in the organization being told by agency officials that they were in violation of their contract and their funding would be revoked. However, according to the FBO, "Three months later, they came back and asked us to take the contract back." While others might experience this situation differently, the person interviewed did not consider this a significant incident. They also implied that they wouldn't consider it out-of-bounds for the government to request that the organization distribute or use different materials. "In hindsight," they explained, "we might not have used those coloring books."[28]

Another organization, which also reported positive relations with the government, noted a similar instance of tension but with a different outcome. This particular organization was involved with AIDS education in Africa. They were approached by the US government after accepting USAID funds to request that the organization distribute condoms. The interviewee explained: "We anticipated such issues. It didn't surprise us. But we were able to navigate this issue and 'come out the other side' with our mission intact." The organization ultimately did not capitulate on the issue, with express support from leaders in the community, and the US government did not push the issue further.[29] "We were able to stay the course," the representative concluded.[30]

The point emphasized by this participant is that if USAID accepts religion as an asset in certain development contexts, then it must also accept that an FBO may have a different view or perspective on certain issues and respect this difference. "The key is to be upfront about your beliefs and where you stand from the start," they said.[31] Another participant also expressed this sentiment, but their experience was vastly different. This organization, too, was asked to distribute condoms as part of its HIV/AIDS work. Though the organization thought this went against the Bible's teaching against premarital sex, the representative explained, "We did the distribution of condoms because we thought it was required." This experience, they explained, led to the organization's decision to draft a new constitution and bylaws that made clear the organization's faith motivations. "If it's already in our constitution," they said, "then we can stand by it before we get the grant."[32]

Other organizations we interviewed took another approach, acknowledging that the US government and FBOs may not "see eye to eye" in certain areas but that FBOs can choose not to apply for grants where there could be tension. Examples provided included programs involving family planning or involving LGBTQ communities.[33] One organization I spoke to explained that being selective about the grants they applied for was a necessary practice to safeguard the organization's mission. In their case, while there were several programmatic fits among USAID grants, the leadership felt only one was so straightforward that it excluded virtually any chance of a conflict of vision. This particular organization was among the minority of USAID-funded FBOs that proselytized, yet it stressed that its food distribution programs did not serve this purpose. "[Our food distribution program] was a demonstration of Christ's compassion," they explained, "there wasn't a sharing of the gospel."[34] They further explained that the decision not to proselytize in this program was not made because of the funding source but was shaped by concerns about what was practical and logistically feasible. They reasoned, "I'm sure because of our distribution of food, there were some people that might have come [to church] as a result, but was it an objective of that process? Absolutely not."[35] This individual also explained that the same philosophy applies to the organization's drilling of water wells—a program not funded by USAID. "We drill water wells not on private property ... but on the property of churches. As a result, there is an impact on the attendance of the local churches, but that's not the objective."[36] With the wells, as with emergency food relief, the organization did not engage in proselytization but prioritized providing tangible goods to those in need and providing opportunities for beneficiaries to see a demonstration of "faith in action."

In the previous case, even the organization's logo does not make it clear that it is a Christian organization, and thus, signage surrounding the well or at food distribution points would not necessarily reveal the organization's motivation for the program. Yet USAID guidelines hold that such signage would be permissible. One of the other organizations interviewed emphasized this point. "If you look around our facility," she explained, "there are crosses everywhere."[37] While she stressed that the facility did not discriminate in the provision of its medical services based on faith, she also clarified that the patients coming to the facility all knew the hospital's faith affiliation. Such overt symbology, she explained, was not a problem in the institution's relations with USAID. In fact, she explained that when a USAID team came to shoot a promotional video highlighting the agency's contribution, the videographer zoomed in on the crucifix on several occasions, and these shots remained in the final footage. The organization was happy to also use the video to highlight the partnership to interested stakeholders, including its private donors.

Donor Impact

The vast majority of FBOs are financed by private donations, and most of these donations are provided by individuals who share the organization's religious beliefs.[38] Public funding, if part of their funding portfolio at all, is, most often, supplemental. If the two funding sources can exist in harmony, the combination can be a net-win for the organization, increasing the organization's resources and potential autonomy and output.[39] This benefit depreciates, however, if government funds begin to displace private donations. The reasons for this can be at least twofold: First, as ample research investigates, donors can see government funding as decreasing the effectiveness of their donation and divert their donation to another organization perceived as more in need of their contribution. This is the so-called crowding-out effect.[40] A second reason, more specific to FBOs, is the donor perception of a conflict of interest.[41] Stephen Hopgood and Leslie Vinjamuri explain that when an FBO accepts public money, "It could potentially lose some of its individual donors, especially those who are more religious, who may see public funding as undermining the organization's faith mission."[42] As discussed in Chapter 5, some FBOs are particularly fearful of this effect, and their perception of its likelihood keeps them from applying for government funds. Yet, all of the organizations we interviewed expressed that this description did not fit their experience. In fact, some indicated that USAID funds likely helped the organization *increase* their private contributions (an effect known as "crowding in").[43]

The varied experience of FBOs concerning their donors' reaction to the receipt of government funds depends, in part, upon whether the donors were first aware of the funding. Nonprofit organizations generally have multiple platforms to relay information to interested stakeholders. These avenues have increased exponentially over the past 20 years. Now, in addition to sending information to donors in the mail, organizations can communicate with donors via email, relay information on an organization's website, post on social media, send updates via text message, create an online video, or tell their story in a podcast.[44] With regard to information on an organization's financial inflows, the only requirement by the Internal Revenue Service is that an organization make available physical copies of its 990 form and provide these to individuals upon request.[45] Many organizations, to promote transparency, go beyond this requirement and include these forms online for both donors and the general public to view. Many also include their organization's current and previous annual reports, which also typically convey financial information.

In addition to making information *available* to donors, an FBO may choose to *advertise* its funding sources by strategically pushing out information to its stakeholders. In terms of an organization's partnership with USAID, this could mean featuring the relationship on the organization's website, social media pages, or in an online newsletter, among other things. Organizations could also email or even text donors, alerting them to the receipt of a grant. Each of these avenues has varying degrees of visibility to the average donor. Because the communication of funding information to donors is a necessary condition to evaluate donor reaction, we asked organizations first if they relied on individual donations and then in what ways, if any, their receipt of a USAID grant was communicated to their donors before asking about donor response.

Approximately one-half of the organizations interviewed indicated that their organization's receipt of government funds was made available to donors, though not advertised.[46] These organizations did not feel it necessary to highlight their relationship with the US government in particular. Reasons varied but included the perception that this information wasn't entirely relevant to donors or that the information might elicit donor questions and criticism.[47] The former perspective is exemplified by an organization that responded, "We have a lot of very generous donors who make very substantial donations, but we never identify a donor or amount of donation, and we treated the funds that came from USAID the same way … ."[48] When asked whether this person expected that some complaints could arise out of a perceived incongruity between the organization's faith identity and the US government, the individual responded, "There's always going to be people who find something to complain about," but they clarified that it wasn't due to the expectation of donor criticism that they didn't promote the information; it was just standard practice. They also explained that if the grant they received had been larger they might have considered it for a fundraising challenge, but as it was, the grant was a very small percentage of the organization's overall contributions. It was also food commodities rather than money, which the individual thought made a difference.

Another FBO chose likewise not to advertise their organization's receipt of US government funds to their private donors. The FBO's representative explained that not everyone in the organization's leadership was initially supportive of pursuing USAID funds, and government grants remained a fairly new income stream for the organization. Current donors might not be aware of this recent choice, they admitted, though if they did some "digging" online, they could find it in the organization's audit reports posted on its website. The interviewee clarified that if this information was made more widely available, the organization might have to dispel some common misperceptions. "A lot of people don't know that Christian nonprofits, or even faith-based in general, can get funding from the US government, so there's probably a stigma there," they explained. To combat this, the representative explained the organization would likely need "to educate [donors] that the government isn't using us, but rather we get to take advantage of their taxpayer dollars, which we think is a good thing."[49]

This organization's suspicions about donor interactions were confirmed in our interviews with several of its peer organizations. In these cases, the organizations more widely communicated their receipt of funds, and, in return, had to field donor questions. One organization, for example, explained that when his organization first received a USAID grant, several donors wanted to know more about the award's implications. "They [donors] have asked questions, direct questions," he said. They ask: "You are taking government dollars, does that mean you are compromising your faith? Do you have to do things that violate your faith?" He explained one phone call in particular:

> I had a pastor once call and ask if we accept government funds and I said "Yes" and he said, "So you are an agent of the government?" and I said "No, we are in a contract with the government," and he said "So you do what they tell you to do?" And I said, "No, only what is in the contract." That was a long time ago. He actually ended up not being a donor.[50]

In this case, the person questioning the organization's relationship with the government was not an established donor but an interested co-religionist. The interviewee did not seem to think that this interaction cost their organization future donations from this individual. He also suggested that such remarks had decreased in frequency. "That was more in the past," he explained, "The donor of today is so much more sophisticated and understands the world we live in. Every once in a while you might get a question, but not much anymore."[51] Another interviewee expressed a similar situation: "When we first got started," they explained, "[the person] who started our organization was reluctant to do it [apply for government funds] ... and we've had questions with older donors, but once you explain it to them ... that our hands aren't tied, that's what they want to know."[52]

While some organizations consider their relationship with the US government separate from their relationship with private donors, other FBOs attempt to use the former to leverage the latter. One organization elaborated: "We blow our horn about it whenever we get it, partly because we use it as a fundraising approach."[53] Another organization thought similarly: "We widely communicate it, because receiving and managing US government funds ... helps our reputation. It proves to others we have good technical management capabilities, and we have the proper systems in place."[54] "It helps our reputation," said another, "... and makes people know they can trust us."[55]

Among the organizations that disclosed their USAID award to their donors, many did so in the hopes that this information would attract or "crowd-in" additional private funds. However, not everyone was successful in this goal. One interviewee described their organization's experience, saying: "We thought maybe people would be excited about the grant and we would get more sponsorships, but that hasn't happened yet. We are still new at this. We might do something different next time."[56] Whether a different approach might yield a different result is unclear, though the experience of other organizations may be informative.

Approximately one-fifth of the organizations interviewed expressed that their private contributions likely increased as a result of their organization communicating its receipt of a government grant. These organizations did not experience the donor skepticism described earlier but instead experienced donor enthusiasm. In one case, the organization actually sought funding because a donor suggested they do so.[57] In other cases, organization leadership made the decision to pursue public funding and then widely communicated it to donors using social media, online and print newsletters and magazines, direct mailers, blog posts, videos, and in-person presentations. The timing of this communication varied by organization.

One of the organizations we interviewed explained that they shared their *intent* to apply for USAID funds with donors in hopes that donors would be willing to cover the upfront costs of grant writing and the later costs of grant administration.[58] The organization was successful in obtaining these private funds and, later, also received the ASHA award for which it had applied. Others expressed that they relayed information about their partnership once they received an award to mobilize donors around a started project. For example, one organization remarked:

> Private money is used as seed money, almost, to leverage larger institutional funding. I know that is something our private donors really like. To be able to show that with that gift, we can start a program that will then receive millions of dollars from institutional funders. It shows that their donation is multiplied.[59]

Another organization attested to a similar approach and effect. "We go to people and say we need your matching funds," they said. "We use it as a lever [and] say for every dollar you raised, we raised $10 with USAID; Our donors think we are pretty smart for doing that."[60] A final example comes from an organization predominately financed through congregational support. "We have ninety-two churches that support us," the representative said, and "when visiting these congregations, I always include government funding in the presentation."[61] When asked how he framed the organization's relationship with the US government with these constituents, he said:

> I ask, "How would you like to know that your tax money is going to faith-based organizations like [ours] to reach people for the cause of Christ? The government has made this money available. We are feeding 250,000 … now with this money.".[62]

This individual and others emphasized that the money seems less threatening if you frame it in terms of donor "taxpayer dollars" and not "government money."

Overall, every organization interviewed seemed to view government funding as an enabler rather than an inhibitor to the organization's faith-based mission and as complimentary to and not in competition with private funds.[63] However, several organizations also cautioned about generalizing their organization's experience. "Our donors are religious, but not really religious," said one organization, "maybe it'd be different if they were."[64] Another organization echoed this thought with specific reference to the spectrum of organizations representing the Muslim faith: "Our work is quite general in terms of religious boundaries," they explained, "We involve many partners, public and private, and we do not experience any [donor] issues. This may not be true of those organizations that provide religious services. Those organizations that accept Zakat and have religious aims."[65]

Both of these statements suggest that the experience of some FBOs cannot necessarily be generalized to all. This may be particularly true about the reaction of donors to government funds. Just as FBOs can be placed along a spectrum from "faith-saturated" to "faith-background," their donor bases also likely vary in their religiosity.[66] The politics associated with specific organizations may well be an additional variable influencing donor response to government funds.[67] An organization with particularly conservative donors, even if from the same faith tradition as one of the organizations interviewed, may have a donor base that is particularly averse to public funding. Donor age is another potential confounding factor. One of the individuals quoted earlier mentioned that it was the older donors who likely came to the organization with more questions relating to its acceptance of government grants. Some suggest that young evangelicals, in particular, maybe more supportive of FBOs that adopt more secular practices and partners.[68] An additional factor could be faith type. Because relatively few non-Christian organizations were included in this sample (and are funded by USAID, generally), it is difficult to judge whether donor response varies significantly between Christian, Jewish, Muslim, Buddhist, and Interfaith organizations.

Partnership Limitations

In his article "A Globalized God," Scott Thomas suggests that US policymakers can choose to see the rise of religion as either a challenge or an opportunity. Concerning the latter, it is Thomas's opinion that if America "can recognize and utilize the worldwide religious resurgence and harness its power, then it can ... better the lives of millions."[69] USAID's partnerships with FBOs are an example of this. The US government can do more with the help of FBOs, and our research shows FBOs can often also do more with assistance from the US government. They can use government funds to scale up work already being done or use it to launch new projects. This is not to say, however, that this relationship is perfect or even easy. FBOs might not experience discrimination or a diminution in their mission or private donations, but they might nonetheless experience frustration, especially as it relates to USAID's increasingly burdensome application procedures and reporting requirements.

The amount of "red tape" involved in the receipt of a US federal grant is well-known, yet many organizations feel it is unnecessary. "We've gotten grants under four administrations now," said one interviewee, "and nothing's changed except that they've made it more difficult ... the bureaucracy gets overwhelming. What they've done is to make it more difficult for small faith-based organizations to get involved."[70] This organization specifically referenced the International Food Relief Partnership (IFRP) program and the new guidelines USAID had implemented, asking organizations to provide hundreds of documents to satisfy a pre-award risk assessment in an abbreviated time.[71] Another IFRP grant recipient explained that the processing time had increased considerably since the organization was first involved in the program and that now the organization judges it to be more efficient to use private funds to directly purchase commodities and shipping containers than to wait for distributions from the US government. Another FBO involved in the ASHA program, which classified itself among the "larger cohort" of FBOs, explained that, in addition to the laborious application process, the administration of USAID grants has become increasingly complex and that "the bar is set so high in terms of compliance and technical requirements" that it is beginning to deter organizations from continuing the partnership.[72]

In addition to complaints regarding USAID's application and reporting procedures, there were complaints of a larger magnitude. One organization, for instance, described a particularly nightmarish experience. This organization was impacted by President Trump's decision in August 2018 to revoke $200 million in assistance planned to go to groups aiding Palestinians. The interviewee explained how this decision impacted the organization's operations: "We had courses. We were committed to people. We had to immediately find other resources to cover our programs. That was a really bad experience." Ultimately, the organization succeeded in raising private funds, but only enough to provide two-thirds of the services they had intended to provide. "And we weren't the only organization affected," they explained. "There were many of us." They continued: "USAID ... puts you under a magnifying glass, and then they stop the contract. It was devastating." Though the organization attributed its hardship to President Trump specifically and not USAID, they still explained how their experience shaped their outlook going forward: "It broke the trust that it will be something you can submit forever," they said, "I am more cautious now that the core operations are not funded by government funds and that anything funded by the government are supplemental and can be turned on and off."[73]

Even with its justified skepticism surrounding US assistance, the organization expressed its intent to apply for future grants and, in fact, was in the process of doing so at the time of the interview. Other organizations, when asked if they would consider applying for future USAID funds, expressed their willingness to do so, but said their organization did not necessarily *plan* to do so. Since this research was conducted primarily before USAID introduced its new Strategic Religious Engagement Policy, it is unclear whether USAID's renewed commitment to engaging FBOs will inspire these organizations to rekindle their relationship and encourage them to seek out additional funding opportunities.

Notes

1 "100+ Christian Leaders Tell Congressional Leadership: Protect Foreign Assistance," *World Vision*, March 16, 2017, www.worldvision.org/about-us/media-center/100-christian-leaders-tell-congressional-leadership-protect-foreign-assistance
2 Richard Stearns, "World Vision Emphasizes the Value of Foreign Assistance, Urges Congress to Reject Cuts to Budget," www.worldvision.org/about-us/media-center/world-vision-emphasizes-value-foreign-assistance-urges-congress-reject-cuts-budget
3 This was the amount provided in new awards by the US State Department, USAID, and the Department of Labor. Data pulled from USASpending.gov.
4 Wilkinson, "Putting the 'Strategic'," 82.
5 Janet I. Tu, "World Vision's Richard Stearns Sets Out to Put an End to Global Poverty," *Seattle Times*, August 23, 2009, www.seattletimes.com/pacific-nw-magazine/world-visions-richard-stearns-sets-out-to-put-an-end-to-global-poverty/
6 Recipient information for FY2006 and FY2007 was unavailable, though it is highly likely these lists contained primarily the same funded FBOs. Taking the data presented in Chapter 4 on the average of newly funded organizations each fiscal year, we can estimate that there could be an additional 22 organizations left out of the full population list. (Though this number is likely to be significantly lower because it assumes all 22 were first-time funders *and* organizations that never again received funding.)
7 The full list could not be contacted because some organizations, especially if they received funding 20 years ago, no longer exist. They either dissolved or merged with another organization. Others, for reasons unknown, had no web presence, no contact information on their website, or nonworking/invalid contact information listed.
8 This list was compiled using the coding procedures outlined in Chapter 1. USASpending.gov does not provide organization website information or contact information, so this was obtained by student researchers using organization names and addresses. Where possible, we tried to first contact someone who was directly involved in institutional giving. If such a person was not listed on the website, we contacted a senior executive or someone most likely to know the broad range of organizational operations. In most cases, we first reached out via a personalized email invitation, though some organizations received a phone call first to determine an appropriate email contact. In both cases, we informed the organization of the intent and scope of the study and the reason for their organization's inclusion. This information was provided alongside a consent form and request for a recorded Zoom interview.
9 For ASHA grant recipients, we spoke only to the direct fund recipient. These were US-based organizations that financially supported a hospital or school operating abroad. USAID refers to these entities as US organizations (USOs) and Overseas Institutions (OSI), respectively.

10 While the sample statistics of the interviewed organizations look similar to those surveyed concerning faith affiliation, the increased number of non-Christian FBOs, while relatively minimal, was the result of a concerted effort to oversample this subset of the population.
11 Table 6.1 lists only those categories representing two or more organizations. The IRS uses National Tax-Exempt Entities (NTEE) codes to categorize non-profit NGOs. All the organizations included in this study generally fall under Q30 or "International Development." The table attempts to show greater specification by identifying organizations that would fall under narrower NTEE codes like Q31 International Agricultural Development, Q32 International Economic Development, Q33 International Relief, Q34 International Educational Development, Q39 International Health Development, Q40 International Peace and Security, and Q71 International Migration and Refugee Issues. Other issue areas represented by interviewees that do not appear in the table include: Q35 International Democracy and Civil Society Development; Q36 International Science and Technology Development; Q38 International Environment, Population, and Sustainability Development; and Q51 International Affairs, Foreign Policy and Globalization. Areas not represented include Q41 Arms Control and Peace, Q42 United Nations Associations, Q43 National Security, and Q51 International Economic and Trade Policy.
12 Karam, "USAID Strategic Religious Engagement Summit," 86.
13 Sider and Unruh, "Typology of Religious Characteristics," 114.
14 Clarke and Jennings, for example, define FBOs as "any organisation that derives inspiration and guidance for its activities from the teachings and principles of the faith or from a particular interpretation or school of thought within that faith." See Clarke and Jennings, *Development, Civil Society*, 6.
15 Dicklitch and Rice, "The Mennonite Central Committee (MCC)," 662.
16 FBO #34, Zoom Interview with Author, July 14, 2023.
17 FBO #40, Zoom Interview with Author, September 11, 2023.
18 Ibid.
19 Ibid.
20 FBO #38, Zoom Interview with Author, September 5, 2023.
21 Ibid.
22 FBO #42, Zoom Interview with Author, October 23, 2023.
23 The idea of FBOs feeling compelled to adopt secular terminology in their interactions with public donors is a well-identified phenomenon. See Haynes, *Faith-Based Organizations at the United Nations*, 23; Koehrsenn and Heuser, *Faith-Based Organizations in Development*; Tomalin, "Religions, Poverty Reduction."
24 FBO #33, Zoom Interview with Author, July 6, 2023.
25 This terminology comes from Emma Tomalin's research, which explains that many FBOs involved in international development have to "shift in register between secular modes of communication with global development actors to religious modes with local faith actors." Tomalin, "Religions, Poverty Reduction," 3.
26 Interestingly, these two actions were often included in the same sentence, though, in reality, one is permitted by the US government (with private funds), and the other is strictly prohibited. This kind of response might reflect the bias discussed in Chapter 5 against development organizations that proselytize.
27 FBO #29, Zoom Interview with Author, July 28, 2021.

28 FBO #24, Zoom Interview with Author, July 26, 2021.

29 The reasons the organization provided for not distributing condoms included that this prevention method was not 100% effective and could potentially impose a financial burden on individuals (if/when the expectation later shifted to promote individual purchases). The organization also felt it encouraged immoral activity—specifically the molestation of young girls.

30 FBO #20, Zoom Interview with Author, June 15, 2021.

31 Ibid.

32 FBO #37, Zoom Interview with Author, August 17, 2023; in this instance, the organization was originally coded as "spiritually ambiguous," because its mission statement and website referenced spirituality obliquely but did not reference a specific religious tradition. This has since changed, and the organization's mission statement indicates it is a Christian organization.

33 Several organizations mentioned that FBOs might avoid grants in this area altogether, while others mentioned that it was "safer" to apply for such grants under certain administrations over others, referencing the Mexico City Policy, which prohibits NGOs from using federal funding for abortion counseling or referrals, advocacy to decriminalize abortion, or the provision of abortion services. Other organizations mentioned the perceived tension that exists between the US government's position on LGBTQ rights and the contrary stance of some Christian denominations/churches. This was not generally framed as something organizations felt they had to compromise on but as a future real or possible impediment to FBOs securing USAID funding.

34 FBO #42, Zoom Interview with Author, October 16, 2023.

35 Ibid.

36 Ibid.

37 FBO #22, Zoom Interview with Author, June 18, 2021.

38 An assessment of the top 71 largest faith-based development organizations in the United States shows that 83% of total revenue was from private contributions. The report further found that 62% of the faith-based development organizations in the United States don't receive any government funds. "Financing of International Development by US Faith-based NGOs 2011–2015," Center for the Faith and the Common Good, March 2017, https://jliflc.com/resources/sources-of-revenue-and-international-expenditures-of-us-faith-based-ngos-fy2011-2016/

39 On autonomy, see Froelich, "Diversification of Revenue Strategies"; On output, see Berrett and Holliday "Effect of Revenue Diversification."

40 Steinberg, "Theory of Crowding Out."

41 Nearly all of the literature on this topic does not consider whether FBOs experience crowding out differently than secular organizations, though research specific to Islamic Relief shows some evidence of the trend among the organization's donor base. See Khan, "Religious Obligation or Altruistic Giving?" 103.

42 Hopgood and Vinjamuri, "Faith in Markets," 38.

43 Research supports this effect, though no one has investigated if the dynamic is different for FBOs. de Wit and Bekkers, "Government Support and Charitable Donations"; Heutel, "Crowding Out and Crowding In."

44 Some of the organizations interviewed for this chapter received grants as early as 2001, and these organizations' donor communication strategies cannot be fairly compared to organizations receiving grants in 2021. This is because many of the now commonplace communication techniques for nonprofits did not exist

20 years ago. In 2005, for instance, one survey revealed that approximately 23% of nonprofits still did not have a website. In contrast, those organizations viewed as especially "tech savvy" were, at that time, just beginning to adopt the "innovative" practice of using emails that linked to an organization's website. Research reveals that most nonprofits did not begin using social media to communicate until 2010. Pope, Isely, and Asamoa-Tutu, "Developing a Marketing Strategy," 192. Holly Minch, "Nonprofit Communications: Fundamental, Strategic – And Chronically Underperforming," *Nonprofit Quarterly*, September 21, 2005, https://nonprofitquarterly.org/nonprofit-communications-fundamental-strategicand-chronically-underperforming/; Young, "Current Status of Social Media Use," 186.

45 USAID does not require awardees to advertise their grants to the public or donor constituencies. Rather, USAID is more concerned with this information being relayed to *beneficiaries*. In the Final Rule, 2 Part 700—Uniform Administrative Requirements, Cost Principles, and Audit Requirements for Federal Awards, published on August 26, 2005, all nonexempt USAID awardees are required to "brand" their program, project, activities, public communications, and commodities provided abroad with the USAID logo and include that it comes "From the American people."

46 In one case, an organization relayed that the specific funding information was not disclosed to donors due to security concerns, and it received the requisite waiver to withhold the information from beneficiaries as well. FBO #4, Zoom Interview with Kayla Wood, March 5, 2021.

47 Another potential reason for not relaying public funding information to private donors is structural. One of the individuals we interviewed, for instance, was involved in her organization's institutional funding, but when asked about private donors, she said it wasn't her area, and she wasn't sure if information from one area made its way into the other area. It was unclear whether this person's position as a grant manager was the limiting factor in knowing about donor communications or if structural barriers existed at the organization separating the two spheres.

48 Ibid.

49 FBO #2, Zoom Interview with Kayla Wood, March 3, 2021.

50 FBO #28, Interview with Author, July 28, 2021.

51 Ibid.

52 FBO #27, Zoom Interview with Author, July 26, 2021.

53 FBO #6, Zoom Interview with Kayla Wood, March 31, 2021.

54 FBO #3, Zoom Interview with Kayla Wood, March 3, 2021.

55 FBO #41, Zoom Interview with Author, September 12, 2023. Note: The minimum number of non-Christian organizations interviewed does not enable me to delineate in what ways, if any, organizations of different faiths perceive that a relationship with the US government helps their reputation, though previous research suggests that Muslim FBOs, in particular, can be advantaged by US government funding, because it signals legitimacy in a space where there can be greater suspicion as to an organization's local connections and finances. See Khan, "Religious Obligation or Altruistic Giving?" 102–103.

56 FBO #40, Zoom Interview with Author, September 11, 2023.

57 FBO #36, Zoom Interview with Author, August 7, 2023.

58 FBO #6, Zoom Interview with Kayla Wood, March 31, 2021.

59 FBO #3, Zoom Interview with Kayla Wood, March 3, 2021.
60 FBO #32, Zoom Interview with Author, July 13, 2021.
61 FBO #25, Zoom Interview with Author, June 28, 2021.
62 Ibid.
63 A separate theme that emerged was that USAID funding helped an organization attract other institutional funds, both public and private.
64 FBO #19, Zoom Interview with Author, June 16, 2021.
65 FBO #35, Zoom Interview with Author, July 30, 2023.
66 Even more complicated on this front is the fact that there could be significant variance even within a given organization's donor base.
67 Jeffrey Haynes also observes this variance in his examination of FBOs involved at the UN. Haynes, *Faith-Based Organizations at the United Nations*, 80.
68 Professor James Wellman quoted in Janet I. Tu, "World Vision's Richard Stearns."
69 Thomas, "A Globalized God," 101.
70 FBO #29, Zoom Interview with Author, June 28, 2021.
71 The assessment requirement is outlined in 2 CFR 200 and USAID ADS 303. Requested documents include copies of an organization's legal incorporation, an organizational chart, a list of board members and their resumes, audited financial statements for the past three years, a marketing and branding strategy, statements on imports being duty-free, confirmation and supporting documentation on the organization's anti-terrorism practices, cash flow projections, bank account statements, financial, procurement, and human resource manuals, third-party performance audits of previous related activities, written descriptions of team members' experience and qualifications, available IT resources, organization procurement and recruitment functions on-site, past-related projects, financial safeguards, accounts payable processes, and plans to meet specified milestones, among other items.
72 FBO #28, Zoom Interview with Author, July 20, 2021.
73 Ibid.

Bibliography

Berrett, Jessica L. and Bradley S. Holliday. "The Effect of Revenue Diversification on Output Creation in Nonprofit Organizations: A Resource Dependence Perspective." *Voluntas: International Journal of Voluntary and Nonprofit Organizations* 29, no. 6 (2018): 1190–1201. www.jstor.org/stable/45105591

Clarke, Gerard and Michael Jennings. *Development, Civil Society and Faith-Based Organizations: Bridging the Sacred and the Secular* (Basingstoke: Palgrave Macmillan, 2008).

de Wit, Arjen and René Bekkers. "Government Support and Charitable Donations: A Meta-Analysis of the Crowding-Out Hypothesis." *Journal of Public Administration Research and Theory* 27, no. 2 (2017): 301–319. https://doi.org/10.1093/jopart/muw044

Dicklitch, Susan and Heather Rice. "The Mennonite Central Committee (MCC) and Faith-Based NGO Aid to Africa." *Development in Practice* 14, no. 5 (2004): 660–672. www.jstor.org/stable/4029894

Froelich, Karen A. "Diversification of Revenue Strategies: Evolving Resource Dependence in Nonprofit Organizations." *Nonprofit and Voluntary Sector Quarterly* 28, no. 3 (1999): 246–268. https://doi.org/10.1177/0899764099283002

Haynes, Jeffrey. *Faith-Based Organizations at the United Nations* (London: Palgrave Macmillan, 2017).

Heutel, Garth. "Crowding Out and Crowding In of Private Donations and Government Grants." *Public Finance Review* 42, no. 2 (2014): 143–175. https://doi.org/10.1177/1091142112447525

Hopgood, Stephen and Leslie Vinjamuri. "Faith in Markets." In *Sacred Aid: Faith and Humanitarianism*, edited by Michael Barnett and Janice Gross Stein (New York: Oxford University Press, 2012): 37–64.

Karam, Azza. "The USAID Strategic Religious Engagement Summit: What Was Not Said." *The Review of Faith & International Affairs* 19, sup1 (2021): 85–91. www.doi.org/10.1080/15570274.2021.1983337

Khan, Ajaz Ahmed. "Religious Obligation or Altruistic Giving? Muslims and Charitable Donations." In *Sacred Aid: Faith and Humanitarianism*, edited by Michael Barnett and Janice Gross Stein (New York: Oxford University Press, 2012): 90–114.

Koehrsenn, Jens and Andreas Heuser, eds. *Faith-Based Organizations in Development Discourses and Practice* (1st ed.) (New York: Routledge, 2019). https://doi.org/10.4324/9780429351211

Pope, Jennifer A, Elaine Sterrett Isely, and Fidel Asamoa-Tutu. "Developing a Marketing Strategy for Nonprofit Organizations: An Exploratory Study." *Journal of Nonprofit & Public Sector Marketing* 21, no. 2 (2009): 184–201. DOI:10.1080/10495140802529532

Sider, Ronald J. and Heidi Rolland Unruh. "Typology of Religious Characteristics of Social Service and Educational Organizations and Programs." *Nonprofit and Voluntary Sector Quarterly* 33, no. 1 (March 2004): 109–134.

Steinberg, Richard. "The Theory of Crowding Out: Donations, Local Government Spending, and the 'New Federalism'." In *Philanthropic Giving: Studies in Varieties and Goals*, edited by Richard Magat (New York: Oxford University Press, 1989): 143–156.

Thomas, Scott A. "A Globalized God." *Foreign Affairs* 89, no. 6 (2010): 93–101.

Tomalin, Emma. "Religions, Poverty Reduction and Global Development Institutions." *Palgrave Communications* 4, no. 132 (2018): 1–12. DOI:10.1057/s41599-018-0167-8

Wilkinson, Olivia. "Putting the 'Strategic' into Strategic Religious Engagement." *The Review of Faith & International Affairs* 19, sup1 (2021): 78–84. https://doi.org/10.1080/15570274.2021.1983361

Young, James A. "The Current Status of Social Media Use Among Nonprofit Human Service Organizations: An Exploratory Study." Order No. 3507810, Virginia Commonwealth University, 2012. www.proquest.com/dissertations-theses/current-status-social-media-use-among-nonprofit/docview/1017535056/se-2

7 Conclusion

Introduction

When the Bush administration published its final report on the Faith-Based Initiative, it suggested the Initiative had ushered in a "quiet revolution" in faith-based organization (FBO)–government relations. As evidence of the change, it highlighted the increased number of government-funded FBOs and the increased amount they had received.[1] Not everyone was convinced, including those who stressed that such numbers were likely insufficient indicators of the Initiative's effects.[2] Fifteen years later, the contours of the conversation remain largely the same, especially at USAID. USAID introduced the concept of Strategic Religious Engagement (SRE) in September 2023, emphasizing the desire to bring new FBOs to the table, and others offered the rejoinder that SRE should be "about quality over quantity."[3] This book examines FBO engagement from both aspects by evaluating the numbers and telling the stories behind them. The overarching narrative is that religious engagement at USAID has looked fairly narrow and shallow over the past 20 years. The numbers show that the Faith-Based Initiative allowed more FBOs to participate in USAID projects, yet the total number of FBOs, especially vis-à-vis the number of USAID's secular partners, has remained consistently low. These FBOs also represent the minority of US-based development FBOs. It also appears that many of the FBOs that partner with USAID do not continue to do so, or at least do not do so with any regularity.

One could look at this dynamic and conclude that USAID has largely failed in its efforts to engage with many FBOs—and they would be correct. Yet the converse is also true—many FBOs do not engage with USAID. After all, FBOs have a *choice* as to whether or not to seek USAID funds. Sometimes, this isn't an easy decision. As shown in Chapter 5, many FBOs avoid government funds for fear of discrimination, mission drift, and donor loss. Meanwhile, other FBOs lean in and choose to apply for funding, sometimes despite having similar fears.[4] Chapter 6 reveals that many FBOs who receive funding have their fears generally abated. They also report receiving a positive return on their investment.

DOI: 10.4324/9781003456704-7

While the partnerships between FBOs and USAID remain imperfect, these arrangements can still prove mutually beneficial. In this chapter, I discuss the specific advantages brought by each party, first discussing how USAID (and other development donors) can benefit by partnering with FBOs and then discussing the ways FBOs can benefit by partnering with USAID. Both of these conversations are informed by the interviews I had with USAID-funded FBOs. I then pivot to provide recommendations for USAID to initiate or sustain impactful relations with FBOs. This is followed by a broader discussion of how other public donors have chosen to engage FBOs and what the available data tells us regarding the success of their efforts.

Why Engage FBOs

At the start of his presidency, George W. Bush argued that FBOs were underutilized resources in the government's fight against poverty. He even stressed, upon occasion, that FBOs could have a comparative advantage over their secular counterparts.[5] Many critics at the time highlighted there was scant evidence to support the president's claims.[6] The story has since changed. USAID may be employing familiar rhetoric to engage FBOs, but it does so atop mounting evidence of their effectiveness in development. In particular, over the past 20 years, researchers have identified several strengths common to FBOs that can optimize their ability to achieve development outcomes. USAID has also come to officially acknowledge and appreciate these common characteristics, going so far as to include them in its official SRE Policy.[7] While different actors have employed different terminology in this conversation, all concur that partnering with FBOs is likely to add an extra dimension to aid, allowing donors to benefit from their long history in developing nations, deep beneficiary relations, and expansive geographic reach.[8]

Long Histories

As discussed in Chapter 2, many modern faith-based humanitarian and development organizations are the institutional progeny of missionaries who went abroad as far back as a century ago. The colonial underpinnings of this history can be severely problematic, yet the long legacy of FBOs in the provision of aid is seen by many to eclipse their origin stories. These institutions remained embedded in their communities and have served generations of individuals. Whether it is a church, synagogue, temple, school, library, or hospital, they have come to be seen, in many cases, as community fixtures rather than Western transplants.

This distinction was highlighted on several occasions during our interviews, with interviewees distinguishing their organizations from those that were "parachuting on the back of an AID contract and closing shop afterward," or committing the "crime" of "bungee jumping" into a country and trying to help without first establishing connections, gaining trust, and understanding the culture.[9] Our interviewees opined that these kinds of organizations can sew suspicion and may leave beneficiaries asking, "What are you getting out of this?" They explained that the same question is asked far less if an organization has long been embedded in the community and has established a reputation for service in the area.[10] There is less doubt in those cases because the organization and its employees are better known and have an established history of care.

Deep Relations

The question "What are you getting out of this?" is also likely to be asked less if an organization's faith identity leads beneficiaries to conclude that its employees are intrinsically, rather than extrinsically, motivated.[11] In other words, if an individual knows an organization is religious, they may feel as though they have some a priori knowledge about why the organization does what it does (to fulfill a spiritual duty) and how it does it (to honor or please a Higher Power). Adherents to Abrahamic religions, for example, all believe in God and an afterlife. They all similarly believe that a believer's actions on earth reflect their spiritual connection to God and impact their experience after death.[12] Good deeds are also prioritized in many nontheistic faiths.[13] Nearly all faiths encourage believers to practice altruism. Thus, even if the organization itself is unknown or relatively new to an area, knowledge of its beliefs can sometimes supplant individual suspicion and allow space for meaningful relationships.

In addition to religion sometimes fostering beneficiary connections, it can also advance an organization's programmatic outcomes, especially if an organization *shares* a spiritual worldview with its beneficiaries—a reality made all the more likely due to the strong number of religious adherents in developing countries.[14] A couple of examples can illustrate the point. One FBO we spoke to, for instance, explained that their organization emphasized abstinence before marriage and sexual fidelity as a way to combat AIDS and that this message was reinforced in the local churches. The area the organization worked in, they explained, was highly religious, and therefore, the organization's instructions were based on a shared spiritual command based on a mutual point of reference.[15] The representative emphasized that the message they were conveying was not foreign but reinforced the values taught in homes and churches in the area.[16] Another example provided to us by an FBO working in sustainability involves how to frame land use. Conversations with farmers, they said, were less effective when centered around the advantages and disadvantages of land management techniques and more effective when centered around the shared spiritual knowledge of God's design for nature and humankind's responsibility to be good stewards of this gift.[17] In both these cases, the hortatory message ultimately can be perceived by beneficiaries to come from a higher authority—an authority already trusted—rather than merely the organization.

Wide Reach

Another known attribute common to FBOs underscored by our interviews and highlighted in the existing literature is their geographic scope. Western organizations with offices in developing countries often position them in more urban and central areas. In contrast, FBOs are often either based in more rural areas or often have partners that reach out into remote locations. One organization we spoke to, for example, mentioned that they benefit by marshaling the resources of "hundreds of local churches." These churches, they explained, are "the best educational network" out there, better than anything the government can hope to create.[18]

These networks can be relational and physical, comprising people and buildings. The interviewee emphasized relationships and knowledge distribution, whereas others underscored physical infrastructure. Even in less populated areas, there can be physical structures that serve as religious meeting areas and places of worship. One interviewee explained:

> We are present in the most remote places. We have the infrastructure with churches ... You don't have to invite people; they are already there for tea after church on Sunday. Other entities have to look for an office, have to establish themselves somewhere, recruit volunteers and attract people.[19]

These three factors, a long history, deep relations, and a wide and penetrating geographic network, are beneficial to USAID and other development donors mainly because they can lead to beneficiary *trust* and *access*. Institutions with deep histories in a given area and those that share the beliefs of those they serve may be more trusted than other institutions, while organizations with sprawling infrastructures and networks are often better positioned to access hard-to-reach communities.[20] FBO vaccination campaigns against COVID-19 provide a poignant example.[21]

COVID-19 is a highly communicable airborne illness that contributed to a global pandemic beginning in March 2020. As the disease swept around the world and global health authorities learned more about its deadly effects, state governments and multilateral institutions began soliciting the support of faith-based leaders and organizations.[22] FBOs were critical allies throughout the pandemic, but their cooperation was especially necessary once a vaccine for the virus became available. Hesitancy surrounding COVID-19 was stronger than initially expected, partly due to rampant misinformation.[23] This misinformation eroded the "trust in authorities" often necessary for vaccine acceptance.[24]

Knowing many people lacked trust in their government and multilateral institutions, those wishing to stop the spread and severity of the disease through vaccination had to consider "non-traditional solutions," including partnering with organizations known to elicit people's trust, like FBOs.[25] The research on these efforts is still forthcoming, but the available evidence suggests that such partnerships directly contributed to a significant increase in vaccine uptake. In the United States, for example, coordination efforts between the Center for Disease Control and the Conference of National Black Churches (CNBC) led to at least 650,000 additional vaccinations.[26] In India, the coordinated efforts of 18 FBOs and 400 religious institutions led to .41 million individuals receiving the vaccine.[27] In both cases, the involved FBOs used their roles as trust agents to dismantle mental barriers and encourage individual vaccination.[28] They also used their physical infrastructure to host vaccination clinics, providing individuals with access to medical intervention while simultaneously allowing the medical community to reach individuals who could otherwise be difficult to reach.

Why Engage USAID

It was the crucible of COVID-19 that essentially pushed religious leaders and institutions from legitimized to *prioritized* actors in international development. The donor community needed the help of FBOs to reach those who did not trust secular institutions and were in more remote locations. Yet the converse also held true in some cases. In the face of a global pandemic, some FBOs found they needed additional support, and they found it from public donors, including USAID. Stories from this time period and others show FBOs benefiting, in particular, from the agency's long and stable history, deep pockets, and wide resources.

Long and Stable History

While "foreign aid" may, at times, become a lightning rod for American political debate, its longstanding prioritization in US foreign policy bespeaks its durability. The United States first committed to providing high levels of international assistance in 1951, and it created USAID in 1964. For 60 years, USAID has operated under a Congressional mandate to distribute and manage America's international assistance, and it has done so across 12 separate presidential administrations. Even as the majority party has changed hands many times over in the executive and legislative branches, USAID's congressional appropriations have been fairly consistent.[29] The US government's funding of FBOs follows a somewhat similar narrative.

America's engagement with FBOs in aid delivery began under Truman, not Bush, and can be traced back to the Public Law 480 food program, which began in 1954. America's response to humanitarian crises, in particular, has always relied heavily on FBOs to deliver food commodities.[30] This practice continued even when USAID began also prioritizing development projects. Under Bush, faith began to have a stronger foothold in American foreign policy, and the president reprioritized USAID's religious engagement. In particular, Bush's establishment of USAID's Center for Faith-Based and Community Initiatives marked the beginning of what Gregorio Bettiza calls America's "Faith-Based Foreign Aid Regime," where FBOs were made increasingly eligible to become implementing aid partners.[31] This regime, as Chapter 4 shows, has continued under four presidential administrations, with the number of funded FBOs remaining relatively constant.

USAID's institutionalized commitment and continuity with regard to engaging religious actors and organizations enables FBOs to consider USAID a viable funding source regardless of the political or economic climate.[32] This is not always true of other funding sources. Most FBOs rely exclusively on private donations, and yet research shows that individual giving can retract significantly during economic downturns or when individuals perceive forthcoming economic instability.[33] This is generally true of both secular and religious giving.[34] Donation trends during COVID-19 provide a compelling example.

Individual giving dropped precipitously in the United States in the early months of the COVID-19 pandemic.[35] Several of the individuals we interviewed expressed that this dynamic caused an especially trying time for their organization. One FBO, in particular, expressed that the organization experienced an unprecedented retraction in individual donations at the precise moment it faced significant demand for its services. In fact, the individual reported operating the only hospital in an area besieged by the illness. It was USAID, they said, that helped the organization meet this need and ultimately sustain the organization's medical operations overseas.[36] At a time when other funding sources were less reliable, the US government presented a solid option.

Deep Pockets

In most cases, individual giving in the United States and elsewhere rebounded as the pandemic progressed, and the amount of private donations given to NGOs in 2020 ended up surpassing that of previous years.[37] This was also true of the amount of aid provided by the US government. The US government spent \$52 billion in foreign assistance in 2020, compared to \$49 billion the year before.[38] Nearly \$15 billion of this was provided by USAID to nonprofit organizations in the form of grants.[39] Even if an FBO did not lose its individual donors, the amount of funding available from the US government then and now can allow for the expansion of an organization's services. This is especially true for smaller organizations or those that have a narrower donor base since, in these cases, there is an effective ceiling on the funds an organization can expect to raise from the private sector within a given period of time.[40] Research shows, for instance, that individual donors give an average of \$556 annually to organizations in international affairs. The median amount for small donors (those under \$1,000) is \$20, while the median gift for larger donors (those in excess of $1,000) is $2,500.[41] The median grant amount provided by private foundations in international affairs, by contrast, is approximately $53,269.[42] Both of these are dwarfed by the median grant amount provided to nonprofits by USAID, which is $4,185,571.[43]

The monetary discrepancy in private and public funding and what it means for an organization was highlighted by one of our interviewees, who expressed that their hospital kept its doors open because of individual donations, but the hospital's *expansion* was made possible only by the US government. What was built in one year with USAID funds, she said, would have taken 30 years if the institution had to rely solely on individual funders.[44]

The limitations of individual donations are not lost on larger organizations either, especially if these organizations face a gradual retraction in their donor base. Research indicates, for instance, that the increased number of FBOs over recent decades has provided individuals with more charitable options and consequently caused many FBOs to work harder to attract and maintain the status quo in their donations.[45] To the extent there exists a finite donor pool, some organizations may benefit from switching their strategies and expending effort on gaining public funding rather than increased individual fundraising.

In other cases, the limit of individual donations may be less related to the number of donors or their dollars and more a factor of what issues donors find salient. For example, one of our interviewees explained that their organization's donors were very generous in response to highly publicized international crises but that mobilizing donors to give to more obscure or protracted crises had proven difficult. Thus, when a locust swarm devastated the area the organization served or when the organization wanted to help those affected by a severe and prolonged drought, they turned instead to USAID.[46]

Wide Resources

In addition to the direct monetary benefits US government grants can provide, the US government also provides funded FBOs with the resources to expand their organizational capacity.[47] In fact, one of our interviewees explained their experience with USAID by saying: "We would not have been successful had we not had their help in setting up our offices, our business plan, strategic plan, and developing the accounting, monitoring and evaluation systems that we could not provide for ourselves."[48] In this instance, the interviewee's remarks seemingly center on the success of a specific project, but the concept of organizational capacity extends beyond project performance to encompass an organization's sustainability and self-renewal.[49] This means that the plans created and the systems put in place in this case, while helpful in achieving the outlined objectives of the funded program, can also be expected to live beyond the duration of the organization's USAID contract and strengthen its performance in future projects. The hope of USAID is that stronger organizations are more likely to apply again for funds, and what might begin as an ad hoc transaction develops into a sustainable relationship. The significant portion of FBOs in our sample that were one-time USAID awardees demonstrates that this vision is not easily realized. However, we did speak to organizations that felt empowered by their relationship with USAID. One FBO emphasized that it isn't just about money changing hands but more about a symbiotic and mutually beneficial relationship. As an ASHA program participant, they explained that the relationship was triangular, involving a US entity, a local entity, and the US government. The organization called this "tripod" arrangement a "miracle machine" for what it allowed the organization to accomplish.[50]

While it may be an overstatement to generally characterize USAID–FBO relations in terms of a miracle, it is also clearly not a mirage. Both parties stand to benefit from the arrangement. USAID can enhance the effectiveness of its aid by capitalizing upon the trust and access that FBOs engender and provide. FBOs, meanwhile, can use USAID to obtain more immediate and more significant sums of money than individual donors can sometimes provide and also gain access to resources to enhance their organization's performance and sustainability. Still, the fact remains that most FBOs do not engage in this mutually beneficial relationship. It thus behooves USAID to better understand why this is the case and to address relevant concerns.

How USAID Can Better Engage FBOs

USAID's new SRE Policy explains that the agency's previous engagement efforts with FBOs were stymied by the misperceptions, myths, and mistrust found prevalent among USAID staff.[51] The policy is the agency's attempt at righting the record and rooting out these fallacious assumptions. It provides a resource for individuals to turn to in case of confusion and is also meant to mitigate inconsistent FBO engagement. Yet my research suggests that FBOs foster their own myths, misperceptions, and mistrust. There is also the joint issue of both entities mishandling their relations. Simply correcting these issues on one side of the equation will likely not yield an adequate solution. Instead, USAID's pursuit of SRE should also include acknowledging and seeking to address the perceived barriers of FBOs.

Myths

Approximately 9% of the development FBOs we surveyed expressed that their religious nature legally prohibited them from receiving government funds. While our survey did not ask further questions relating to why an organization held this belief, one could hypothesize that the US Supreme Court's previous prohibition of the government subsidizing religious entities and the introduction of Jefferson's now ubiquitous statement regarding the "separation of church and state" is likely to blame. This is all the more likely since the constitutionality of the Faith-Based Initiative was heavily debated in the press and among politicians when it was first introduced. In fact, one analysis shows that a full 40% of the news coverage of the Faith-Based Initiative discussed whether or not the program comported with the First Amendment, with many of these stories appearing on the front page.[52] The majority of the stories implied that the program may not meet constitutional muster. The national conversation and the president's priorities changed drastically after 9/11. In the subsequent years, the Supreme Court supplied answers to many of the earlier questions surrounding the constitutionality of the Initiative and the funding of FBOs generally, yet these stories were less sensational and largely remained eclipsed by the shadow of the nation's ongoing war on terror. When Obama continued the Faith-Based Office at the White House, for example, far fewer stories were published, and those that were, focused primarily on procedural matters.[53] Therefore, if one wasn't looking for the information, it could be relatively easy to conclude that the federal government doesn't fund FBOs—or at least not certain types of FBOs.

Faith-saturated FBOs, in particular, may be more likely to think they are ineligible to receive federal dollars. This could be because this type of FBO was among the last groups made eligible for government funds by the Supreme Court. It could also be due to the separate debate that encompassed proselytizing organizations when the Faith-Based Initiative first began. Research indicates that 15% of the early news coverage on the Faith-Based Initiative specifically discussed whether federal funds could go toward organizations that proselytize, with the majority implying this exchange was likely unconstitutional.[54]

In fact, FBOs from across the spectrum are eligible for government awards. The Bush administration considered the Initiative to be on solid constitutional ground, and the Supreme Court later effectively agreed. Our research shows, however, that there is a contingent of FBOs that remain unaware of the jurisprudential history of faith-based federal funding. While not every faith-saturated FBO is eligible, the question of their eligibility lies not in their faith status or even in their faith programs but in the nature of the specific program for which they seek funding.

This information is currently relayed to USAID staff through USAID's SRE, International Religious Freedom, and Establishment Clause trainings, but it is *not* similarly relayed to USAID's prospective partners.[55] The ideal home for such information would be the newly launched site WorkwithUSAID.org, which serves as a comprehensive resource hub for the agency's current, past, and potential partners. The site houses a publicly accessible resource library that includes documents, audio recordings, toolkits, and videos. Topics covered include everything from proposal writing to public speaking to financial reporting. There are also videos clarifying specific agency policies. Currently, however, there is nothing that speaks directly to FBOs. At a minimum, USAID should make available to its potential and current faith-based partners the same level of training available to its staff, outlining the implications of the Court's interpretation of the First Amendment's Establishment Clause on USAID's funding partners and strategies and clarifying for partners' permissible and prohibited activities.

Misconceptions

USAID's SRE Policy admits that "FBOs may feel they need to hide their religious identity or compromise core values to be eligible for USG [US Government] partnership."[56] My research shows that this accurately describes the beliefs of some FBOs, and this belief causes them to avoid US government funding. The SRE Policy labels this a "myth," because The Rule provides FBOs with legal protection.[57] However, my conversations with FBOs indicate this perception may be less due to a misunderstanding of fact or law and more a matter of generally perceiving that the US government remains biased against religious institutions. In other words, even if an FBO is aware of its de jure eligibility for federal funding, it may still question the de facto likelihood of receiving such funds.

Our findings suggest there is no institutionalized pattern of the US government denying funds to FBOs; however, this does not foreclose the possibility of individual instances of discrimination. USAID's new SRE Policy admits as much, explaining that an interagency survey revealed that some aid officials did, in fact, harbor reservations about working with FBOs due to perceptions of them potentially proselytizing with federal funds and discriminating in their provision of goods and services.[58] FBOs may have experienced this kind of bias directly, either in seeking funds or in other interactions with the agency. Alternatively, those FBOs that have not had direct encounters with USAID (which our survey shows is the majority) may think of USAID as one of many government actors, all of whom are likely to exhibit "anti-religious animus." High-profile instances of such cases may contribute to FBOs reaching this conclusion.[59]

In this case, rather than highlighting the relevant regulations that govern FBO–USAID relations, prospective faith-based partners are more likely to be influenced by seeing these principles in action. Hearing directly the stories of USAID-funded FBOs—especially those that are lesser known—may prove instrumental in this effort. These stories could be shared in the resource hub alongside the legal training videos and documents but should also be disseminated more broadly. The key would be to reach the organizations that have not yet established contact with USAID.

In addition to the stories, USAID should share statistics. As discussed in Chapter 4, USAID does not routinely collect information on the faith status of its grant applicants or awardees. It, therefore, cannot share information on the number of faith-based applicants it receives or the number it funds. In the absence of numbers, the suspicion of bias can grow. USAID needs to collect this information and report on it. The FY2022 Localization Progress Report, published one year after the announcement of USAID's Localization Targets, is a good example to follow.[60]

Mistrust

In addition to the FBOs that are deterred from applying for USAID funds for fear that their time will be wasted and they won't receive an award, there are those who fear they *will* receive an award and that this award will come with unintended consequences. This belief speaks less to the legal criteria governing FBO–USAID relations and more to the power dynamics of the relationship. If an entity thinks it will likely *change* its values and identity as a result of entering into a relationship with the US government, then this shows that the organization is wary of the influence the government has over it and it mistrusts its ability to "maintain the course" in this dynamic.

In this case, sharing the legal safeguards available to FBOs may be a critical component in further engagement. In particular, USAID can add to its resource hub documents and videos that explain the protections FBOs are afforded under The Rule, the International Religious Freedom Act, and the "Conscience Clause" for those organizations implementing grants relating to HIV and AIDs.[61] One FBO I spoke to explained the need for such information:

> We hope, especially since we were a prime partner before and there were no challenges ... and USAID is now pushing localization ... we hope to be well situated for future funding ... and we hope to properly negotiate the Conscience Clause, though, I've read it, but I don't know how to apply it. I don't have that information. I don't know where to get it. I have the clause and I need a lawyer to interpret it.[62]

The organization explained that they learned about the Conscience Clause by reading the training material they were given about grant management, but they'd never been told more about it. As USAID looks to prioritize FBOs, more resources should be made available that are directly relevant to this constituency. These should be loaded to the hub but also highlighted to current and prospective faith-based partners. Mission officers, in particular, should be able to discuss these issues with partners in a way that leaves them empowered and not bewildered.

Mishandling

Discussions of FBO–USAID engagement are shallow if they do not acknowledge that institutional relationships are built atop interactions between individuals. USAID's SRE Policy acknowledges that the myths, misperceptions, and mistrust displayed by some aid officials have caused the agency's religious engagement efforts to stall. Yet aid officials also sometimes mishandle these relations, sometimes by dropping the ball completely. This is a fairly minor point in the USAID policy document but one that Olivia Wilkinson has previously identified and addressed as an issue. According to Wilkinson: "Development professionals cycle through the sometimes quickly revolving doors of a development organization."[63] As a result, she explains, FBOs that have strong relationships with an officer can be left out in the cold when that person leaves the agency or transitions to a different post. "The burden can fall on the religious partners to renegotiate relationships and brief the new staff members on their own organization's partnership history, leading to repetition and duplication," she says.

Wilkinson suggests that USAID can combat this trend by not leaving religious engagement solely in the hands of specific individuals, but rather, institutionalizing the agency's knowledge and practices relating to religious engagement. This ensures the relationships are deeper and broader than just a few individuals. USAID's SRE Policy appears, prima facie, to adopt Wilkinson's recommendations. Among the changes it suggests is for agency officers to develop "transition plans" to ensure the continuity of knowledge between position changes. The same advice could benefit FBOs.

In at least half a dozen instances when I reached out to FBOs, I was told by the person I contacted that they did not have any knowledge of the organization ever receiving government funds. In most cases, at least five years had passed since the organization received the award. In other cases, I was told, "That was Jim's thing, and he's not with us anymore," implying that while the person I contacted knew of the award, they associated it with a past employee more than with the organization and could not speak about it.[64] Such responses suggest that Wilkinson's words describing USAID mission officers can equally apply to some FBOs. The "revolving door" metaphor, in fact, aptly describes both government officials and nonprofit development professionals.[65] One study even found that half of all fundraising directors at nonprofit institutions anticipate leaving their current positions in two years or less, and those at smaller institutions likely look to leave even sooner.[66] This means that even if USAID were to follow Wilkinson's recommendation and carry out the vision of the SRE Policy in implementing transition plans among its mission officers, and even if USAID were to employ officers dedicated to religious outreach—another valuable practice suggested in the SRE—its religious engagement efforts would likely still stall if FBOs do not adopt a similar practice. The fluidity of USAID *and* FBOs threatens the continuity of their relations, and therefore, both parties should prioritize creating processes for transferring their employees' institutional and relational knowledge upon exit. Fixing this issue could go a long way in transforming the many "short-term ad hoc transactional interactions" that now exist between FBOs and USAID into the "enduring relationships" the agency desires.[67] Again, the data shows approximately 82% of the new faith-based partners USAID has attracted since it changed its regulations only received one award from USAID.[68]

Because USAID often has more institutional resources than its FBO counterparts, this may be an area where the agency can provide assistance. USAID can do this in at least two ways: It can deepen its relations with prospective faith-based partners and also deepen its relations with its present partners. Already, USAID has made it easier for organizations seeking to partner with the agency to better understand their eligibility and to "connect" in a low-risk environment. WorkwithUSAID.org was launched in late 2021 and provides current, past, and potential partners with a comprehensive resource of information. It also allows them to create an organizational profile with the agency. The profile is relatively straightforward, and while individual users supply their first and last names, the rest of the information consists of organizational attributes. What this means for USAID is that it may have only one point-of-contact and one email associated with a registering organization.[69] This may prove problematic in the future, especially since the site does not require information relating to registrant title. As a result, the connection made with the directory can be fairly tenuous and able to be severed when an individual at an FBO leaves the organization.[70]

Deepening relations means ensuring that connections between FBOs and USAID are not reliant upon only a couple of individuals. The same is true of current partners. Just as USAID commits to developing "transition plans" for its officers, it can also ensure that transitions in FBO staff do not disrupt the organization's relations with FBOs. Having an online partner platform that stores communication and that is regularly updated by both sides with appropriate and relevant points-of-contact could be an important and practical bridge in this process.

The myths, misperceptions, mistrust, and mishandling prevalent among FBOs have thus far impeded USAID's Religious Engagement efforts. USAID's SRE Policy is aimed at rooting these out among its staff, but if it wishes to truly advance its relations with FBOs, then it also needs to acknowledge and address how FBOs perceive engagement and why many are reluctant to do so. Addressing this side of things will take considerably more time and attention than addressing issues in-house, though one can begin the process by taking some of the same steps.

USAID's SRE Policy was a product in large part of the agency's Evidence Summit on SRE held in 2020. At the Summit, USAID surveyed its staff on their experiences and perceptions of religious engagement. Conducting a similar survey of USAID's current faith-based partners and the prospective partners now in its directory would be a significant step in the right direction.[71] (Though it would only include those organizations that have chosen, on their own accord, to first establish contact with the agency.)

At the time of this publication, there are 205 FBOs that have registered with USAID on its new partner platform, three-quarters of which have never partnered with USAID. This provides the organizations with an unprecedented opportunity to engage prospective partners directly and to ask them what has previously kept the organization from applying for funds. It can supplement this data with survey data on existing partners.[72] Another place to turn is to other donors. After all, as discussed in Chapter 2, America is not the only development donor to recognize and seek to capitalize on the value of faith-based actors and organizations in development. Other multilateral and bilateral institutions have also done so, to varying effect. Looking at the efforts and outcomes of other public donors may further inform their actions.

Comparable Donors

Chapter 2 explains that America's religious engagement did not occur in a vacuum but was part of a global narrative. The Westphalian state system and the rationalism of the Enlightenment caused Western states to long define development in terms of state economic growth and neglect considerations of sociocultural context, human experience, and religion. This changed with the growth of religious fundamentalism and its collision with state power at the turn of the 21st century. As religion became globalized, weaponized, and politicized, its relevance and importance became unmistakable. The United States and others took note. Over the next two decades, in addition to USAID, multilateral actors like the European Union (EU) and United Nations, as well as the state aid agencies of Britain, Germany, Canada, Switzerland, the Netherlands, Denmark, and Sweden, all began to engage with FBOs at various levels. Quantitative benchmarks of these efforts are sparse (with most donors, like USAID, not collecting the faith status of its applicants), but the available data suggests that America is not necessarily an outlier in its engagement outcomes. It may have been the state harbinger of religious engagement in development, but it did not take the lead.

Between 2008 and 2021, 13% of all the nonprofits receiving USAID assistance were faith based. This number is higher in other countries. In Canada, research reveals that approximately 17% of the organizations funded by Canada's International Development Agency (CIDA) between 2005 and 2010 were faith based.[73] Research by Kristy Schroeder on Britain's religious engagement in development also generally follows this pattern. According to Schroeder, FBOs accounted for 19% of all UK Aid Direct grants between 2011 and 2016 and 12% of the more select Programme Partnership Arrangements (PPA)-holders.[74] In the EU, data from 2017 reveals that FBOs made up a quarter of the organizations funded by the European Community Humanitarian Office.[75]

Greater variance is exhibited in levels of FBO funding. My research indicates that FBOs received approximately 9% of USAID's allocated assistance between 2008 and 2021. This is the same proportion of funding provided by the EU to FBOs between 2007 and 2016 through the Thematic Program on Civil Society Organizations and Local Authorities under the Development Cooperation Instrument.[76] In Canada and Britain, by contrast, this number was doubled. allocated 20% of its funds to its faith-based partners between 2005 and 2010 and DFID provided FBOs with 21% of available grant funding between 2011 and 2016.[77]

In contrast to the United States, both Canada and Britain produced early policy papers anchoring their relations with FBOs in development. Particularly instructive for the US case is DFID's Faith Partnership Principles Paper (FPPP). Though published a decade earlier, DFID's FPPP parallels USAID's new SRE Policy in many ways. Both documents identify the value of FBOs in development, and both documents commit to more expansive and deeper religious engagement. Both documents also identify barriers or challenges to engagement and propose solutions for overcoming them.

Yet, USAID's new SRE Policy differs in several important respects from DFID's FPPP. First, the FPPP is, as the name implies, a *paper* written in conjunction with FBOs and DFID staff meant to serve as "a clear statement of intent."[78] The SRE Policy, by contrast, is a *policy* codified by USAID. The latter is clearly more authoritative. It is also intentionally designed to connect and advance the agency's broader development agenda, including, importantly, its efforts at localization.[79] Relatedly, while the FPPP appeared to some to lack an "institutional home" at DFID, the SRE Policy comfortably resides at USAID's Center for Faith-Based Initiatives, whose staff will presumably see to its implementation. Both of these differences suggest the SRE Policy may be better situated to make an impact. However, another critical difference remains—one that this book speaks to directly. Unlike the FPPP, the primary audience for USAID's SRE Policy is USAID staff, and the solutions the document proposes are all internal.[80] It is silent on the measures that may be necessary to encourage "secular engagement" among FBOs. The FPPP, in contrast, acknowledges that the "estrangement" between FBOs and development donors "is not just one-sided." FBOs hold their own reservations, admit the FPPP, and some, in fact, want "nothing to do" with public donors.[81] The FPPP explains this separation in terms of perceived positionality, with some FBOs desiring to stand apart from entities that represent "a secular and materialistic world."[82] My research suggests there may be more to the divide in the United States, including perceptions of government discrimination.

Conclusion

World Vision once characterized USAID as the nation's "best kept secret."[83] The reference was meant to highlight the general public's ignorance of America's international benevolence, yet this description takes on multiple meanings in light of the present research. While World Vision is not shy about its relationship with USAID, the relationship between USAID and FBOs, broadly, is not well understood—especially among FBOs. Instead, myths, misperceptions, mistrust, and the mishandling of relations continue to cloud the narrative and keep many FBOs from seeing the potential benefits and opportunities of partnership.

My research indicates that nearly half of all eligible development FBOs in the United States believe they either cannot legally receive funds from the US government due to their religious nature or that the US government is unlikely to fund them for this reason. Others are reticent because they anticipate that the acceptance of government funds will come at the cost of their organization's religious mission or identity or their organization's religious donors. The stories of the FBOs that have partnered with USAID show these fears to be largely unfounded. This disconnect could be attributed to the historic interpretation of the US Constitution and the "separation of church and state" now emblazoned on the nation's collective memory. The Courts effectively created a chasm that USAID now seeks to bridge. Its SRE Policy presents a viable blueprint, but solid construction will require both parties. Both parties must build trust. Both parties must have faith in one another's intentions and abilities. There's little utility in building a bridge if one side is unwilling to cross it.

Notes

1 While the report relied upon numbers to tell its story, it also admitted that the numeric data was, at best, a *proxy* measure for religious engagement. "Any quantitative measure," the report said, "[is] limited in capturing the full scope of change [in FBO-government relations]." Nevertheless, it concluded, "If government was truly being transformed and new partners were being welcomed, the change would undoubtedly be reflected in an expansion of government partnerships with faith-based organizations." The White House, Office of the Press Secretary, *The Quiet Revolution*, 86.

2 Melissa Rogers, who served as the director of the Faith-Based and Neighborhood Partnerships Program under President Obama, also eschews quantitative measures. Rogers and E.J. Dionne Jr. expressed, "The mission … is serving people in need … the metrics for evaluation should focus on whether vulnerable people's lives are being improved, not on whether the amount of government funding that flows to faith-based organizations increases." See Melissa Rogers and E. J. Dionne, *A Time to Heal, a Time to Build* (Washington, DC: Brookings, 2020), www.brookings.edu/wp-content/uploads/2020/10/A_Time_to_Heal_report.pdf

3 Olivia Wilkson specifically contends that USAID should not focus on increasing the number of its faith-based partners but rather spend efforts ensuring that all funded partners fit the agency's mission. Wilkinson, "Putting the 'Strategic'," 82.

4 This is exemplified by an FBO representative we interviewed who said: "There are perceptions about having to yield to government … there's a real fear. We had to face that too and overcome it because the need was so overwhelming."

5 Hefferan, Adkins, and Occhipian quote Bush as describing FBOs as "the best, most efficient purveyors of social services … since they often worked with low overhead and volunteer labor" (*Bridging the Gaps*, 6).

6 Chaves, "Six Myths About the Faith-Based Initiatives," 21; Farnsley II, "Faith-Based Action," 12; Gilman, "Fighting Poverty with Faith," 415. Peter Steinfeis, "Despite a Decade of Controversy, the Faith-Based Initiative Endures," *New York Times*, July 31, 2009, www.nytimes.com/2009/08/01/us/01beliefs.html

7 USAID's new SRE Policy frames FBO contributions in terms of history and presence, trust and influence, access and reach, and social capital. USAID, "Building Bridges in Development," 8.
8 It is important to emphasize what ample research shows—that these characteristics are NOT unique to faith-based organizations and are, in fact, also present among many secular NGOs.
9 FBO #18, Zoom Interview with Author, June 16, 2021; FBO #24, Zoom Interview with Author, June 28, 2021.
10 FBO #18, Zoom Interview with Author, June 16, 2021.
11 The idea of "intrinsic religiosity" and its connection to individual behavior was first explored in Allport and Ross, "Personal Religious Orientation and Prejudice."
12 In Judaism, believers prepare for *Olam Ha-Ba* (the World to Come) by studying the Torah and doing *mitzvot*, which translates to "commandments of the law," but which is commonly understood to encompass any good actions done on earth in obedience to God's will. Similarly, in the Muslim faith, believers seek *raza-e-ilahi* (to please God) to receive rewards in the afterlife. In Christianity, while scripture says deeds are not enough to get one into heaven, they are still seen as an earthly manifestation of one's faith and relationship with God and included in one's final judgment.
13 In Buddhism and Hinduism, a good deed, or karma, is believed to elevate the quality of one's life in the next incarnation.
14 A 2010 Gallup survey showed that in countries where people made, on average, less than $2,000 per year, 95% say religion is important in their daily lives. This is compared to 47% of people who supplied the same answer in countries with average per capita incomes above $25,000. Steve Crabtree, "Religiosity Highest in World's Poorest Nations," Gallup, August 31, 2010, https://news.gallup.com/poll/142727/religiosity-highest-world-poorest-nations.aspx
15 FBO #20, Zoom Interview with Author, June 15, 2021.
16 The representative further made the point that, in some cases, while the organization and beneficiaries shared a Christian faith, their faiths were experienced and translated through their respective cultures. The interviewee expressed that the Christian concept of "faithfulness," for instance, was often equated with monogamy in Western contexts but that the organization had to accommodate its understanding and teach the concept as it applied to communities where polyamorous relationships were the norm. This led them to stress being faithful and committed to the partners one is with.
17 FBO #43, Zoom Interview with Author, June 9, 2021.
18 FBO #27, Zoom Interview with Author, July 26, 2021.
19 FBO #30, Zoom Interview with Author, June 30, 2021.
20 While not necessarily commonplace, the *opposite* can also be true—an organization's religious status or operations may prohibit it from accessing and aiding certain areas. The Eritrean government's campaign to shut down health clinics operated by the Presbyterian Church is one example. The government justified its decision by saying that "Religious organizations may fund but not initiate development projects." Thaut, "Role of Faith in Christian Faith-Based Humanitarian Agencies," 325.
21 On the positive effect of FBOs in vaccine uptake for other illnesses, see Syed et al., "Role of Faith-Based Organizations."

22 The importance of FBOs was clear from the onset of the pandemic. One of the first recommended strategies for containment was to limit large gatherings. Since weekly and sometimes daily, communal worship and instruction are a regular feature of nearly every faith, this strategy necessitated the cooperation of religious leaders and groups. This was made all the more pressing the following month as many faith communities anticipated celebrating their annual religious holidays, including Passover, Easter, Ramadan, Vaisakhi (Vesak), and Ridván. In light of these known celebrations, UN Chief António Guterres issued a special appeal to religious leaders in April 2020, calling for reflection and continued commitment by religious groups to defeating COVID-19. "UN Chief Calls on Religious Leaders to Unite in the Fight against COVID-19," April 11, 2020, https://news.un.org/en/story/2020/04/1061512
23 Zimmerman et al., "Misinformation and COVID-19 Vaccine Hesitancy."
24 Joshi et al., "Predictors of COVID-19 Vaccine."
25 Soni et al., "Engaging Faith-Based Organizations."
26 Centers for Disease Control and Prevention, "Using Faith-Based Initiatives to Increase Vaccination Coverage among African Americans," *Health Equity in Action Projects*, March 14, 2023, www.cdc.gov/healthequity/whatis/healthequityinaction/topics/faith-based-vaccine-initiatives.html
27 Soni et al., "Engaging Faith-Based Organizations."
28 In the case of CNBC, this took the form of hundreds of leader trainings and thousands of public service announcements, printed materials, social media posts, and in-person and virtual public information sessions encouraging vaccination. Evans, Webster, and Flores, "Partnering with the Faith-Based Community," 609.
29 Since the establishment of USAID, foreign aid funding has remained below 1% of US GDP. Since 1979, it has consistently been between .2% and .5% of the nation's GDP. Emily M. Morgenstern and Nick M. Brown, "Foreign Assistance: An Introduction to US Programs and Policy," *Congressional Research Service*, updated January 10, 2022, 31–32, https://crsreports.congress.gov/product/pdf/R/R40213
30 As discussed in Chapter 3, most of the NGOs that served as conduits for American food delivery abroad were faith-based, including Catholic Relief Services, Hadassah, Lutheran World Relief, Church World Service, American Friends Service Committee, and the American Jewish Joint Distribution Committee. McCleary, *Global Compassion*, 76.
31 Bettiza, *Finding Faith in Foreign Policy*, 97–136.
32 I use the word "viable" and not necessarily "reliable" here on purpose. As was made painfully clear by one of our interviewees, FBOs, as well as secular NGOs, cannot be guaranteed that USAID's program priorities will remain the same year after year, especially as administrative agendas shift. However, even if specific routes to funding are foreclosed, the institution's *ability* to fund FBOs has generally remained consistent.
33 Meer, Miller, and Wulfsberg, "The Great Recession and Charitable Giving."
34 Khan, Jain, and Cameron, "Analysing the Donor Behaviour," 388–389.
35 This trend did not continue as the year progressed. In fact, studies show global philanthropic giving *increased* in 2020 compared to previous years. www.cafonline.org/docs/default-source/about-us-research/caf_world_giving_index_2022_210922-final.pdf

36 FBO #9, Interview with Dexter Woods, March 5, 2021; the experience of FBOs varied broadly during COVID-19 (a topic discussed more in this chapter), but surveys indicate that most experienced an initial decline in donations. "Nonprofits Hit by 6% Decline in Giving Due to COVID-19," Association of Fundraising Professionals, June 22, 2020; Michael Theis and Dan Parks, "Giving Plunges by 6% in First Quarter, Signaling $25 Billion in Lost Revenue for Nonprofits," *Chronicle of Philanthropy*, June 22, 2020; Dan Parks, "73% of Charities Worldwide See Decline in Contributions," *Chronicle of Philanthropy*, May 18, 2020; Michelle Boorstein, "Church Donations Have Plunged Because of the Coronavirus. Some Churches Won't Survive," *Washington Post*, April 24, 2020.

37 Soskis, "Norms and Narratives," 13; "World Giving Index 2022: A Global View of Giving Trends," Charities Aid Foundation, www.cafonline.org/docs/default-source/about-us-research/caf_world_giving_index_2022_210922-final.pdf

38 Agency Profile: United States Agency for International Development, FY2020 summary, USASpending.gov.

39 Ibid.

40 Hopgood and Vinjamuri, "Faith in Markets," xx.

41 "Charitable Giving Report: Using 2021 Data to Transform Your Strategy," The Blackbaud Institute. February 2022, 7, https://institute.blackbaud.com/wp-content/uploads/2022/03/BBI_CGR_2022.pdf

42 "The State of Global Giving by U.S. Foundations, 2022 Edition," Council on Foundations, 2022, 11, https://cof.org/sites/default/files/documents/files/private/2022-state-global-giving-US-foundations.pdf

43 Figure calculated from USASpending.gov download data for USAID grants and cooperative agreements to nonprofits in FY2022 (excludes multilateral institutions).

44 FBO #22, Interview with Author, June 18, 2021.

45 In this situation, donors have more charitable options, and FBOs have to work harder to attract and maintain donations (Hopgood and Vinjamuri, "Faith in Markets," 57).

46 FBO #30, Interview with Author, June 30, 2021.

47 Of course, this organization, like other USAID prime award recipients, had already been judged by USAID to have sufficient capacity to successfully steward the agency's funds. What they are describing is thus not the creation of capacity but the *growth* of their organizational capabilities made possible by accompanying project support.

48 FBO #20, Interview with Author, June 15, 2021.

49 While USAID does not adopt a specific definition for organizational capacity, it references the definition adopted by Alan Fowler and Jan Ubel's in *Capacity Development in Practice*, which defines capacity as "the ability of a human system to perform, sustain itself, and self-renew." United States Agency for International Development, "Organizational Capacity Development Measurement," 2, www.usaid.gov/sites/default/files/2022-05/Capacity_Development_Measurement_Recommendations_Final_Draft_5.11.2017_1.pdf

50 FBO #25, Zoom Interview with author, June 28, 2021.

51 USAID, "Building Bridges in Development," 5.

52 Pew Research Center, "Media Coverage of the Faith-Based Initiative in the First Six Months of 2001 and 2009," August 12, 2009, www.pewresearch.org/religion/2009/08/12/the-starting-line/

53 Ibid.
54 Ibid.
55 USAID, "Building Bridges in Development," 16.
56 Ibid., 6.
57 In addition to 22 CFR 205.1 Rule on Participation of Religious Organizations in USAID Programs, FBOs are also covered by the 1998 and 2016 International Religious Freedom Acts and the 2013 US National Strategy on Integrating Religious Leader and Faith Community Engagement into US Foreign Policy.
58 USAID, "Building Bridges in Development," 7.
59 The Supreme Court has ruled in favor of religious (Christian) entities in several widely reported cases in recent years, finding they were constitutionally discriminated against by government actors. See *Masterpiece Cakeshop, Inc. v. Colorado Civil Rights Comm'n*, 138 S. Ct. 1719 (2018); *Roman Catholic Diocese of Brooklyn v. Cuomo*, 141 S. Ct. 63 (2020); *Fulton v. Philadelphia*, No. 19-123, 2021 WL 2459253 (2021); and *Tandon et al. v. Newsom*, 141 S. Ct. 1294 (2021).
60 I'm not suggesting that USAID should approach SRE like Localization and establish a funding target, but rather that it should collect and disclose the data as it has done with its Localization efforts. The Localization Progress Report for FY2022 provides both the monetary amount ($1.6 billion) and the proportion of total obligation (10.2%) that went to local entities in FY 2022, noting the progress the agency has made toward its 2030 goal of a quarter of funding going toward local partners. The report also tracks how much USAID has allocated over the past ten years. (United States Agency for International Development, "Moving Toward a Model of Locally Led Development: FY 2022 Localization Progress Report," 2022, www.usaid.gov/sites/default/files/2023-06/FY%202022%20Localization%20Progress%20Report-June-12-23_vFINAL_1.pdf)
61 The so-called Conscience Clause is a safeguard available to FBOs receiving funds to combat HIV/AIDs included in the Leadership Act, Section 301(d). See Chapter 3, endnote 106, for complete legal language.
62 FBO #37, Zoom Interview with Author, August 17, 2023.
63 Wilkinson, "Putting the 'Strategic'," 82.
64 The name was changed for anonymity purposes.
65 Nicole Rizkallah, "Shutting the Revolving Door of Development Turnover," *Philanthropy Daily*, February 3, 2020, https://philanthropydaily.com/shutting-door-development-turnover/
66 Eddie Adkins, "Half of All Fundraisers Flee," *The Nonprofit Times*, July 9, 2013, https://thenonprofittimes.com/npt_articles/half-of-all-fundraisers-flee/
67 United States Agency for International Development (USAID), "Building Bridges in Development," 17.
68 Since the data collected is limited to only awards and not applications, I cannot measure how many of these FBOs applied again for an award and were denied.
69 Additional "users" can register and be associated with the organization, but this is not required, and information relating to who this person is at the registering organization is limited.
70 At present, the profile asks only if a user is an "administrator" (of the account) or a "collaborator."

71 Prospective partners can now register with USAID through the WorkwithUSAID.gov site.
72 The latter may be particularly helpful in identifying why a large number of FBOs remain what USAID calls "underutilized" partners. It can also identify why a significant number of FBOs chose to engage with USAID only once or twice over a 20-year period. USAID's new SRE Policy recognizes that "One-time engagements to achieve short-term objectives might yield particular accomplishments, but risk becoming transactional in nature. Episodic encounters can instrumentalize our stakeholders, bring harm to communities, and jeopardize our reputation."
73 Zaag, "Canadian Faith-Based Development," 327–328.
74 Schroeder, *Religion and Secularism in Development*, 33–34.
75 Berkley Center for Religion, Peace, and World Affairs and the Edmund A. Walsh School of Foreign Service at Georgetown University, "Faith-Inspired Organizations," 10.
76 Perchoc, "The EU and Faith-based Organisations," 11.
77 Schroeder, *Religion and Secularism in Development*, 33, 34. These figures were collected via Schroeder's independent analysis, though they align with one of the only official statistics provided by DFID. In its Faith Partnership Principles Paper, DFID reported that 10 of the 53, or 18.86%, of the organizations it funded through the Global Poverty Action Fund in 2012 were faith based (Department for International Development, "Faith Partnership Principles," 4).
78 Department for International Development, "Faith Partnership Principles Paper," 6.
79 The SRE Policy is nestled amidst a constellation of other related agency policies, including USAID's Local Capacity Strengthening Policy, its Policy on Promoting the Rights of Indigenous Peoples, its Nondiscrimination Policy, and its guidance on Integrating Inclusive Development Across the Program Cycle.
80 These include encouraging USAID staff to conduct "religious landscape surveys" to account for the FBOs operating in their area, highlighting legal trainings and resources available to USAID staff relevant to FBO engagement, requesting that staff build relationships with area FBOs, and promoting staff to take a proactive approach to faith-based partnerships, evaluating what works, what doesn't, and having the flexibility to pivot together if necessary.
81 Department for International Development, "Faith Partnership Principles Paper," 6.
82 Ibid.
83 Marian V. Liautaud, "USAID: Our Country's Best Kept Secret?," *World Vision*, April 28, 2017, https://live-advocacy.d2.worldvision.org/2017/04/28/usaid-countrys-best-kept-secret/

Bibliography

Allport, Gordon Willard and J. Michael Ross. "Personal Religious Orientation and Prejudice." *Journal of Personality and Social Psychology*, 5, no. 4 (1967): 432–443. DOI:10.1037/h0021212

Berkley Center for Religion, Peace, and World Affairs and the Edmund A. Walsh School of Foreign Service at Georgetown University. "Faith-Inspired Organizations and Global Development Policy: A Background Review 'Mapping' Social and

Economic Development Work in Europe and Africa." Report presented at the Institute of Social Studies in the Hague, 2008, 10. https://s3.amazonaws.com/berkley-center/090101FaithInspiredOrganizationsGlobalDevelopmentPolicyBackgroundReviewMappingSocialEconomicDevelopmentWorkEuropeAfrica.pdf

Bettiza, Gregorio. *Finding Faith in Foreign Policy: Religion and American Diplomacy in a Postsecular World* (Oxford: Oxford University Press, 2019).

Chaves, Mark. "Six Myths About the Faith-Based Initiative." *The Christian Century*. (September 12–19, 2001): 20–23. www.religion-online.org/article/six-myths-about-faith-based-initiatives/

de Wit, Arjen and René Bekkers. "Government Support and Charitable Donations: A Meta-Analysis of the Crowding-Out Hypothesis." *Journal of Public Administration Research and Theory* 27, no. 2 (2017): 301–319. DOI:10.1093/jopart/muw044

Evans, Anthony, Joseph Webster, and Glenn Flores. "Partnering with the Faith-Based Community to Address Disparities in COVID-19 Vaccination Rates and Outcomes Among US Black and Latino Populations." *JAMA* 326, no. 7 (2021): 609–610. DOI:10.1001/jama.2021.12652

Farnsley II, Arthur E. "Faith-Based Action." *The Christian Century*. (March 14, 2001): 12–15. www.religion-online.org/article/faith-based-action/

Gilman, Michele E. "Fighting Poverty with Faith: Reflections on Ten Years of Charitable Choice." *Journal of Gender Race & Justice* 10 (2007) (symposium): 395–438. https://scholarworks.law.ubalt.edu/cgi/viewcontent.cgi?article=1252&context=all_fac

Hefferan, Tara, Julie Adkins, and Laurie A. Occhipint. *Bridging the Gaps: Faith-Based Organizations, Neoliberalism, and Developments in Latin America and the Caribbean* (Lanham, MD: Lexington Books, 2009).

Heutel, Garth. "Crowding Out and Crowding In of Private Donations and Government Grants." *Public Finance Review* 42, no. 2 (2014): 143–175. DOI:10.1177/1091142112447525

Hopgood, Stephen and Leslie Vinjamuri. "Faith in Markets." In *Sacred Aid: Faith and Humanitarianism*, edited by Michael Barnett and Janice Gross Stein (New York: Oxford University Press, 2012): 37–64.

Joshi, Ashish, Mahima Kaur, Ritika Kaur, Ashoo Grover, Denis Nash, and Ayman El-Mohandes. "Predictors of COVID-19 Vaccine Acceptance, Intention, and Hesitancy: A Scoping Review." *Front Public Health* 9, 698111 (2021). DOI:10.3389/fpubh.2021.698111. PMID: 34485229; PMCID: PMC8414566

Khan, Aila, Siddharth Jain, and Bruce Cameron. "Analysing the Donor Behaviour of a Muslim Diaspora in Australia." *Voluntary Sector Review* 13, no. 3 (2022): 376–395. DOI:10.1332/204080521X16377818399015

McCleary, Rachel. *Global Compassion: Private Voluntary Organizations and U.S. Foreign Policy since 1939* (New York: Oxford University Press, 2009).

Meer, Jonathan, David H. Miller, and Elisa Wulfsberg. "The Great Recession and Charitable Giving." National Bureau of Economic Research Working Paper No. 22902. December 2016. www.nber.org/system/files/working_papers/w22902/w22902.pdf

Perchoc, Philippe. "The EU and Faith-Based Organisations in Development and Humanitarian Aid." European Parliament. November 2017. www.europarl.europa.eu/thinktank/en/document.html?reference=EPRS_BRI(2017) 608800

Santibañez S., Davis M., and Avchen R.N. CDC Engagement with Community and Faith-Based Organizations in Public Health Emergencies. *American Journal of Public Health* 109 (2019): S274–S276. DOI:10.2105/AJPH.2019.305275

Schroeder, Kristy Bergman. *Religion and Secularism in Development: Trends in the Approaches of Bilateral Donors in Canada and the United Kingdom* (Winnipeg: Department of Religion, the University of Manitoba, the University of Winnipeg, 2016).

Seidel, Timothy, "Development, Religion, and Modernity in Palestine-Israel." *CrossCurrents* 62, no. 4 (2012): 424–441. www.jstor.org/stable/24462297

Soni, Gopal Krishna, Anumegha Bhatnagar, Anil Gupta, Amrita Kumari, Sonal Arora, Surbhi Seth, Apurva Rastogi, Natasha Kanagat, and Rebecca Fields. "Engaging Faith-Based Organizations for Promoting the Uptake of COVID-19 Vaccine in India: A Case Study of a Multi-Faith Society." *Vaccines (Basel)* 11, no. 4 (2023): 837. DOI:10.3390/vaccines11040837. PMID: 37112749; PMCID: PMC10140837.

Soskis, Benjamin. "Norms and Narratives that Shape US Charitable and Philanthropic Giving." *Urban Institute*, March 2021. www.urban.org/sites/default/files/publication/103772/norms-and-narratives-that-shape-us-charitable-and-philanthropic-giving_0.pdf

Syed, Uzma, Olivia Kapera, Aparajita Chandrasekhar, Barbara T. Baylor, Adebola Hassan, Marina Magalhães, Farshid Meidany, Inon Schenker, Sara E Messiah, and Alexandra Bhatti. "The Role of Faith-Based Organizations in Improving Vaccination Confidence & Addressing Vaccination Disparities to Help Improve Vaccine Uptake: A Systematic Review." *Vaccines* 11, no. 2 (2023): 449. DOI:10.3390/vaccines11020449

Thaut, Laura. "The Role of Faith in Christian Faith-Based Humanitarian Agencies: Constructing the Taxonomy." *VOLUNTAS: International Journal of Voluntary and Nonprofit Organizations* 20 (2009): 319–350.

The White House. Office of the Press Secretary. *The Quiet Revolution: A Seven Year Progress Report* (Washington, DC: U.S. Government Printing Office, 2008).

United States Agency for International Development (USAID). "Building Bridges in Development: USAID's Strategic Religious Engagement Policy." September 2023. www.usaid.gov/sites/default/files/2023-09/USAID-Strategic-Religious-Engagement-Policy-9-6-23_1.pdf

Vander Zaag, Ray. "Canadian Faith-Based Development NGOs and CIDA Funding." *Canadian Journal of Development Studies/Revue canadienne d'études du développement* 34, no. 2 (2013): 321–347. DOI:10.1080/02255189.2013.792726

Wilkinson, Olivia. "Putting the 'Strategic' into Strategic Religious Engagement." *The Review of Faith & International Affairs* 19, sup1 (2021): 78–84.

Zimmerman, R.K., A. Hoberman, M.P. Nowalk, C.J. Lin, D.P. Greenberg, S.T. Weinberg, F.S. Ko, and D.E. Fox. "Improving Influenza Vaccination Rates of High-Risk Inner-City Children Over 2 Intervention Years. *Annual of Family Medicine* 4 (2006): 534–540. DOI:10.1370/afm.612

Zimmerman, Tara, Kristina Shiroma, Kenneth R. Fleischmann, Bo Xie, Chenyan Jia, Nitin Verma, and Min Kyung Lee. "Misinformation and COVID-19 Vaccine Hesitancy." *Vaccine* 41, no. 1 (2023): 136–144. DOI:10.1016/j.vaccine.2022.11.014

Index

Note: Endnotes are indicated by the page number followed by "n" and the note number e.g., 99n58 refers to note 58 on page 99. Page numbers in **bold** refer to tables and those in *italic* refer to figures.

For Product Safety Concerns and Information please contact our EU representative GPSR@taylorandfrancis.com
Taylor & Francis Verlag GmbH, Kaufingerstraße 24, 80331 München, Germany

www.ingramcontent.com/pod-product-compliance
Lightning Source LLC
LaVergne TN
LVHW021247011026
849160LV00010BA/933
* 9 7 8 1 0 3 2 5 9 8 7 9 6 *